CHRISTMAS: A COOK'S TOUR

CHRISTMAS
A
COOK'S
TOUR

Ingeborg Relph
&
Penny Stanway

ILLUSTRATIONS BY
Linda Smith

A LION BOOK
Oxford · Batavia · Sydney

Text copyright © 1991 Ingeborg Relph and Penny Stanway
Illustrations copyright © 1991 Linda Smith
This edition copyright © 1991 Lion Publishing

Published by
Lion Publishing plc
Sandy Lane West, Oxford, England
ISBN 0 7459 2028 4
Lion Publishing Corporation
1705 Hubbard Avenue, Batavia, Illinois 60510, USA
ISBN 0 7459 2028 4
Albatross Books Pty Ltd
PO Box 320, Sutherland, NSW 2232, Australia
ISBN 0 7324 0523 8

First edition 1991

The three verses from Sir John Betjeman's poem 'Christmas'
on page 14 are reproduced by kind permission of John Murray
(Publishers) Ltd, London

British Library Cataloguing in Publication Data
Applied for

Library of Congress Cataloging-in-Publication Data
Applied for

Printed and bound in Italy

DEDICATION

*To our mothers, Lis and Joan, and to all those who
lovingly continue to weave the golden threads of tradition
into our modern lives.*

CONTENTS

CONTENTS

CONTENTS

Acknowledgments

Friends and acquaintances from around the world have helped this book to come about. In particular we would like to thank Doug and Olga Abraham, Christiana Efua Addo, Marjan Adlington, Sue Allpass, Elisabet Baldwin, Pamela Banks, Marianne Bauchet, Carmen and Sandy Bjerre, Käthi Bolt, Adelita Broome, Edita Camm, Judy Catt, Anne Cook, Rosalie Cooper, Christine Core, Elena Court, Kathrin Fielder, Birthe Fraser, Linda Ginsberg, Jorid Holm, Helen Holmes, Monsignor Hook, Chizuko Katakabe, Inger and Dirk Laan, Shannon Latham, Carin Lowenborg, Jane Manfield, Kate Medlachlow, Anne Mehrling, Pierre Michel, Maya Moor, Sharyn Nicholls, Nadean Nixon, Lisette Nollner, the Parish Priest of the Russian Orthodox Church in London, Hilda Perham, Inma Phelip, Swantje Postlethwaite, Danielle Robinson, Joan Russell, Lydia Saharova, Stephanie Smith, Diana Stanway, Leonie Starink, Theresa Sundt, Christina Swift, John Taylor, Brigitte Tongue, Marcela Turpin, Ann Urban, Maarit Verkki, Doreen Watson, Marlene Webber, Dorothy Wedel-Nilssen, Denise White, and the Women's Institute of Canada.

We would also like to thank Doreen Montgomery for her continued encouragement, our families for their willingness to eat Christmas food all year round, Rebecca Winter for her clear-sighted enthusiasm for the project, Linda Smith for her delightful illustrations, and Lois Rock and Jeanette Cotterill for their patient editing.

About the Recipes

QUANTITIES
For all recipes, quantities are given in metric, imperial and American cup measures. Follow one set of quantities only; they are not interchangeable.

SPOON MEASUREMENTS
Standard spoon measurements are used in all recipes.

1 tablespoon — one 15ml spoon
1 teaspoon — one 5ml spoon
All spoon measures are level, unless otherwise specified.

INGREDIENTS
Where an item is known by a different name to American cooks, the US term is given in brackets. Names of specialist food suppliers can usually be obtained from embassies.

Unless otherwise stated, recipes are for four people.

INTRODUCTION

Living in our own small corner of the world, steeped in familiar customs, it is easy to forget that Christmas is celebrated by millions of people, in many different countries, in an infinite variety of ways.

Astoundingly, the birth of a baby in a stable in Palestine 2000 years ago is honoured by people in countries as culturally diverse as Ghana and Finland, Australia and Mexico. Folklore and commercialism may play their part at Christmas, but wherever you go you find people celebrating the birth of Christ.

The seeds of this book germinated as the two of us discussed how we celebrate Christmas. With Danish, English, Polish and South African strands in our families, there were many contrasts, yet so much in common. Our conversation aroused a curiosity to explore further what people in other countries did at Christmas and, in particular, what foods they ate and why these foods were specially chosen. The idea blossomed as people enthusiastically shared their experiences, recipes and customs with us.

We found it remarkable that, despite the pressures of a modern, mobile society, many Christmas rituals and symbols have survived relatively unchanged. Digging deeper, we discovered a mixture of myth and ancient pagan superstition woven into the Christian celebrations. Christmas was not celebrated as a festival at all until AD353. When it was introduced, it either superceded or took its place alongside the pre-existing ancient and almost universal winter solstice festivities. Constant themes surrounding Christmas are the contrast between good and evil, light and dark, old and new, death and rebirth; and the universal need for a message of hope.

As we continued our research, we became aware of just how strong is the urge, conscious or unconscious, to have a link with the past, and how important it is that we pass our cultural heritage and traditions to future generations.

Feasting and festivals go hand in hand the world over and nourish both body and soul. Beliefs are mirrored in celebration meals; symbolic, traditional foods; families and friends coming together. Whilst our own customs will always be special, an insight into how other people celebrate can broaden our understanding of the festival and give us a sense of celebrating with them.

Many of the recipes in this book are family favourites handed down from generation to generation and are published here for the first time. They vary from the simple to the sophisticated and will appeal to both the beginner and the experienced cook.

Perhaps you'll want to ring the changes this year by celebrating in the style of one of the twenty-two countries featured in this book. Or perhaps you'll simply want to enjoy an armchair journey round the world at Christmas time. We hope this book excites a renewed sense of wonder at Christmas, and that it inspires you to look afresh at how and why you celebrate.

For us the Christmas mystery is summed up in the words of the poet Sir John Betjeman:

And is it true? And is it true?
This most tremendous tale of all,
Seen in a stained-glass window's hue,
A Baby in an ox's stall?
The Maker of the stars and sea
Become a Child on earth for me?

And is it true? For if it is,
No loving fingers tying strings
Around those tissued fripperies,
The sweet and silly Christmas things,
Bath salts and inexpensive scent
And hideous tie so kindly meant,

No love that in a family dwells,
No carolling in frosty air,
Nor all the steeple-shaking bells
Can with this simple Truth compare—
That God was Man in Palestine
And lives today in Bread and Wine.

AUSTRALIA

CHRISTMAS: A COOK'S TOUR

Australia was first visited by Christians when Spanish and Dutch explorers landed in the seventeenth century. *The English sailor, Captain James Cook, explored the east coast in 1769, and in that year ate what was perhaps Australia's very first Christmas dinner: he shot several Solan geese and made a goose pie.*

Christmas Day 1788 saw 1350 people, men and women, sailing in eleven ships towards Botany Bay. These were Australia's first European settlers. They came from Britain, in the British government's attempt to relieve the population pressure in its prisons. Known as 'poms' (Prisoners of Mother England), they brought Christianity—and Christmas—with them.

Wrote Private John Easty on board the *Scarborough*: 'O God Grant that I was at home with you to eat of your Goose and Apple Pie for I shall have only a Poor dinner here'. Sergeant Scott on the *Prince of Wales* was luckier with his Christmas dinner. He wrote: 'Being Christmas day, Dinned off a pice of pork and apple Sauce a pice of Beef and plum pudding, and Crowned the Day With 4 Bottels of Rum, Which Was the Best Wee Vitr'ens Could Afford.' Captain Walton on the *Friendship* went so far as to kill a sheep.

The English immigrants to this vast, empty land joined the earlier immigrants, the Aboriginals, who had lived there for forty thousand years. Over the next two hundred years or so there was a flood of people eager for opportunity and sunshine. They came from Great Britain, Italy, Asia, Greece, Yugoslavia, Germany, Holland, Poland, Africa, the United States, Canada, China and Vietnam, and they brought with them many different customs. Today, out of the more than seventeen million inhabitants, one in five was born overseas!

There is no state religion in Australia, but there are around four million Roman Catholics, nearly as many Anglicans, one and a half million members of the Uniting Church of Australasia, and half a million Greek Orthodox, among others. With such variety it's hardly surprising that Christmas celebrations, traditions and food differ from family to family so much.

Christmas in Australia is very different from a northern hemisphere Christmas because, of course, it is celebrated in summertime. December is the beginning of the long, hot Australian summer, and is also the start of the school summer holidays. It's a time for being outside and a time for exploring the country and for visiting people. About a third of the continent has a tropical climate and the temperature can soar in a heat wave. Because of this, Christmas is the time of the big bush fires and, in the North, of the 'big wet'—sudden torrential rains. In spite of the climate, the Christmas traditions brought from Europe and America are closely followed and people travel sometimes thousands of miles to be with their families at this special time.

The shops display Christmas wares and decorations well before the holiday, and most department stores have a fairy grotto with a Father Christmas for children to visit. Christmas trees may be beautiful Australian pines or expensive synthetic ones. Put in a window and strewn with fairy lights they light the way of passers-by at night. Some families even light trees in their gardens. Houses are decorated with greenery and flowers such as nasturtiums, wisteria and honeysuckle. The yellow-flowered Christmas bush is out at this time of year, as are Christmas bells—bell-shaped flowers with bright green stamens.

The traditional Father Christmas of the northern countries has little use for a reindeer sleigh in such a sunny climate. He comes to homes in Australia by helicopter, landing on the roof to leave presents in pillowslips on Christmas Eve; he water-skis down rivers in red bathing trunks; he sails a boat into Bondai Beach; and he lands by plane in the outback. However Father Christmas comes, he brings the thrill and excitement of Christmas gifts with him.

An Australian tradition which began about thirty years ago is outdoor carol singing in the big cities and smaller communities on Christmas Eve. Lit by torches and special candles sold in aid of charity, people sing around a large Christmas tree. In Melbourne, where carols by candlelight began, crowds gather in a vast outdoor 'music bowl' or auditorium similar to the Hollywood Bowl. Well-known show-business and other personalities join in and all the proceeds go to a good cause. Australian carols include those familiar all over the world but also some special ones, such as the 'Melbourne Carol', 'Once Upon a Hillside'—the story of the angel and the shepherds on the hills by Bethlehem, set to the music of 'Waltzing Matilda', and carols with their imagery drawn from the bush such as the 'Carol of the Birds'.

Children wake to bright Christmas Day sunshine and open their presents before breakfast. Breakfast itself is quite a grand meal in many homes. Ham cut off the bone is fried in a pan with eggs and butter and eaten with toast and tea or coffee.

After the church service in the morning, lunch is prepared. In the heat some prefer a cold meal but it's surprising how many enjoy a

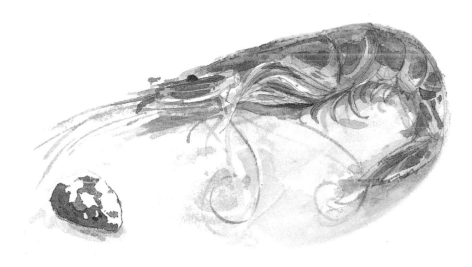

hot cooked Christmas lunch. Some families prepare a barbecue, while others save their Christmas meal for the cool of evening.

According to Vogue Australia's *Wine and Food Cookbook*, a national cuisine is evolving that takes the best of everything—European, Asian and American—and takes it a little further, to suit Australians, their way of life and their climate. This evolving cuisine is greatly helped by the

abundance of natural ingredients. Australians eat well and traces of the multicultural background are to be found in the daily cooking of most families who have lived there for more than one generation.

Australia's shellfish can be put to good use to make a delicious starter. Prawns stir-fried with spring onions and thin slices of Chinese red ginger, then flamed with gin, make a spectacular dish. Those who wish to have part of the meal pre-prepared might make a rich crab mousse, decorated with caviare and sprays of fresh thyme. Dainty sandwiches of wholemeal bread with a filling of herbs go well with a crab mousse.

Meat for the main course varies from roast turkey, pork, ham, beef, duck, quail or chicken to kangaroo, the latter being the choice of members of the Warrabri tribe. It's purely a matter of choice and individual family tradition. In the days of the first European settlers, stuffed mutton often took the place of the roast goose of their homeland. Today, 'colonial goose' may still scent the Christmas morning kitchen, though nowadays it is more likely to be a succulent leg of lamb stuffed with kidneys and herbs, as lambs aren't as precious now as they were then. In with the roasting meat go pieces of pumpkin and par-boiled potatoes and parsnips—delicious accompaniments with no fuss for the cook.

Some prefer to have a selection of salads—potato, bean, Waldorf, macaroni, or green—with their meat, while others like hot vegetables such as cauliflower, carrots, green beans, peas or greens. Because it's summertime, the choice is wide. Tiny pickling onions candied in the oven with sugar, cinnamon and red wine, or crisp heads of lettuce heated quickly in butter are recipes well worth trying.

Other people prefer barbecued meat or fish or a simple picnic. A more elaborate Australian idea, suitable for a large family party, is cold stuffed turkey with pickled pears. Easy to prepare the day before, this is best served with hot crusty bread and salads. You might like to make salad baskets with Greek *kataifi* pastry and fill them with dressed fruit and vegetables.

A traditional flaming Christmas pudding complete with charms or old coins inside and served with custard, cream or brandy butter is popular with many. In the days of the gold rush in Queensland in the 1860s, people even baked their Christmas puddings complete with gold nuggets in the middle! Some prefer a lighter, cold dessert. Christmas pudding ice-cream, flavoured with rum and chestnuts, is wickedly rich, and brown bread ice-cream is enjoyed by most, young and old. By such clever devices the Christmas feast, like the festival itself, adapts the customs of the old countries to a new world.

In their food and their festivities, Australians draw together traditions from the many lands from which they have come. In proclaiming the Christmas message they link the good news of Jesus' birth with their new homeland.

AN AUSTRALIAN CHRISTMAS LUNCH

A hot lunch
FLAMING GINGERED PRAWNS

~

'COLONIAL GOOSE' *Stuffed lamb*
ROAST PUMPKIN, POTATO AND PARSNIPS
HOT LETTUCE
CANDIED ONIONS

~

BROWN BREAD ICE-CREAM

or

CHRISTMAS PUDDING ICE-CREAM

A cold lunch
CRAB MOUSSE AND CAVIARE
HERBY WHOLEMEAL SANDWICHES

~

STUFFED TURKEY
PICKLED PEARS
KATAIFI SALAD BASKETS WITH
HONEY-LIME DRESSING

~

RASPBERRIES OR STRAWBERRIES WITH
CREAM

Flaming gingered prawns

King prawns are made especially delicious for Christmas by cooking them with ginger and spring onions. This light starter can be flamed at the table for a dramatic start to your festive meal.

prawns (or shrimp) (preferably medium-sized king prawns)	575g	1lb 4oz	1lb 4oz
butter	50g	2oz	1/2 stick
spring (or green) onions, finely sliced	4	4	4
Chinese root ginger, finely chopped (Chinese red ginger, if available, from oriental food shops)	10ml	2tsp	2tsp
salt and pepper to taste			
gin	100ml	4fl oz	1/2 cup

Peel and clean prawns, then wash in cold water, drain and dry. Melt the butter in a large frying pan then add the spring onions. Gently fry, stirring, for half a minute. Add the prawns and ginger and fry for a few minutes until the prawns are cooked. The time will depend on the size of the prawns. Season to taste. Flame by pouring the gin over the prawns and putting a match to the vapours from the pan. This can be done at the table if you like.

'Colonial goose'
STUFFED LAMB

Unable to cook a Christmas goose, early Australian settlers chose a more than adequate substitute—fragrant stuffed boned roast mutton—stuffed lamb is even better.

Pumpkin, parboiled potatoes and parsnips can be roasted in the fat around the lamb to add to the treat.

leg of lamb with bone	2.5kg	5lb	5lb
butter	75g	3oz	3/4 stick
medium onion, finely chopped	1	1	1
lamb's kidneys	2	2	2
fresh white breadcrumbs	100g	4oz	1/2 cup
fresh rosemary, chopped OR	10ml	2tsp	2tsp
dried rosemary	5ml	1tsp	1tsp
fresh sage, chopped OR	10ml	2tsp	2tsp
dried sage	5ml	1tsp	1tsp
fresh parsley, chopped	30ml	2tbs	2tbs
salt and pepper to taste			

Ask your butcher to bone the leg of lamb, and to save the bone for you.

Melt the butter in a large pan and gently cook the onion until translucent. Skin, core and chop the kidneys. Add to the pan and cook, stirring, until lightly browned. Remove from the heat and add the breadcrumbs, herbs and seasoning. Mix well and use to stuff the leg of lamb. Tie the leg into a neat shape with string at intervals. Put on a rack in a roasting pan and cook in a pre-heated oven at 180°C (350°F/Gas 4) for up to 2 1/2 hours, for well done lamb, basting occasionally with the pan juices. Cover with foil and allow to rest in a warm oven for 20 minutes before removing the string and carving.

Boil the lamb bone in water for half an hour and use this stock when making the gravy.

Hot lettuce

Perhaps you've never thought of cooking lettuce but it does make a delicious hot vegetable.

butter	125g	4oz	1 stick
lettuce, large, tight heads, coarsely shredded	2	2	2
salt and pepper to taste			

Melt the butter and add the lettuce and seasoning. Toss for 3–4 minutes until the lettuce is hot. Serve immediately.

Candied onions

These sweet, cinnamon-flavoured onions cooked in red wine are a mile away from plain boiled onions and are easy to prepare at any time of year, let alone for a Christmas treat. Peel the onions the day before and store in an air-tight container in the fridge.

pickling onions	450g	1lb	1lb
cooking oil	15ml	1tbs	1tbs
brown sugar	100g	4oz	1/2 cup
red wine	225ml	8fl oz	1 cup
cinnamon stick	1	1	1
butter	15ml	1tbs	1tbs

Heat the oil in a frying pan and add the onions. Toss the onions in the oil for about 7 minutes, until lightly browned. Remove from the heat and add the sugar, wine, cinnamon stick and butter. Stir well and pour into a casserole dish. Place, uncovered, into a pre-heated oven at 180°C (350°F/Gas 4) for 40 minutes.

Brown bread ice-cream

If you've never had this ice-cream before, you're in for a treat because it's unusually delicious. Brown bread is actually not as good as proper wholemeal bread, which gives a lovely nutty taste.

wholemeal breadcrumbs (or brown)	75g	3oz	1/3 cup
soft brown sugar	75g	3oz	1/3 cup
milk	300ml	1/2 pint	1 cup
egg	1	1	1
egg yolk	1	1	1
caster sugar (US: granulated)	25g	1oz	2tbs
double cream (US: whipping)	150ml	1/4 pint	1/2 cup
brandy or rum	15ml	1tbs	1tbs

Mix the breadcrumbs and soft brown sugar together and spread out evenly on a baking tray. Cook at 190°C (375°F/Gas 5) for about 5 minutes. Remove from the oven and stir, then cook for a further 5 minutes or until lightly and evenly coloured. Watch carefully to avoid burning. Leave to stand at room temperature and when cool crumble the caramelised breadcrumbs with your fingers.

Make a custard with the milk, egg, egg yolk and caster sugar as follows. Warm the milk to almost boiling. Whisk the egg, egg yolk and sugar in a bowl and pour the warm milk into the mixture, stirring as you do so. Put the mixture into the top of a double pan and heat over boiling water, stirring until the custard thickens. Remove from the heat and cool. Add the cream and brandy or rum, and stir well. Put into a shallow tray and freeze until half-frozen. Remove from the freezer and stir in the breadcrumbs. Return to the freezer until firm.

Christmas pudding ice-cream

This rich, fruity ice-cream is flavoured with chocolate and chestnut and is the perfect substitute for Christmas pudding on a hot day.

Any combination of the following: sultanas (golden raisins), raisins, currants, glacé orange and lemon peel, glacé cherries, angelica, marrons glacés, glacé pineapple	175g	6oz	³/₄ cup
dark rum or brandy	60ml	4tbs	4tbs
egg yolks	5	5	5
caster sugar (US: granulated)	150g	5oz	²/₃ cup
single cream (US: light)	300ml	¹/₂ pint	1¹/₄ cups
canned chestnut purée	100g	4oz	¹/₂ cup
plain chocolate, (or baking chocolate) broken into small pieces	100g	4oz	¹/₂ cup
double cream (US: whipping)	300ml	¹/₂ pint	1¹/₄ cups
double cream, (US: whipping), for piping	50ml	2fl oz	¹/₄ cup
sprig of holly to decorate			

Chop the dried and glacé (candied) fruit. Put the fruit in a bowl and pour the rum or brandy over it. Put the egg yolks and sugar into a separate bowl and whisk well. Heat the single cream to nearly boiling point. Pour it over the yolks and sugar mixture. Stir well and return to the pan. Heat gently until the custard thickens, but do not boil. Remove from the heat. Add the chestnut purée and chocolate and stir until dissolved, returning to the heat if necessary. Allow to cool. Whip the double cream and add this and the soaked fruit to the cooled custard. Mix well. Put the mixture into a shallow container and freeze until half-frozen. Remove from the freezer and stir well. Line a pudding basin (or gelatine mould) with foil and add the half-frozen mixture. (The foil makes it easier to turn the frozen ice-cream out when ready to serve.) Replace in the freezer. Allow the ice-cream to thaw for about an hour in the fridge before you want to eat it.

Whip the remaining cream and use it to pipe rosettes around the base of the 'pudding'. Bring the ice-cream to the table with a sprig of holly stuck in the top.

Crab mousse and caviare

An exotic dish for a special occasion, unless you are lucky enough to live in an area where crabs are plentiful and cheap. Serve this mousse with caviare sprinkled on top and with herby wholemeal sandwiches handed separately.

mayonnaise	300ml	¹/₂ pint	1¹/₄ cups
single (half and half) or whipping cream	300ml	¹/₂ pint	1 cup
fresh thyme OR	10ml	2tsp	2tsp
dried thyme	5ml	1tsp	1tsp
pinch of salt			
pinch of cayenne pepper			
crab meat, flaked	450g	1lb	1lb
gelatine	10ml	2tsp	2tsp
cold water	15ml	1tbs	1tbs
black caviare or lumpfish roe	50g	2oz	¹/₄ cup
sprays of fresh thyme			

In a large bowl whisk together the mayonnaise, cream, thyme, salt and cayenne pepper. Fold in the flaked crab gently. Soak the gelatine in the cold water in a cup until soft, then place the cup in a pan containing a little hot water and heat gently until the gelatine has dissolved.

Add the gelatine to the crab mixture and mix well. Pour into a mould or serving dish and chill. When set, loosen the mousse by running hot water over the outside of the mould and turn out on to a serving dish. Decorate with caviare and sprays of thyme.

Herby wholemeal sandwiches

These dainty herb-flavoured sandwiches go well with the rich crab mousse.

fresh wholemeal bread, thin slices, per person	2	2	2
butter			
Marmite or Vegemite			
parsley, chives, tarragon, or other fresh herbs to taste			
lettuce			

Soften the butter and carefully spread it over the slices of bread, taking care not to break the bread. Add a very thin layer of Marmite or Vegemite to half the slices. Wash the herbs and strip off the leaves, then chop roughly. Sprinkle the herbs over the Marmite or Vegemite-coated slices of bread, then cover with the other slices. Remove the crusts with a sharp knife and cut each sandwich in half. Cut each half into three strips and arrange on a bed of lettuce on a plate.

Stuffed turkey

This can be eaten hot or cold. Both pear, celery and pistachio nut stuffing and pickled pears complement the rich flavour of turkey perfectly and can be made days in advance. Don't forget to arrange for your butcher to bone the bird for you. You may like to stuff the boned bird well in advance of Christmas and store it in the freezer, but only do this if the bird had never been frozen before you stuffed it. Cook the bird the day before you eat it, so it can chill overnight.

turkey, boned (and opened down its back)	1	1	1
salt and pepper to taste			
pear, celery and pistachio nut stuffing (see recipe below)			
butter, melted	175g	6oz	1 1/2 sticks

Spread out the boned turkey on a clean surface, skin side down. Sprinkle with salt and pepper. Pile the stuffing (see below) in a sausage shape down the middle of the flattened bird. Fold each side of the turkey over the stuffing and secure with skewers. Fold up each end of the bird and secure with skewers. Shape the stuffed bird into a roll.

Pre-heat the oven to $200°$ C ($400°$ F/Gas 6). Stand the turkey on a rack in a roasting tin (or pan). Pour the melted butter over the turkey. Cover loosely with foil and cook for 30 minutes. Baste from time to time with the butter and drippings. Lower the oven temperature to $180°$ C ($350°$ F/Gas 4) and cook for a total of 15–20 minutes per $1/2$ kg (1lb).

Pear, celery and pistachio nut stuffing

butter	75g	3oz	3/4 stick
onion, finely chopped	300g	11oz	1 1/3 cups
oranges	3	3	3
fresh white breadcrumbs	350g	12oz	1 1/2 cups
dried pears, cut into fine strips	450g	1lb	1lb
celery, chopped	175g	6oz	2/3 cup
pistachio nuts shelled and halved	100g	4oz	1/2 cup
eggs, beaten	2	2	2
seasoning to taste			

Melt the butter in a frying pan and fry the onions until translucent. Meanwhile pare the oranges, taking care not to include any of the white pith in the peelings. Cut into fine strips. Place the onions in a large bowl with the breadcrumbs, pears, celery, pistachio nuts, orange peel, eggs and seasoning, and mix well.

Pickled pears

dried pear halves	350g	12oz	1 1/2 cups
white wine vinegar	100ml	4fl oz	1/2 cup
sugar	150g	5oz	3/4 cup
salt	2ml	1/2 tsp	1/2 tsp
cinnamon stick	1	1	1
cloves	4	4	4
oranges	3	3	3
peeled fresh ginger, cut into tiny strips	10ml	2tsp	2tsp

Soak the pears in water for one hour. Place the vinegar, sugar, salt, cinnamon stick and cloves in a large pan and bring to the boil. Boil for 3 minutes. With a sharp knife pare the peel from the oranges, taking care not to include any of the white pith in the peelings. Cut into fine strips. Add the drained pears, ginger and orange peel to the pan and simmer until most of the liquid is absorbed by the pears. Remove the cinnamon stick. Store in a covered jar.

Kataifi salad baskets with honey-lime dressing

The many Greek immigrants to Australia, and particularly to Melbourne, brought *kataifi* pastry to Australian cooking. You can buy *kataifi* pasty ready-made in Greek grocery shops and it doesn't take long to shape little baskets and bake them. The cooked baskets look unusually festive on the table and can carry any combination of fruit and vegetables you like. The quantity given is for one basket, enough for one person.

Basket

kataifi pastry	25g	1oz	2tbs
melted butter	20g	3/4 oz	1tbs

Filling

Any combination of 3–4 fruits and vegetables chosen for colour, texture and flavour from the following: papaya, melon, tomato, apple, avocado, Jerusalem artichoke, grapefruit, orange, pineapple, cucumber, cauliflower florets, mango

Honey-lime dressing

honey	5ml	1tsp	1tsp
lime juice OR orange and lemon juice, mixed	10ml	2tsp	2tsp
olive oil	10ml	2tsp	2tsp

Sprinkle the pastry with melted butter and shape into a basket. Place on a greased baking tray and bake in a pre-heated oven at 180°C (350°F/Gas 4) for about 15 minutes or until a pale golden colour. Cool.

Prepare the fruit and vegetable mixture by peeling as necessary and cutting into slices, chunks or matchsticks small enough to fit into the basket. Cut each fruit or vegetable into differently shaped pieces.

Prepare the dressing by putting the honey, juice and oil into a bowl and whisking with a fork until the oil is emulsified.

Pour the dressing over the fruit and vegetables in a bowl and stir gently. Arrange the fruit and vegetables in the basket just before serving.

PAPUA NEW GUINEA

Papua New Guinea

is part of a large tropical island in the sun. At Christmas time the coconut palms sway gently in the breeze, heralding the imminent monsoon season.

This island off the northern coast of Australia has been called 'the last unknown'. Although cities are developing fast, much of the island is unspoilt. It is divided into two halves: Indonesian Irian Jaya on the left and Papua New Guinea on the right. About 700 languages are spoken, so the people in one village may not necessarily understand their neighbours. Pidgin (a charming language combining some English and German) and English are both used as a *lingua franca*.

The people of Papua New Guinea have been exposed to Christianity by missionaries. The island was roughly split by the government into London Missionary Society (now United Churches), Anglican, Roman Catholic and Lutheran areas. Today the church plays an important part in village life, as a large number of the people have become Christians. Many islanders combine Christianity with ancestor and spirit worship, in the same way that Norse and Roman paganism still linger in Europe.

In the coastal villages, there is remarkably little commercialization, even at Christmas. There is no long build-up to the festival, in spite of the coming of radio. On Christmas Eve the children decorate the church in preparation for the great day ahead. Palm leaves are made into archways at the church door, down the centre aisle and around the altar. There are no pews as such but plenty of logs on the sand floor to sit on. The children thread flowers in and out of the latticework of plaited brown coconut leaves which make up the walls. Over the last few days they have laid banana leaves out to dry in the sun until they go white and now these leaves are shredded, tied with flowers and hung in fringes at the window to waft in the breeze.

Fragrant frangipani is a flower they use a lot because its waxy white, yellow or pink flowers last well even without water. Red hibiscus is picked in bud and put round the altar in the late afternoon. By the next morning—Christmas morning—the buds will have burst open, only to last for that one special day before wilting.

Once the church is finished the children turn their attention to the village, for everything must look as lovely as possible for the celebration of Jesus' birthday. Frangipani flowers are strung into garlands with thread or string made by rubbing vines, and then hung around the lower branches of the trees around the houses. Similar garlands are worn as *leis* around the villagers' necks as they feast and dance the next day.

The houses need little decoration as they are highly decorated already with intricate traditional designs woven with sago or coconut palm leaves into their outer walls of plaited bamboo. Sometimes these leaf patterns are emphasized with coloured paints. Standing on stilts, the houses are extremely practical for the tropical conditions in which they were built.

The women leave the village at dawn to collect vegetables from their gardens, which may be some distance away. As the sun rises higher in the sky, flocks of brightly coloured parrots and cockatoos fly from the trees and call to them. Sweet potato is a favourite vegetable, as is pumpkin. *Taro* is a highly prized starchy root vegetable of the arum family. It has greyish flesh and is often cooked for a special occasion as a treat. The women get home around nine o'clock before the day becomes too hot, and the vegetables are stored under their houses until the next day.

While the children are titivating the village and the women are collecting vegetables, the men are out fishing. They are especially keen to have a good catch for the feast to come, so they are more than usually attentive to the signs of fish in the water. Fishing is mostly done from the coral reefs with spears, lines, or nets and is a very skilful business as fish are not as abundant as one might suppose: the hot tropical waters provide little plankton on which to feed. Sometimes they are lucky and catch large fish such as barramundi. At other times they have to make do with smaller varieties. The younger boys may help by collecting oysters from the mangrove swamps, or mud crabs, rock lobsters, freshwater whitebait and prawns from the streams. If they go out to the reef they may catch octopus and collect clams. Octopus must be beaten hard to make it tender and it must have its ink sac removed. It is a popular food, as is squid.

Fish is the usual dish at Christmas time: pork is more often reserved for other celebrations such as weddings, though some villages kill and cook a pig at Christmas. In some areas the village may organize an inland hunt to find a cassowary which, although tough, makes a good soup. The fine, silky feathers are highly prized, and so are the eggs.

When the day grows cooler, the children collect various green leaves which they put into water ready to be cooked for the feast the next day.

At midnight, everyone goes to a church service. At the same time on Christmas evening as people in cooler climes are wrapping themselves up in warm coats, hats and boots for their chilly expedition, the village folk in Papua New Guinea are filling their church. It is warm in the balmy night, there is sand between their toes and the fragrant smell of frangipani lingers in the air.

The temperature at night is never less than 25° C (77° F) and usually about 30–32° C (86–90° F).

In the church there is a small nativity scene with a plastic or home-made doll representing the Christ child. If there is no priest, a village elder reads the evening service.

After church everyone goes back to their houses to sleep on mats made of woven *pandanus* leaves. The children sleep easily at night—the babies and toddlers nestling against their mothers' breasts and having a sleepy nuzzle for milk from time to time, and the older ones cuddled up together like puppies, with no need to be afraid of the dark. Men and women in some clans sleep in separate houses, the men with the older boys and the women with the girls and children, but customs vary as much as the languages.

Dawn comes suddenly in the tropics and people rise with excitement on Christmas morning. Breakfast may be some cold cooked yam or sweet potato from the previous evening's meal. Housework comes next, for all must look good for the dancing later. The women shake out the sleeping mats and put the clay cooking pots neatly away on shelves. They straighten the grass skirts hanging on the walls and sweep the floors and the ground around the house with a broom made of midribs or 'bones' of coconut leaves. Later, families return to the decorated church for a Christmas morning service.

Lunch is a simple affair—just a green coconut collected by boys who climb up the palm trees to knock them down. Little pieces of coconut 'meat' keep children's hunger pangs at bay. The daytime is spent preparing food for the evening feasting. After midday the women go to the creek or spring to fill their coconut bottles or clay pots with water and to wash and peel their vegetables. Some of the knives they use are made from sharpened, polished blacklip pearl shells, while others are bought from the trade store. The prepared vegetables are carried back to the village on lovely wooden platters or, nowadays, on bold enamel dishes from Hong Kong.

As important as the food is personal adornment and decoration. The men wear loin clothes made out of cloth from the bark of the tapu tree. They may have feather head-dresses and the feathers from the bird of paradise are most valued. The women wear grass skirts—sometimes more than one. These skirts are lovingly cared for because of the hours of work involved in making each one from coconut leaf veins or dried banana leaves. Blue dye from carbon paper spirited to the village from the city offices and purple and dark red vegetable dyes transform the skirts with bands of rainbow colour. Hair is teased and coaxed into elaborate styles according to the local custom and it may be bleached in patches. Feathers stuck in the hair are from the cockatoo or cassowary. Cassowary feathers have long bluish-black, iridescent fronds and the women often carry them in their hands and wave them in rhythm to the dancing later in the evening.

Coconut oil scented with the crushed leaves of an aromatic scrub plant makes hair and bodies gleam. Faces are painted in amazing and often fearsome patterns with white clay, black charcoal and red and yellow plant dyes. Some make-up is bought from Chinese stores in the towns. Shell and seed beads threaded into long strands are worn round necks and arms, and sweet-smelling herbs collected from the scrub are stuck inside the bracelets. Later, as people dance, the heat of their bodies releases an evocative, chamomile-like scent from these herbs.

Amidst all this activity the feast is cooked.

All village feasts are communal—one lot of food is prepared and shared out when cooked. The fish and vegetables are cooked in a pit (an earth oven or *mumu*) or in cooking pots over a fire. For large fish such as they hope to catch at Christmas, pit cooking is more appropriate. The villagers fill a large pit with flat round stones then light a fire on top of them. When the stones are sizzling hot, the villagers rake out the fire and lay banana leaves across them. Next, they arrange the fish, vegetables and greens on top of the leaves, then pour coconut milk over them. Coconut milk isn't just the liquid in the middle of the coconut. It's made by scraping the coconut meat from the nut, soaking this in water, then squeezing it. The resulting sweet white liquid percolates through the food and tenderizes it as it cooks. Banana leaves are laid on top of the food, more hot stones are placed over them, then the pit is filled with earth. The heat from the stones gently steams the fish and vegetables soaked in coconut milk. The principle of pit cookery is similar to that of the hay box: the food is kept hot by superb insulation so that it can go on cooking slowly.

The starchy, greyish *taro* roots are cooked separately. First they are grated, then they are put into a clay pot with some water and root ginger and cooked over an open fire to make a soup. The pot is supported by three upright stones which retain so much heat themselves that only a few burning sticks are needed underneath. Another pot holds pit-pit—the creamy flower buds of a rush—which is cooked in a little water. Large orange or pink bananas are either roasted in their skins or cooked in a clay pot.

Sunset comes as quickly as did dawn and suddenly all is dark. Now is the time for the anopheles mosquitos to descend, but the smoke and heat of the little flickering 'smudge' fires dotted around keep most at bay. Plaited coconut leaf mats are laid out for people to sit on and banana leaves are put in front of each family ready for the food. When the food is ready, it's shared out by the men and the feasting begins, illuminated perhaps by a hurricane lamp or two as well as the firelight. The food seems bland to a person unused to it, because it contains little salt or spice. People eat the feast with their fingers or with bamboo spoons. There is an abundance of fresh fruit to finish off with. Mangoes ripen at Christmas time and are much enjoyed, together with pineapples, pawpaws and bananas.

The people take their pick from beer drunk from the bottle or coconut liquid drunk straight from a green 'drinking' coconut. Green coconut liquid is delicious—slightly fizzy, sweet and very refreshing. Cool drinking water from clay pots is drunk from thick bamboo containers.

Men, women and children enjoy chewing betel nuts when they've had enough to eat. These nuts grow on feather palm trees by the coast and are dipped into lime made by roasting coral, then stored in a sealed gourd. The villagers carry their lime and betel nut supplies in little bags called bilums, made from dyed vine string. Betel juice is tastier with lime added. It is notorious for staining teeth brown and saliva red. Betel nuts contain a stimulant (and addic-

tive) drug which aids digestion and kills intestinal worms as a bonus.

The feasting is leisurely—there's no need to hurry. Children can snooze or stay wide awake but are never sent to bed. They sing carols translated into their own language and learnt at mission school. Gradually the pace of the music hots up and the little kundu drums join in to make the rhythm stronger. Dancing begins and may continue all night. The men are the main performers, dancing well-known steps peculiar to their clan over and over again to the beat of the drums under the starlit sky. Women and children dance a little but only at the periphery, waving their feathers in the air as they move to the beat.

Gradually the children drop off to sleep, unable to keep their eyes open any more and lulled by the music. Only when the last people have danced enough do the drums cease. The little ones are carried inside and a few hours of sleep are snatched at the end of another Christmas.

The customs may seem strange to the visitor, accustomed to the trappings of a westernized Christmas. But in its refreshing simplicity the message of the angels is particularly clear: 'I am here with good news for you, which will bring great joy to all the people.' The Christmas message is for all the world.

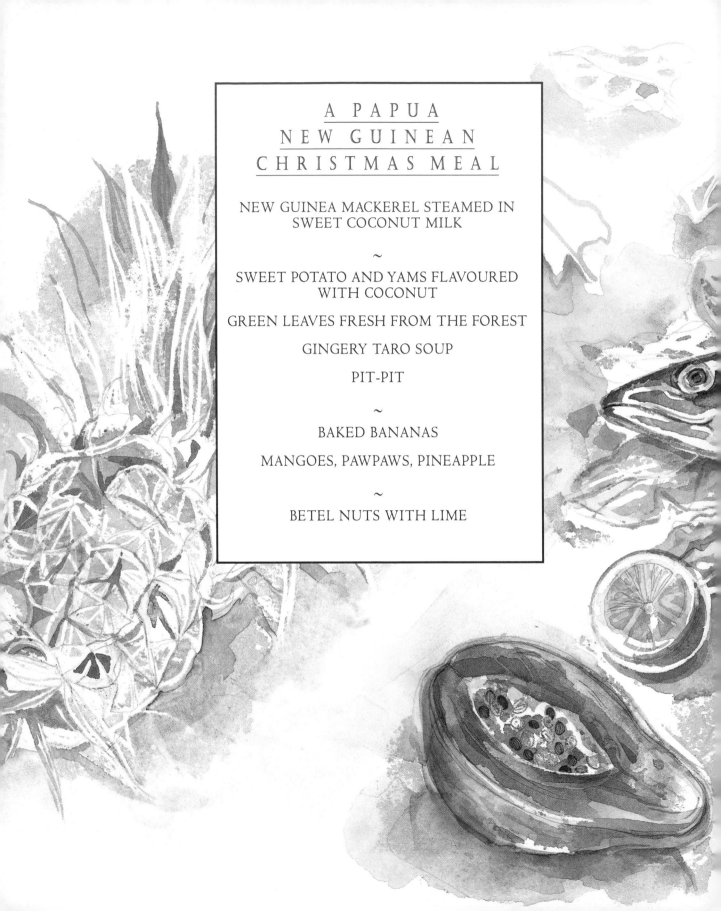

A PAPUA NEW GUINEAN CHRISTMAS MEAL

NEW GUINEA MACKEREL STEAMED IN
SWEET COCONUT MILK

~

SWEET POTATO AND YAMS FLAVOURED
WITH COCONUT

GREEN LEAVES FRESH FROM THE FOREST

GINGERY TARO SOUP

PIT-PIT

~

BAKED BANANAS

MANGOES, PAWPAWS, PINEAPPLE

~

BETEL NUTS WITH LIME

New Guinea mackerel steamed in sweet coconut milk

Mackerel steamed in sweet coconut milk over succulent orange sweet potatoes makes a dish fit for a king. The sweet potatoes soak up the flavour of the coconut and ginger and provide an unexpectedly delicious treat for Christmas Day.

sweet potato or yam (or both)	1kg	2lb	2lb
green cabbage or spinach leaves	100g	4oz	4oz
mackerel	675g	1 1/2 lb	1 1/2 lb
root ginger, grated OR dried ginger	25g / 5ml	1oz / 1tsp	1oz / 1tsp
water	300ml	1/2 pint	1 1/4 cups
coconut	1	1	1

Peel and slice the sweet potato into 12 mm (1/2 in.) slices. Lay these in a heavy casserole and place the washed leaves on top. Gut the mackerel and leave it whole if your casserole dish is large enough, otherwise cut it into as few pieces as possible. Put the fish on to the leaves. Sprinkle the grated ginger over the fish.

Bore 2 holes through the coconut eyes and pour the liquid into a bowl. Put the coconut into a hot oven for 10–15 minutes. Break open the coconut with a hammer. Carefully remove the meat and cut the brown skin away. Either mince or grate the coconut meat or put it in the blender. Add the minced coconut to the coconut liquid and mix. With clean hands, squeeze the milky fluid from the meat, a handful at a time.

Pour the coconut milk plus the water over the mackerel. Bring the contents of the casserole to boiling point then cover tightly and transfer to the oven. Bake at 180°C (350°F/Gas 4) for at least an hour, till all the liquid has been absorbed and the sweet potato is tender, adding a little more water if necessary to prevent burning. Serve the mackerel with the pieces shaped into a whole fish and surrounded with the vegetables attractively laid out.

Gingery taro soup

The swollen brownish underground stems of the *taro* plant are usually called roots. In West Africa they are also known as *cocoyams*. Other names used in foreign marketplaces are *dasheen*, *eddo*, and *Chinese eddo*. If you can't get *taro* use ordinary yams instead. Starchy roots such as yams are a staple food on Pacific islands such as Papua New Guinea. *Taro* is rather more highly prized than yam, which is why it is eaten at feasts.

taro, peeled and grated	1 kg	2 lb	2 lb
root ginger, peeled and grated	25 g	1 oz	2 tbs
water to cover			

Put the grated *taro* and root ginger into a large saucepan and cover with water. Bring to the boil, cover the pan, and cook for about 25 minutes or until tender. You can serve this soup as it is, seasoned to taste, or you might like to blend it for a smoother consistency.

JAPAN

Based on a Japanese lacquer document box - late 14ᵗʰ.

Japan consists of four main islands and many smaller ones. This island location has enabled the people to keep a strong cultural identity. While happy to import foreign beliefs, practices, ideas and foods, the Japanese assimilate them only slowly into their culture and in so doing change— or japanize—them subtly.

The original religion in Japan was Shintoism (or *Kami-no-michi*—the way of the gods). Buddhism was introduced in AD587, and was harmoniously taken on board by the Japanese. Today many are both Shintoists and Buddhists and see no conflict in having a dual religion.

Christianity came to Japan relatively recently—in 1594, to be exact, when it was introduced by a Portuguese Jesuit, St Francis Xavier. However, the ruler Hideyoshi and his successors the Tokugawa Shoguns cruelly stamped out the new religion and closed Japan to the outside world for two centuries. Every Japanese person was required to register as a Buddhist and people were forced to stamp on plaques bearing the Christian symbols of Mary and Jesus. Only in 1873 did the government finally allow freedom of religion.

Christian missionaries flocked to Japan as soon as they were allowed but the growth of Christianity there has remained slow. Less than one per cent of the Japanese are nominal Christians today and far fewer than this are 'committed' Christians, so Christmas is an important spiritual event to only a tiny minority of people. However, throughout the country large numbers enjoy the commercial trappings of Christmas which have been imported from the West and superficially it looks as though Christmas has really caught on. Customs vary from place to place, and especially from town to village. More changes are constantly taking place.

The Christmas period coincides with preparations for the celebration of the New Year: the *osoji* or big clean-up, the card-sending and the cooking. New Year is a very important festival with a Shinto emphasis and is celebrated by almost all the Japanese, with a two-day holiday.

Christmas in Japan seems more like a commercial carnival than a religious occasion. In early December the shops are decorated with tinsel and garlands as in any Western city. In the department stores Father Christmases dole out presents to queues of children against a background of Christmas music ranging from 'Silent Night' to 'Jingle Bells' over the loudspeakers. A large spruce tree may decorate the store's main lobby and Christmas cards and gifts are on sale.

The Japanese have for a long time exchanged presents at this time of year: they call it giving *oseibo*. This is an old tradition which originally had nothing to do with Christmas but has been incorporated with the commercial celebration. Hoteiosho, one of their gods, acts as Father Christmas.

Holly and mistletoe are familiar to many now and some homes are decorated with a Christmas tree, though real ones are rarely seen except in public places. Plastic or tinsel trees are numerous, as are gaudy decorations. Somehow an artificial tree seems strangely out of place in a traditional Japanese home with its paper screens and elegant lack of furnishings. Even though many Japanese families now live in larger suburban houses or in city centres in concrete blocks of flats, and Western furnishings are becoming popular in many households, many houses still have at least one typically sparsely furnished *tatami* (woven rice-straw mat) room with a low table and no chairs.

Japanese flower arrangements (*ikebana*) are

famed. At Christmas time and around the New Year one of these beautiful and carefully arranged creations might contain the 'three friends of winter': pine (for long life), bamboo (for endurance and devotion to duty) and plum (for its courage in blossoming while the snow is still on its branches). Flowers used include chrysanthemums and camellias. White blossoms are chosen for their purity and red because this is the colour of celebration. Traditionally the arrangement is placed in the *tatami* room, in the *tokonoma*—a recess in the wall used for flower arrangements and scrolls.

On Christmas Eve it has become a national custom for fathers to take home a 'decoration cake'—a sponge cake with elaborate butter or cream icing—which is eaten that evening with the family.

It is in this frenetic lead-up to the New Year festival that Japanese Christians celebrate their own festival. The Christian message is spread by personal friendship. Handel's 'Messiah' is sung in many places. Mission schools are busy with nativity plays performed by children in national costume. Friends are invited to church services and special Christmas programmes and there may be a communal meal at church after the Christmas Eve service.

On Christmas Day in a Christian home the mother gets up early to prepare *miso* soup for breakfast and for the evening meal. This is a fish-based clear soup containing chopped-up vegetables, *tofu* (bean curd), or small clams, and flavoured with *miso*—a salty product made from fermented cooked soya beans which smells like very ripe cheese and has a strong taste like nothing else, though very pleasant. There is rice for breakfast with beaten raw egg and Japanese soy sauce (*shoyu*). Some people wrap their rice in a sheet of dried *nori* seaweed, which

quickly softens in contact with the moist rice. Other breakfast foods include pickled vegetables, omelette and grilled fish, and tea is the usual accompaniment. Some people nowadays choose a Western breakfast of toast and coffee but many still prefer traditional Japanese foods.

After breakfast the family may attend an early-morning church service, before the working day. There is no time allowed for festivities until the evening. Lunch is naturally kept very simple.

A family evening meal may consist of five separate dishes all served at once, though for a special occasion there could be more. Japanese food is quicker to cook than many Western foods, so this isn't as time-consuming as it sounds. The Japanese love variety and have an old saying, 'If you have the pleasant experience of eating something new, your life will be lengthened by seventy-five days.' There are many take-away or send-out shops in Japan and the send-out shops will deliver food and collect dirty dishes from the front doorstep later.

To eat its evening meal, the family kneels on large flat cushions (*sabuton*) in front of a low table. The evenings can be cold at Christmas time and the wooden houses rather draughty. In northern Japan there is snow from October right through to April or May. In many homes there is no central heating and the only heating is from an electric heater (*kotatsu*) under the top of the table. Sometimes there is a heater below floor level under the table. An eiderdown quilt (*kotatsu futon*) is draped over the table and the family sits or kneels with its feet in the warm under the quilt to eat.

Chopsticks (*hashi*) are used to eat most foods, though *chawan mushi* (savoury egg custard), for instance, is eaten with a china spoon. The foods are served in small decorated bowls. Most families have a variety of china or lacquer bowls and they choose them according to the season or the colours and shapes of the food.

The Japanese like their food to be a visual treat and appreciate complementary or contrasting colours. Their food is always attractively presented in small portions and the individual foods are usually apparent rather than being mixed together. The aim is to alter the food as little as possible from its natural state so that its quality and flavour are fully appreciated. For a festive occasion such as Christmas, food may be presented in the shape of an animal or a flower—for example, carrots may be cut to resemble plum blossom—and a fresh, edible flower may adorn each bowl.

Their Buddhist and Shinto backgrounds influence the eating habits of the Japanese and give them respect for their oneness with nature and for the sacredness of the food they prepare and eat. This is evident from the 'grace' they say before eating: 'Itadakimasu', which means roughly, 'I shall receive this food.' To the Japanese, 'you are what you eat' and food is considered best when kept as raw as possible. Foods reflect the changing seasons and the garnishes always include some reference to the season too.

The basic Japanese diet, unchanged for centuries, consists of rice, fish and vegetables. As Japan is a series of islands, fish, shellfish and seaweed are always readily available. Over recent years more meat and dairy produce has been creeping into the diet but meat, and particularly beef, is expensive because of the scarcity of suitable pasture ground for the cattle in such a mountainous country. For this reason, beef might well be chosen for the special Christmas meal, as may sea bass (suzuki) or tuna, both delicious and highly prized fish. The Japanese know their different cuts of fish just as Westerners distinguish between different cuts of meat. The choicest parts of a fish would be bought for special occasions. The fat part of a tuna (mauro) known as toro takes pride of place over the leaner red flesh, and resembles meat when cooked. The firm, oily meat from the belly of the bonito is considered a special delicacy.

For a meal on Christmas Day, bowls of cashew nuts, delicious deep-fried seaweed tangle (popular with children and made of very finely sliced cabbage) dried fish or crunchy ginkgo nuts may be served before the cooked part of the meal is placed on the table. Ginkgo nuts are small, green and decorative and they have the consistency of chestnuts. They are boiled first, then fried to give them a crunchy texture.

Oysters are a particularly good winter delicacy, as are red salmon eggs (ikura). Tempura consists of pieces of at least six different kinds of fish and vegetables dipped into a light batter (koromo) and fried. The cooked foods are served immediately and each person dips theirs into a bowl of savoury sauce. Tempura is a famous Japanese dish and is said to have been imported by the Portuguese traders centuries ago. The Portuguese, as good Catholics, rejected meat on Ember Days, which they called by the Latin name of Quattuor Tempora, the 'four times' of the year. They asked for fried seafood instead, and so this became known as tempura.

Beef is served in the equally well-known if somewhat modern dish sukiyaki, which means 'grilled on the blade of a plough' as this is how hunters used to cook their meat over an open fire in the field. Sukiyaki today isn't grilled but simmered in a heavy pan.

Japanese buckwheat noodles (soba) or wheat noodles (udon) are among the most popular foods and would certainly be part of the meal, as would rice. Noodles are dipped into soy sauce, or into a broth containing spring onions. The name for rice, *gohan*, means 'meal', and it is the staple food of Japan. Most people have rice two or three times a day and it can be served separately or sometimes combined with raw fish as *sushi*, in which case it is mixed with vinegar.

Extra-special *sushi* can be ordered in from a *sushi* shop, when the pieces of raw fish (*sashimi*) on top of tiny cakes of vinegared rice appear in exquisitely colourful and artistic forms arranged beautifully on a large platter. *Maki sushi* are sliced sushi rolls made by putting a piece of raw fish, such as red tuna fish or sea bass (*suzuki*) or green cucumber inside some vinegared rice, then wrapping this in a small sheet of *nori* seaweed and slicing across the roll. *Sushi* are eaten with soy sauce, Japanese horseradish (*wasabi*) and thin slices of *gari* (ginger pickled in vinegar), which is a lovely pink colour.

Sashimi—raw fish—is an unexpectedly delicious treat. Besides the popular tuna, flounder, bonito, shrimp, abalone, squid, eel, salmon, cuttlefish, sole and sea bream are eaten raw, as is blow-fish (*fugu*), a delicacy which in its original state contains a poison safest removed by an expert. This is why it is usually only eaten when prepared by a licensed *fugu* chef.

There is a salad on the table, such as one of spinach and sesame seeds garnished with dried *bonito* shavings, and there might be some *chawan mushi*, hot savoury egg custard popular with children and made from eggs, chicken, prawns or shrimps, mushrooms, fish-cake, fish or chicken stock and celery or other greenstuff.

Throughout the meal there is *miso* soup to drink, kept hot in a lidded lacquered bowl. Green tea and perhaps *sake* (rice wine) or Japanese beer are popular drinks. *Sake* is said to be named after the city Osaka, the centre of *sake* production.

Desserts are not common at Japanese meals though nowadays city housewives are more likely to buy one, perhaps a cheesecake or some pretty pressed rice cakes covered with sweetened red bean paste and cut into the shape of snowflakes. Fruit is much appreciated and the Christmas meal is likely to be rounded off with satsumas or tangerines. Traditionally the satsuma represents the flame-coloured rising sun that will return in spring to warm the earth and its people. This human yearning for life and light to triumph over death and darkness reveals just how relevant the message of Christmas is to all people.

A JAPANESE
CHRISTMAS MEAL

CASHEW NUTS/PEANUTS/GINKGO NUTS/
DRIED FISH

~

MISO SOUP

~

IKURA IN NORI CONES
Salmon eggs in seaweed cones

~

TEMPURA TAUYU *Tempura with tempura sauce*

or

SUKIYAKI *Beef and vegetables in soy sauce and sake*

or

CHIRASHIZUSHI *Vinegared rice cakes with raw fish*

~

GOHAN *Rice*

~

UDON OR SOBA *Wheat or buckwheat noodles*

~

HORENSO NO HITASHI
Spinach and sesame seed salad

~

CHAWAN MUSHI *Savoury egg custard*

~

MIKAN *Satsumas or tangerines*

Miso soup

This fish, seaweed and fermented soya bean (*miso*) soup is a popular part of the traditional Japanese diet, both on the Christmas table and at all other times of the year. Many women make their own *miso* from cooked soya beans, rice or barley, and a starter mould to set off the process of fermentation. Salt stops it going bad. They store the mixture in a pottery jar with a wooden lid and leave it to ferment for up to 2 to 3 years. The finished *miso* is a brown paste with a consistency of blended split peas and smells of over-ripe cheese. At Christmas time *miso* soup is made using red *miso*, while in summer it would be made from white *miso*. If you can't easily get the seaweed called kelp (*kombu*), you can use one small leek instead. Aubergines (eggplants) and potatoes are often included in the soup.

piece of dried kombu (kelp) 5cm (2in.) square	1	1	1
water	1.2 litre	2 pints	5 cups
dried bonito fish shavings (katsuobushi)	10ml	2tsp	2tsp
red miso (red soya bean paste)	30ml	2tbs	2tbs
tofu (soya bean curd)	100g	4oz	1/2 cup

Decoration

carrot, sliced	1	1	1
white radish, sliced	10cm	4 in.	4 in.
spring onion, sliced	1	1	1

Soak the dried *kombu* for several hours or overnight. Drain it, put it into a large pan, add the water, bring to the boil, then remove and discard the piece of *kombu*. Add the bonito shavings and simmer for 3 minutes.

Remove from the heat and leave to stand for about 5 minutes, or until the shavings have sunk to the bottom. Pour this fish-and-seaweed flavoured stock into another large pan. Add 45ml (3tbs) of the stock to the *miso* paste in a small bowl, stir well, then add this creamed paste to the pan of stock to make the *miso* soup. Cut the *tofu* into small cubes and add to the *miso* soup. Heat through without boiling, and serve in small bowls.

Float some pieces of carrot, radish and spring onion on the soup in each bowl before serving.

Tempura tauyu

TEMPURA WITH TEMPURA SAUCE

This recipe serves four as a main dish. If you are making a full Japanese meal, make correspondingly less.

Tempura satisfy the Japanese love of beauty because the individual shapes of the foods are clearly visible through the thin crispy batter coating. Foods such as the lotus root look particularly attractive. The colours of the foods also show through faintly. It's no wonder that *tempura* have been adopted by the Japanese.

There are four parts to the preparation of *tempura* but it is not long-winded. First make the dipping sauce, then prepare the garnish and the foods for the *tempura*, and lastly make the batter to coat the foods, and deep-fry them.

Savoury dipping sauce

water	600ml	1 pint	2 1/2 cups
piece dried kelp (kombu)	1	1	1
dried bonito fish shavings (katsuobushi)	15g	1tbs	1tbs
sweet sake (mirin) or medium sherry	45ml	3tbs	3tbs
Japanese soy sauce (shoyu)	10ml	2tsp	2tsp

salt to taste

sugar to taste

A fish-and-seaweed flavoured stock, *dashi*, forms the basis for most Japanese soups and many other dishes. You can use stock cubes or powder to save time. Bring the water and kelp to the boil in a saucepan, then remove the kelp and add the bonito shavings. Leave to stand until the shavings settle at the bottom of the pan, then strain the liquid and return 450ml (3/4 pint) to the pan. Heat the sweet sake in a small saucepan until lukewarm. Remove from the heat and ignite the sake with a match, then shake the pan gently until the flames die away. Add the soy sauce, fish stock and salt and sugar (only a little) to taste. Bring to the boil, then allow to cool to room temperature.

Garnish for sauce

spring onion, finely chopped OR	15ml	1tbs	1tbs
fresh ginger root, grated	15ml	1tbs	1tbs
Japanese white radish or mooli (daikon), grated	90ml	6tbs	6tbs

This garnish is served separately so that each person can mix in as much or as little of the onion (or ginger) and white radish as they like with the sauce. White radish is often served with fried food to counteract the fatty nature of the food.

Tempura

Any combination of the following ingredients:	575g	1 1/4 lb	2 1/2 cups

shelled prawns or shrimps, strips of white fish, scallops, courgettes (zucchini) in 5mm (1/4 in.) slices, aubergine (eggplant) in 5mm (1/4 in.) slices, cauliflower or broccoli broken into florets, mushrooms—small button ones or large ones sliced, blanched French beans, onion rings, lotus roots (renkon) in 5mm (1/4 in.) slices (these are available in tins from oriental food stores and have a pretty shape), red or green pepper cut into matchsticks, asparagus stalks cut into 5cm (2in.) lengths, carrot sticks, sweet potato, peeled and sliced 5mm (1/4 in.) thick

vegetable oil for deep frying (corn oil has a good flavour)

Batter

egg, beaten	1	1	1
water	175ml	6fl oz	2/3 cup
plain white flour	100g	4oz	3/4 cup

Beat the egg and water together. Add the flour and mix roughly together. The batter does not have to be smooth.

To cook *tempura*, heat about 5cm (2in.) depth of oil in a large pan until a drop of batter dropped in immediately rises to the surface bubbling. Using either chopsticks or tongs, dip the first batch of *tempura* pieces into the batter one by one and then lower them into the oil. Too many pieces will mean they stick together while cooking and so look unattractive when served. Fry for about two minutes or until pale golden brown, turning once while cooking. Lift out with a perforated spoon and drain on kitchen paper. Skim off any loose bits of batter from the oil and cook the next batch. *Tempura* have to be cooked in relays and you can either give everybody a little at a time or cook for one person at a time. Serve the *tempura* in a wicker basket. They are dipped into the savoury dipping sauce before they are eaten.

Sukiyaki

BEEF AND VEGETABLES IN SOY SAUCE AND SAKE

B eef was only introduced into Japan towards the end of the nineteenth century and in many areas chicken is used instead of beef in this dish. Choose a tender cut of beef lightly marbled with fat, and serve the finished *sukiyaki* with a dip of beaten egg. *Sukiyaki* is usually cooked at the table in a frying pan over a portable burner.

tender beef (such as fillet or rump)	450g	1lb	1lb
canned shirataki (long 'noodles')	225g	8oz	1 cup
water	250ml	9fl oz	1 cup
canned bamboo shoot (takenoko)	1	1	1
strip of beef fat 5cm (2in.)	1	1	1
spring onions, cut into three	6	6	6
onion, thickly sliced	1	1	1
mushrooms, thickly sliced	6	6	6
cakes of white tofu (bean curd) canned or fresh, cut into 2.5cm (1in.) cubes	2	2	2
watercress, Chinese leaves or Chinese chrysanthemum leaves	50g	2oz	$1/4$ cup
Japanese soy sauce (shoyu)	100ml	4fl oz	$1/3$ cup
sugar	75g	3oz	$1/3$ cup
sake (rice wine)	100ml	4fl oz	$1/3$ cup

Chill the beef for 30 minutes in the freezing compartment of your fridge to make it easier to slice. Cut it against the grain into $1/2$ cm ($1/8$ in.) slices, the cut each slice across. Put the water into a pan, bring it to the boil, drop in the *shirataki* (noodles), return to the boil, then immediately drain the noodles and cut them into thirds.

Scrape the bamboo shoot at the base, cut it in half lengthways, then slice it thinly and wash in cold running water.

Arrange the beef, noodles, bamboo shoot slices, spring onions, onion, mushrooms, *tofu* and watercress or leaves attractively on a plate.

Heat the frying pan and rub the beef fat over the bottom. Put half of the beef slices and half of the soy sauce into the pan, and sprinkle the beef with half of the sugar. Cook for 1 minute, then turn the beef over and push to one side of the pan. Add half of the bamboo shoot, noodles, spring onions, mushrooms, *tofu* and watercress or leaves to the pan, sprinkle them with half of the *sake* (rice wine) and cook for 5 minutes.

Serve the cooked *sukiyaki* at once and cook the rest of the beef in the same way.

Chirashizushi
VINEGARED RICE CAKES WITH RAW FISH

Use Japanese sticky rice to make *sushi* because you'll find it holds together well. Lay thin slices of *sashimi* (raw fish) on top of the rice cakes and dip the *sushi* into soy (*shoyu*) sauce as you eat them. Japanese horseradish (*wasabi*) paste is usually added to the vinegared rice cakes by the cook but, because it is extremely hot, you might prefer to serve it separately. Pickled ginger (*gari*) also makes a wonderful accompaniment. Many types of fish can be eaten raw, including tuna, salmon, sea bream, porgy (black sea bream or dorado), lemon sole, bonito and flounder. Make sure you choose top quality, extremely fresh fish. If you have never eaten *sashimi* before you are in for a lovely surprise and an added benefit is that, according to the Japanese, raw fish makes you full of energy.

sashimi (raw fish)	350g	12oz	12oz
'sticky' short grain rice	275g	10oz	$11/4$ cups
water	450ml	$3/4$ pint	$13/4$ cups
pinch of salt			
rice vinegar (cider vinegar will do if you can't get rice vinegar)	60ml	4tbs	$1/4$ cup
sugar	30ml	2tbs	2tbs

salt	10ml	2tsp	2tsp

wasabi paste	15ml	1tbs	1tbs
(green Japanese horseradish paste), made with wasabi powder and water			

Clean the fish, remove the scales, and wash it well. Put it in a bowl and cover it with warm water. Leave it to soak for one hour. Using a thin, sharp knife, remove the skin and cut the meat of the fish from the bone. Chill to make it easier to slice, then cut diagonal slices about 4cm ($1^1/_2$ in.) wide and $^1/_2$–$1^1/_2$ cm ($^1/_4$–$^1/_2$ in.) thick.

Wash the rice with several changes of water until the water is clear, and put it into a heavy-based pan. Cover with water, add a pinch of salt and leave it to soak for $^1/_2$–1 hour. Bring to the boil and simmer, covered, for 20 minutes. Remove the pan from the heat and leave the rice to stand for 5–10 minutes. Put the rice vinegar, sugar and salt into a large saucepan and heat, stirring, to dissolve the sugar. Remove from the heat, add the rice and toss it carefully, so as to coat the grains of rice without breaking them up.

Take a ball of about 15ml (1tbs) of the vinegared rice and form it into a firm flattened cake with your hands. Put it on to a serving dish and use the rest of the rice to make similar cakes.

Put a smear of *wasabi* paste on each cake and cover with a thin slice of *sashimi*, or cover the rice cake with *sashimi* and serve the *wasabi* separately.

Horenso no hitashi

SPINACH AND SESAME SEED SALAD

This winter salad combines two delicious flavours and also looks attractive. Sesame seeds, roasted dry, are a popular Japanese flavour. For bonito shavings buy a dried, smoked fillet of bonito fish (*katsuobushi*) from a Japanese food supplier and shave it thinly with a sharp knife. You may also be able to buy shavings ready prepared.

spinach, washed	450g	1lb	2 cups

white sesame seeds	30ml	2tbs	2tbs
(goma) plus a few more to garnish			

Japanese soy sauce (shoyu)	30ml	2tbs	2tbs

bonito shavings	15ml	1tbs	1tbs
to garnish			

Cut the spinach into strips and cook with a little boiling water for 3 minutes. Drain well. Roast the sesame seeds in a dry pan over a moderate heat for a few minutes, stirring to make sure they don't burn. The pan must be covered to prevent the seeds from popping out while roasting. If the pan is small enough, it can be shaken to prevent the seeds burning. Crush the roasted sesame seeds with a little soy sauce, using a pestle and mortar or a food grinder. Mix the spinach with the crushed seeds and the remaining soy sauce and serve in individual bowls. Garnish with bonito shavings and a few whole sesame seeds.

Chawan mushi

SAVOURY EGG CUSTARD

A Japanese meal often includes food steamed or cooked over boiling water. A savoury egg custard is one of the most popular of such dishes and is eaten hot in winter and cold in summer.

small prawns or shrimps	6	6	6
OR			
larger ones, shelled	4	4	4
sweet sake (mirin)	15ml	1tbs	1tbs
or medium sherry			
eggs, beaten	4	4	4
dried mushrooms	4	4	4
(shiitake) soaked in boiling water for 30 minutes and sliced			
fish-and-seaweed stock*	600ml	1 pint	2 cups
or chicken stock			
Japanese soy sauce (shoyu)	10ml	2tsp	2tsp

raw chicken breast, diced	100g	4oz	1/2 cup
slices Japanese fish cake (kamaboko), optional	4	4	4
chopped spring onions or spinach	15ml	1tbs	1tbs
small strips lemon rind	6	6	6

Sprinkle the prawns with the sake and leave for half an hour. Sprinkle the soy sauce over the chicken and leave for another half an hour. Heat the stock and pour on to the eggs, stirring well. Take four bowls and arrange in each a portion of the prawns, mushrooms, chicken, fish cake, greenstuff and lemon rind. Divide the egg mixture between the bowls. Put the bowls into a large roasting pan and pour boiling water into the pan so that it comes half-way up the sides of the bowls. Bake in a pre-heated oven at 110°C (225°F/Gas 1/4) for 20–25 minutes or until just set but not browned. Serve at once.

See the recipe under tempura.

RUSSIA

Russia, one of the most influential states within the Soviet Union, has a wide variety of Christmas traditions. Some of these were suppressed in the harsh times following the revolution but are now being reclaimed; others have changed with time. Russia is a vivid example of a country in which the religious festival exists side by side with many traditions which have ancient, pre-Christian origins.

In the tenth century, Vladimir the Great, prince of Russia, sent envoys 'shopping' for a religion. He was impressed by the Byzantine form of worship which was full of symbolism and mystery, and chose it for his country in preference to Roman Catholicism, Islam or Judaism.

Although some Christians celebrate Christmas on 25 December, many celebrate on 6 January and 7 January—the date set by the Julian calendar. Thanks to *glasnost*, preaching of the message of Christianity is no longer restricted. Over 70 million Russians are Christians and Christmas is celebrated by all Russian believers. It's interesting that there are three times as many Christians in Russia as there are card-carrying communists.

Freedom of worship is recognized for all citizens but the church is quite definitely separate from the state. Because of this a second, non-religious celebration called the Festival of Winter has been officially recognized and this takes place at the New Year.

Undoubtedly the traditions associated with Christmas and with the Festival of Winter are inextricably linked in many people's minds. One example is the fir tree, which is a common sight in many homes and is sometimes called a Christmas tree and sometimes a New Year tree. The family tree is decorated with lights and baubles and has a star on top. Schoolchildren may take home a branch of the school tree which they have decorated with toys and sweets. Children on their school holidays enjoy troika rides and are entertained by clowns in city centres, where steaming tea is made with water heated in samovars.

Grandfather Frost (*Ded Moroz*, a character out of old Russian folklore and based on St Nicholas, *Kolya*, the patron saint of Russia), leads the winter celebrations, usually arriving by sledge on New Year's Eve. Grandfather Frost is said to come from an ice-cave in the little Norwegian town of Budo and, accompanied by the Snow Maiden (*Snegurochka*), he puts a present and sweet gingerbread biscuits for each child under the tree. The Snow Maiden wears white and blue and sparkles with snowflakes. The daughter of Grandfather Frost and Fairy Spring, she has been deprived of happiness, according to legend, until she learns the meaning of love. Grandfather Frost wears a cossack's hat of white fur. He has long white hair, a bushy beard, carries a staff and wears a coat made from or trimmed with fur.

Contrasting with these festivities are the Christmas celebrations enjoyed by Russian Christians. The majority are Russian Orthodox and their celebration focuses strongly on the nativity.

For most Russian Orthodox families the celebration begins on 6 January after weeks of mounting excitement. The children help their parents lay the table for the special meal called the apostles' supper, which is the last meal of the long, meatless pre-Christmas fast. The meal and its setting are full of symbolism. The family puts a little hay under the tablecloth to represent the manger, and on the floor to evoke the atmosphere of the stable.

Following an old Ukrainian custom, the father goes out into the street at some stage during Christmas Eve to see if he can find anyone with nowhere to go for Christmas. If he does, the person is invited to join his family's celebration.

An extra place is always laid at the head of the table and an extra glass of wine is poured to remind people that Christ is the unseen head of the house. The father of the family sits to the right of this place. The best table linen, china and crystal glasses are used, to show that the occasion is a very special one.

The children watch from the window for the first star to appear in the sky. Sunset marks the beginning of Christmas. The Orthodox Church reckons its day from sunset to sunset, so sunset on Christmas Eve signals the beginning of 7 January and Christmas Day. Everyone helps decorate the Christmas tree, Christmas hymns are sung and then the family sits down to eat.

Twelve meatless dishes are served. Tradition says that they are in honour of the twelve apostles and they frequently include *borshch* (the delicious, dark pink beetroot soup loved all over the world and originating in Russia), roast carp, dried fruit compôte (*uzvar*) and *kutya*, the sweetened porridge eaten in much of eastern Europe. These twelve dishes are eaten in memory of the dead.

The recipe for *kutya* varies from area to area. In southern Russia it is made from boiled rice, raisins, honey and walnuts, while in central Russia wheat grains, sultanas (golden raisins), honey, walnuts and poppyseeds are used. Each person's bowl represents the crib, into which is put the rice or wheat which represents the straw. A place is made in the porridge with a spoon for the baby Jesus. Fruit is added (to represent his body), and honey (to represent his blood and

the sweetness of everlasting life with him).

In some Ukrainian families a spoonful of *kutya* is thrown up to the ceiling. If it sticks, it is said that the bees will swarm. This is probably a custom best forgotten if young children are around!

After this meal, the whole family goes to church for a long service of hymns and prayers. The priest begins by singing the '*Z-namy Bog*': 'God is with us, understand all ye nations, for God is with us.' When they come home, the children rush in to find a present on the table, given in memory of Jesus, God's special gift to everyone.

Some families tell their children the legend of Baboushka, the kindly grandmother so similar to la Befana of Italy. One version of the story is that the wise men visited her on their way to find Jesus. She decided to go with them but was so busy cleaning her house that they left without her. The snow covered their footprints, and by the time she found her way to Bethlehem the holy family had gone. The only gift she had for the baby was some black bread she had made, so she laid that in the manger. She went to sleep, disappointed, but was awakened by a beautiful golden light from the far corner of the stable. 'Baboushka, I am here. Come, rise and greet me,' said a child's voice. 'Who are you?' cried Baboushka in fright. 'Do you not know, have you not been looking for me? I am the one they call the Christ Child.' 'Oh Child, I have waited so long to see you.' 'Then walk into my light, Baboushka, and let us hold hands,' said the voice softly. The next day they found Baboushka dead, curled up in the straw with the donkey and the ox.

Children who hang up a stocking for their presents may find a piece of black bread at the bottom, wrapped in coloured paper, in memory of Baboushka's gift. The children are told that Mother Christmas, or Baboushka, has filled their stockings.

On Christmas morning the family goes to the service at the church. Young country girls traditionally bring boughs from flowering cherry trees to church and place them in front of the icons that cover the walls. The boughs are cut on St Catherine's Day (7 December) and kept in water so that they will bloom in time for Christmas.

After church everyone gathers for Christmas lunch. Unlike at Easter, the most important religious festival in Russia, there is no traditional meal, but the menu consists largely of party dishes.

Zakuski are appetizers very like the Finnish voileipäpöytä (smörgåsbord) and are a much-loved part of Russian meals. They are served in crystal bowls grouped round a basket of different kinds of bread. The decanters of vodka and other drinks are placed in the centre of the table along with any table decorations, and by each person's plate is a small glass for vodka and a larger one for wine or sweet Soviet champagne.

Typically Christmas *zakuski* include smoked salmon, salted herring, canned fish such as sprats, liver pâté, salami, ham, hot boiled potatoes with dill, chives or spring onions and sour cream, pickled cucumbers, radishes, marinaded mushrooms, bean salad and various winter salads made from vegetables dressed in sour cream, mayonnaise or sunflower oil. Pink potato salad (*vinegret iz kartofelya i svyokly*) looks suitably festive. Caviar (*ikra*) is a real luxury because most of it is exported from Russia. It is served ice cold with ice-cold vodka and white bread, toast or *blini*, the famous Russian buckwheat flour pancakes. Small open sandwiches (*buterbrody*) or hot titbits on toast (*tartinki*) are

tasty and easy to prepare.

Pirozhki are a favourite part of the meal. They are delicious little pies made from a dough pastry or a short or flaky pastry, and they can have many sorts of fillings. Their name comes from the word *pir*, meaning 'feast', and savoury *pirozhki* are an integral part of most special Russian meals. At Christmas they are often served with other *zakuski* and at other times with soup as a separate course.

Recipes for *zakuski* were originally brought to Russia from Scandinavia by Peter the Great in the eighteenth century. This enterprising tsar made several tours of Europe and the modern *zakuski* owe their being to his delight in these foods he tasted abroad. They were introduced to France in the nineteenth century as *hors d'oeuvre*. Traditionally *zakuski* are washed down with small shots of vodka as the many good-natured and often long-winded toasts are made. In fact, the Russian verb *zakusit* means both to bite into something and to follow a drink down with some food.

After the *zakuski*, large families or gatherings may be served with several roast or cold joints of meat, such as cold spiced ham or roast pork, in addition to goose. The goose is stuffed with chopped cooking apples, which are removed from the cooked bird and served as apple sauce. A special dish of sugared baked apples is eaten with the goose, along with *kasha* or potatoes.

To the Russian, *kasha* refers to any grain dish, whether cooked in water, milk, cream or stock. *Kasha* is usually cooked on top of the cooker (stove) for speed but it is best when baked slowly in the oven. Some Russian women have a special way of cooking *kasha*. Once the water has disappeared, they wrap the covered pot in newspaper, blankets or pillows and let it finish cooking by itself. One Russian granny surprised her foreign guests by getting up from the table and saying 'I go now to get the *kasha* from my bed.'

The sweet dishes in any special Russian meal are usually served later with tea when appetites have returned. The samovar is a familiar and attractive sight in many Russian homes. The word simply means 'self boiler', and a samovar has a central tube which holds charcoal. The burning charcoal heats water in the body of the urn surrounding the central tube, and the teapot stands on top. The most beautiful samovars are made of brass. Mass-produced electric samovars really don't have the same appeal, which perhaps explains why charcoal ones are still popular. Tea is made in the teapot by pouring just a little boiling water on to the tea leaves and leaving the mixture to infuse. A little of this infusion is run from a tap in the teapot into a glass held in a decorative filigree holder, then the glass is filled with water from a tap in the samovar.

Many Russians enjoy drinking their tea with a lump of sugar held between their teeth. Others have a small dish of jam by the glass and either eat this with a spoon or else add it to their tea, giving it a fruity aroma and flavour. Milk isn't usually added to Russian tea.

Russians enjoy lovely desserts. The rum baba is said to be the invention of the Polish king Stanislas Lesczinski, who dipped his *kugelhopf*

into rum and set it alight. He was in Lemberg (Lvov) at the time. Lemberg was Polish but is now Russian, and Polish and Soviet historians disagree as to whether rum baba is rightly a Russian or a Polish speciality. Anyway, rum baba is now so famous that it is an international menu item. *Baba* is the Russian for 'granny' and the cake is called a *baba* because when cooked in the traditional mould—a tall, cylindrical one with a depression in the top—it resembles a granny's skirts.

Toffee torte (*tort tyanuchki*) is a great favourite, and particularly so with Russian expatriates living in Finland, who like it so much that Finland's largest confectionery firm now makes it commercially. This exquisitely flavoured cake, made with ground almonds, is covered with caramel and decorated with almonds. The cake is moist without being heavy.

Khvorost or *Kreschalski* (Christmas 'twigs' or crunchies) are deep-fried biscuits which look like twigs covered with snow. They are delectable, with crisp golden-brown outsides and soft centres, and they are a popular Christmas treat.

So much luxury after so long a fast! But such a splendid feast in the lean days of a dark northern winter helps evoke the real, spiritual joy of Christmas itself: the promise of a life filled with riches now that Jesus has come to show us the way to God.

A RUSSIAN
CHRISTMAS DAY MEAL

PIROZHKI *Tiny savoury pies*

and

VINEGRET IZ KARTOFELYA I SVYOKLY
Pink potato salad

~

GUS S YABLOKAMI *Roast goose stuffed with apples*

SUGARED BAKED APPLES

GRECHNEVAYA KASHA *Buckwheat groats*

~

ROMAVAYA BABA *Rum baba*

or

TORT TYANUCHKI *Toffee torte*

~

KHVOROST (KRESCHALSKI)
Christmas 'twigs' (crunchies)

NUTS, DRIED FRUIT, CHOCOLATE

Pirozhki

TINY SAVOURY PIES

The filling for *pirozhki* is immensely variable, and Russian women sometimes make *pirozhki* in order to use up leftover vegetables or meat. For Christmas, several different fillings may be made and recipes are given here for beef, mushroom and onion fillings. Other fillings might be minced, spiced beef or potato and bacon or cabbage, onion and caraway—a favourite for Lent. The recipe for the dough pastry makes 24 *pirozhki*. This might sound a lot but the mouthwatering little pies are not much bigger than bite-sized and an adult might easily get through four or five along with other *zakuski*. It may seem surprising to find sugar in a recipe for pastry for savoury pies but its very slight sweetness makes this pastry even more delectable.

Drozhzhevoye testo *Dough pastry*

dried yeast	10ml	2tsp	2tsp
warm water	50ml	2fl oz	3tbs
milk	225ml	8fl oz	1 cup
butter, cut into pieces	100g	4oz	1 stick
sugar	25g	1oz	2tbs
egg	1	1	1
egg yolks	2	2	2
plain flour	500g	18oz	4¾ cups
egg, beaten, to brush over pastry	1	1	1

Sprinkle the dried yeast on to the warm water and stir with a fork. Leave till bubbly. Heat the milk until lukewarm and stir in the butter. Mix the milk and butter, the yeast mixture and the sugar, egg and egg yolks. Gradually stir in the flour to make a soft dough. Knead the dough until smooth and elastic and place in a greased bowl. Cover the bowl and leave in a warm place until the dough doubles in size, about I–I½ hours. If you want to make the dough earlier in the day, put it into the fridge after kneading and remove it about two hours before you want to use it. This will give it time to rise.

Knock down the dough and divide it into 24 equal pieces on a floured table or board. Shape each piece into a ball and then flatten it with your fingers. Either using your fingers or a rolling pin, shape each flattened ball into a circle of roughly 8cm (3in.) diameter. Put a heaped teaspoonful of the filling into the centre of each circle, then using a pastry brush or your fingers moisten half the edge of the circle with water. Press the edges of the circle firmly together, then sit the little pie on a greased baking sheet with its sealed edge uppermost and flute the edges with your fingers to make it look attractive. Leave the *pirozhki* until well risen, about 40 minutes.

The *pirozhki* can either be baked in the oven or deep fried in oil. To bake, brush each pie with beaten egg to give it a shiny brown glaze when cooked. Place in an oven pre-heated to 180 C (350 F/Gas 4) and bake for 20 minutes. To deep fry, heat the oil until a crumb of bread thrown in bubbles and immediately rises to the surface of the oil. Cook a few *pirozhki* at a time until golden-brown, about 5 minutes. Drain on kitchen paper and serve hot.

Gribnaya nachinka *Mushroom filling*

butter	100g	4oz	1 stick
medium onion, finely chopped	1	1	1
mushrooms, finely chopped	225g	8oz	1 cup
egg, beaten	1	1	1
rice, cooked	40g	1½ oz	¼ cup
fresh parsley, finely chopped OR	25g	1oz	2tbs
dried parsley	15ml	1tbs	1tbs

freshly ground black pepper to taste			
fresh dill, finely chopped OR	15ml	1tbs	1tbs
dried dill	5ml	1tsp	1tsp

Melt the butter in a frying pan and gently cook the onion until soft. Add the mushrooms and cook for a further 5 minutes. Remove from the heat and stir in the egg, rice, parsley, pepper and dill.

This makes enough filling for 24 *pirozhki*.

Nachinka iz rublenogo myasa *Beef filling*

large onion, chopped	1	1	1
butter	25g	1oz	2tbs
olive oil	10ml	2tsp	2tsp
minced beef	225g	8oz	1 cup
large pinch of salt			
pepper to taste			
fresh dill OR	15ml	1tbs	1tbs
dried dill	5ml	1tsp	1tsp
egg, hard-boiled and finely chopped	1	1	1
sour cream	15ml	1tbs	1tbs

Melt the butter with the oil and gently cook the onion until softened. Stir in the minced beef and cook until brown. Add the remaining ingredients and mix well.

Machinka iz zelonogo luka *Onion filling*

medium onions, finely chopped	4	4	4

butter	175g	6oz	1¹/₂ sticks
fresh parsley, finely chopped OR	25g	1oz	2tbs
dried parsley	15ml	1tbs	1tbs
hard-boiled eggs, finely chopped	2	2	2
fresh dill, chopped OR	15ml	1tbs	1tbs
dried dill	5ml	1tsp	1tsp
freshly ground black pepper to taste			

Melt the butter in a frying pan and gently cook the onions until soft. Remove from the heat and stir in the parsley, eggs, dill and pepper. This recipe makes enough filling for 24 *pirozhki*.

Vinegret iz kartofelya i svyokly
PINK POTATO SALAD

This winter salad combines several typically Russian ingredients—dill pickle, potatoes, beetroot, garlic and sour cream. Dill and parsley are favourite herbs and are used in many recipes for added flavour and colour. The salad's pink colour makes it especially suitable for the Christmas table and it has the advantage of improving if kept in the fridge overnight.

potatoes, boiled	450g	1lb	2 cups
medium beetroot, boiled	1	1	1
medium cucumber, diced	1/2	1/2	1/2
dill pickles (small pickled cucumbers), diced	3	3	3
medium onion, chopped	1	1	1
large cloves garlic, crushed	2	2	2
capers, chopped	10ml	2tsp	2tsp
olive oil	15ml	1tbs	1tbs
white wine vinegar	15ml	1tbs	1tbs
freshly ground black pepper to taste			
pinch of dried dill OR fresh dill, chopped	10ml	2tsp	2tsp
sour cream	75ml	3fl oz	1/3 cup

Cut the potato and beetroot into chunks and put into a large mixing bowl. Add the cucumber, dill pickle, onion, garlic and capers and mix well. Stir in the olive oil, vinegar, pepper and dill and lastly the sour cream. Mix well, cover and chill.

Gus s yablokami
ROAST GOOSE STUFFED WITH APPLES

Roast stuffed goose is very popular at Christmas in Russia and some people add sauerkraut to the apples for the stuffing. If you are also cooking a dish of sugared baked apples, you'll need some of the large amount of goose fat produced as the goose is being cooked.

lard OR cooking oil	25g 25ml	1oz 1fl oz	1/8 cup 2tbs
small onions, peeled and chopped	2	2	2
cooking apples, peeled and sliced	900g	2lb	4 cups
caraway seeds	15ml	1tbs	1tbs
allspice	5ml	1tsp	1tsp
streaky bacon	200g	7oz	7oz

Heat the lard or oil in a large frying pan and gently sauté the onions until softened. Add the apples, caraway seeds and allspice and mix well. Use this mixture to stuff the goose. Put the goose in a deep roasting tin and cover with streaky bacon. Cook in the oven at 190°C (375°F/Gas 5), allowing 20 minutes per 450g (1lb) stuffed weight, plus 20 minutes extra.

Grechnevaya kasha
BUCKWHEAT GROATS

Grechnevaya kasha is a nutty-flavoured porridge made from the groats (hulled, or de-husked, and crushed grains) of buckwheat. It is often eaten plain, but you can add mushrooms or onions, lightly sautéd in butter, herbs or even curd cheese before cooking if you wish. Buckwheat groats taste best if they are first dry-fried in a frying pan in order to brown them. You can buy pre-roasted buckwheat groats in some health food shops and delicatessens. Choose coarser groats rather than the finer ones if both are available.

buckwheat	200g	7oz	³/₄ cup
salt	2ml	¹/₂ tsp	¹/₂ tsp
pinch of grated nutmeg			
stock or water	300ml	¹/₂ pint	1 cup

Stir the groats in a large frying pan over a medium heat for about 5 minutes, until each groat begins to brown. Grease a large casserole with butter and place in it the browned groats, salt and nutmeg. Boil the stock or water and pour over the groats. Cover the casserole and cook in a pre-heated oven at 180°C (350°F/Gas 4) until the liquid is absorbed and the groats are tender, about 30–45 minutes. Check towards the end of the cooking time whether more water is required. If the groats are tender but some liquid remains, cook for a further 5 minutes or so with the casserole uncovered. Serve the *kasha* with plenty of butter for those who like it.

Sugared baked apples

cooking apples	4–6	4–6	4–6
sugar	100g	4oz	¹/₂ cup
fat (from the cooking goose)	100ml	4fl oz	¹/₃ cup

Slice each apple and lay the slices overlapping in a shallow greased baking dish. Sprinkle the apples with sugar and pour the fat over them. Cover with a lid or with foil and bake in a moderate oven 180°C (350°F/Gas 4) for 50 minutes.

Romavaya baba

RUM BABA

This is an international favourite today but will ruin the waistline unless eaten only on special occasions. The rum-flavoured syrup soaks into the yeasty sponge cake to give a melt-in-the-mouth consistency.

dried yeast	15ml	1tbs	1tbs
warm water	50ml	2fl oz	3tbs
eggs, beaten	3	3	3
butter, softened	50g	2oz	1/2 stick
sugar	25g	1oz	2tbs
plain white flour	350g	12oz	2²/₃ cups
double cream (US: whipping)	150ml	5fl oz	1/2 cup
butter to grease the mould	25–50g	1–2oz	2–4tbs

Syrup

sugar	225g	8oz	1 cup
water	175ml	6fl oz	²/₃ cup
rum	100ml	4fl oz	1/2 cup
juice of half a lemon			

For a flaming *baba*

rum	50ml	2fl oz	3tbs

For a cream-filled *baba*

apricot jam	225ml	8oz	1 cup
whipping or double cream	300ml	10fl oz	1¹/₄ cups

First choose your mould. This recipe when cooked will fill an 900ml (1¹/₂ pint/3 cup) mould. Traditionally, a tall cylindrical *baba* mould is used for a celebration cake, but for home use a plain cake ring is ideal. The mixture will tend to stick to a fluted mould unless you're very careful about turning the cake out. Sprinkle the yeast on to the water and stir with a fork. Leave till bubbly. Mix the yeast mixture, eggs, butter, sugar, flour and cream. Work the dough with your hands for five minutes, then cover the bowl and leave in a warm place for up to an hour until well risen. Butter the mould generously and carefully, then spoon in the mixture, which should come only half way up the mould. Leave in a warm place until doubled in size. Bake in the oven at 190°C (375°F/Gas 5) for about 25 minutes or until a skewer comes out clean. Larger amounts of mixture take longer to cook. Turn the *baba* out of the mould after 30–45 minutes on to a wire rack.

Make the syrup by adding the sugar to the water and lemon juice and boiling to dissolve it. Then boil rapidly until the mixture is of a syrupy consistency. Add the rum. While still hot, put a plate under the wire rack holding the *baba* and pour the syrup over the *baba*. Any syrup that runs on to the plate can be poured back over the *baba*.

To serve. A flaming *baba* makes a dramatic dessert for Christmas. Warm the rum in a small pan and pour it over the *baba* at the table. Light it immediately with a match and it will flame for 20 seconds or so.

To serve the *baba* cold, warm the apricot jam and pour it over the *baba*, spreading it evenly to make the *baba* look shiny. When cool, whip the cream and either fill the centre of the *baba* or pipe it round the outside.

Tort tyanuchki

TOFFEE TORTE

This toffee-covered cake is brown and shiny with a deliciously different centre. Keep the toffee topping thin or you'll find it too chewy!

butter	100g	4oz	1 stick
sugar	175g	6oz	3/4 cup
eggs, separated	3	3	3
ground almonds	150g	5oz	1/2 cup
potatoes, cooked and mashed	700g	1 1/2 lb	3 cups

Topping

double cream (US: whipping)	75ml	3fl oz	1/3 cup
sugar	100g	4oz	1/2 cup
golden (dark corn) syrup	45ml	3tbs	3tbs
butter	25g	1oz	1/4 stick
vanilla essence (extract)	2ml	1/2 tsp	1/2 tsp
blanched almonds to decorate			

Filling

apricot jam	

Cream the butter and sugar and beat in the egg yolks. Add the ground almonds and potatoes and beat well. Beat the egg whites and fold them into the mixture. Grease and flour two 20cm (8in.) diameter cake tins. Cut circles of grease-proof (or waxed) paper to fit the tins and grease and flour the paper. Put the cake mixture into the tins and bake for 1 hour in an oven pre-heated to 180°C (350°F/Gas 4), until a skewer comes out clean.

Prepare the topping while the cake is in the oven. Heat the cream, sugar and syrup in a heavy saucepan until the sugar has dissolved, then cook slowly for 50 minutes until the mixture is thick and brown. Remove from the heat and stir in the butter and vanilla essence. Cool slightly.

Turn out the cakes and allow to cool. Sandwich the two layers together with apricot jam. Pour the toffee topping over the cake, spreading it thinly over the top and sides. It's best to do this with the cake still on the rack, so that the toffee doesn't thicken as it runs down the sides of the cake and so stick it to the plate. Mark the cake into slices with a knife and decorate with almonds.

Khvorost or kreschalski

CHRISTMAS TWIGS OR CRUNCHIES

These deep-fried biscuits are made of a sweet yeasty dough. They resemble *klenäter*, the Swedish Christmas biscuits. *Khvorost* is Russian for twigs—an apt name for these biscuits which look just like bare twigs sprinkled with snow.

plain white flour	225g	8oz	2 cups
single cream (half and half) or tinned evaporated milk	50ml	2fl oz	3tbs
brandy	50ml	2fl oz	3tbs
egg yolks	3	3	3
icing sugar (confectioner's sugar)	50g	2oz	1/4 cup
oil for deep frying			
icing (confectioner's) sugar for dusting			

Mix all the ingredients (except frying oil and dusting sugar) and stir well. Knead the dough on a floured board and roll out thinly—less than 2cm (3/4 in.) thick. Cut strips 1/2 cm (1/8 in.) wide and 8cm (3in.) long. Cut a slit in the centre of each strip and twist one end through, making a loose loop. Fry in deep oil a few at a time, at about 190°C (375°F) until light brown. They should rise to the surface of the oil immediately if the oil is hot enough. If you haven't a thermometer, put one twig in first as a test. Each batch of biscuits takes only a minute or so to cook, so don't leave them. Turn them with a perforated spoon while frying, then use this spoon to remove them from the oil when ready. Drain on kitchen paper, then transfer them to a plate. Dust generously with icing (confectioner's) sugar. Pile in a heap to serve and eat while still hot. Makes 36.

FINLAND

Finland and Christmas seem to be made for each other, not least because Finland has become the home of Father Christmas himself. Way back in 1927 the Finnish Broadcasting Company officially made a three-peaked hill in Lapland called Korvantunturi his abode. Lapland is also the natural territory of many thousands of reindeer!

Finland's eastern border with the USSR runs across the middle peak of Korvantunturi. This spot, Savukoski, is uninhabited except for *Joulupukki*, as the Finnish Father Christmas is known. His name—'Christmas Goat'—originated because presents were once given to children in Finland by a horned figure reminiscent of the masked dancers of the Roman Kalends. *Joulupukki*'s residence has been modernized for, although there was once only a small café, he is now the proud possessor of a new, larger and more commercial home in Santa Claus village, seven kilometres (4½ miles) north of Rovaniemi on the Arctic Circle. There he continues making toys for children the world over and, even more important, reading and answering their letters, care of the Finnish Post Office with its excellent translation service.

Lapland has the largest virgin wilds in Europe and it is there that the reindeer graze by digging with their spade-shaped hooves for lichen hidden under the winter snow on the fells. Thirty-seven per cent of the Finnish Lapps rely on reindeer-breeding for their income and some reindeer meat finds its way—usually smoked—on to the Christmas table in Finnish homes. Reindeer meat is purplish-brown and more tender than beef, with less fat. Salty and strong, the Lapps consider it a food for feasts.

The Finnish Christmas celebrations owe a lot to the Lutheran Church to which the vast majority of the people belong. A little over one per cent of the population are members of the Orthodox Church of Finland, a church akin to the Greek and Russian Orthodox churches. The first Sunday in Advent sees the official opening of the Christmas season, with Advent concerts all over the country and the sound of G. J. Volger's 'Hosanna' ringing from the churches and from the TV and radio.

Even before Advent the Christmas bazaars begin and soon the season of the *pikkujoulu* or 'little Christmas' parties is in full swing. Since the 1920s these gatherings have been popular both at home and at work. There may be music, seasonal delicacies to eat, a talk or a sketch. If there are presents they are likely to be small but amusing.

On each Sunday throughout Advent another candle is lit and the excitement mounts as the children help make decorations. A complicated mobile made of straw tests the cleverest fingers but the Christmas cross, or cross of St Thomas, is easier and can be hung in the window when finished.

Made from recipes passed down for generations, fragrant gingerbread is baked in the shape of stars, moons, hearts, pigs and even whole houses. Cakes full of dried fruit are becoming popular, but the traditional Christmas bread—saffron-coloured, cardamom-scented *pulla*—is still made all over Finland. *Joulutortut*, or Christmas stars, are rich pastries (also popular in Sweden) filled with sweetened prune purée. They freeze well, as does fig cake.

The Sunday before Christmas is the time to cut down the Christmas tree earmarked in the forest long before the snow fell in the autumn. City dwellers can choose their tree from the market. The tree is kept outside until Christmas Eve.

Christmas Eve is the most important day in the Finnish calendar and it's a time when families try to get together to celebrate in a homely, old-fashioned style. There's work as usual in the morning, but only until midday. By then Christmas cooking is always well under way, for it's a custom that as little food preparation as possible is done over the Christmas period. Flowers are brought in to make the home look and smell lovely. Tulips and lilac, hyacinths, Christmas roses, poinsettias and lilies of the valley are available in the markets and are often displayed in baskets in the living-room. Everlasting flowers and sprigs of juniper and lingonberry stand on the window-sills.

At 12 noon the start of the Christmas festivities is signalled by the ringing of bells and the proclamation of the 'Christmas Peace', broadcast from the cathedral in Turku, Finland's oldest city and former capital. This is a custom which dates back to the middle ages. Christmas time is precious in this country and, to help maintain an atmosphere of peace and tranquillity, any crime is doubly punished if committed between 24 December and 13 January.

Christmas Eve lunch usually begins with a *riisipuro* (rice pudding) or a *pito-je-joulupuro* (wholegrain barley pudding) made with milk and baked in the oven for hours until the lactose (milk sugar) turns the pudding pinkish-red. The pudding is unsweetened but sugar or jam are served separately and perhaps also cinnamon, ginger and butter. A raisin and prune purée makes a delicious accompaniment too. An almond is added to the pudding before baking and the finder is supposed to have a wish granted as long as he or she makes the wish while chewing the almond. Mothers have been known to hide as many almonds as there are

children in the family to avoid disputes! If a woman finds the almond, it's said that she'll have a child within the year.

The afternoon is spent decorating the tree. Some Finns loop a string of tiny paper flags of different countries on their tree, while others prefer tinsel and baubles, with a star on top. Real candles still burn on some trees, though most people prefer electric fairy lights.

Another feature of Christmas Eve is the Christmas sauna. Most detached houses in Finland have their own private sauna. Indeed there are as many saunas as there are cars in this country! Families without a sauna go to the nearest public one. After the sauna when everyone feels serene and relaxed there's coffee or *kalja* (home-made, non-alcoholic beer) and Christmas stars or *pulla*.

Before sunset the Christmas ham is prepared and put into the oven to bake and the whole family makes its way to church for a service that starts at around 5 p.m. and lasts only 30–45 minutes. Candles are lit on the graves of departed loved ones, making a moving sight in the darkness of Christmas Eve.

After church there's a drive or a walk home through the snow. Finland is one of the northernmost countries in Europe, a third of it lying north of the Arctic Circle. Luckily its shores are warmed slightly by the Gulf Stream, taking some of the edge off the winter bitterness. Finland is one of the lands of the midnight sun, when daylight reigns in the north from May to July. This means that, in the north, in the middle of winter the daytime hours are as dark as night.

Back home, with the resinous scent of pine needles from the Christmas tree and the sweet smell of hyacinths and lilies of the valley wafting through the house, it's time for Father Christmas to appear. And appear he does, in person! A Father Christmas is often hired for a small fee to come and distribute presents, or else a relative or neighbour plays the part.

The children dress up as Father Christmas' little helpers in red tights, a long red cap and a grey cotton suit decorated in red. When the children are young, their presents are hidden outside in a sledge ready for Father Christmas to collect and bring to the door. The older ones' presents are under the tree. The children sing and play games with *Joulupukki*, who then asks, 'Are there any good children here?' Unknown to them, a friendly gnome or *tomtar* may have been looking through the windows before Christmas to watch how they behave. However, whatever the *tomtar* might say, the children reply with a resounding *YES* and then they are given their presents.

The climax of this special day is the Christmas Eve supper, served at about 7 o'clock. The Christmas table-cloth is decorated with stars and little embroidered Father Christmases. A nativity scene made by the children at school out of paper is placed on the table. Red and white candles are often stuck into a pretty container filled with sand and there may also be red and white flowers on the table.

A traditional grace, 'Thank my God for the food and for the gift of his son, Jesus,' is usually said, then the eating begins. All the food is put on the table at once, arranged in many shallow dishes. Inevitably there's the popular Finnish Christmas food—baked lutefish with white sauce and boiled potatoes fragrant with chopped dill. Finland has an abundance of lakes and sea inlets, and the lye-treated dried ling called lutefish is an old-established dish.

There's a *voileipäpöytä* (*smörgåsbord*) of freshly-salted, dill-flavoured salmon, often prepared at home; Glassmaster's herring marinaded in spicy vinegar, Swedish-style; beetroot salad; cold meats; liver pâté served with cranberry jam; and cheeses—perhaps including some home-made baked cheese served with yellow cloudberry conserve. There is usually a baked ham—either glazed with honey and studded with cloves or else cooked with a stuffing of prunes, apple and onion tucked into a pocket. Some cooks prefer to cook their ham in a rye dough crust to keep it moist. Particularly Finnish are the carrot, swede and potato casseroles which are served hot and are good re-heated over the next few days too. *Karjalanpiiraat* (little savoury rice pasties) originating from Karelia over the Russian border have a place on the table too, along with melted butter and bread of various kinds.

The Christmas desserts include Christmas stars, gingerbread and Christmas *pulla* in one of the many traditional shapes such as animals, people, 'S' shapes, 'priest's hair' and knots. The *Viipuri* twist is a knotted loop of sweet, spicy bread which has little gingerbread biscuits and fancy cakes decoratively nestling into its curves. It is said that the *Viipuri* twist was first baked for Christmas in a Finnish monastery in 1433. Some families have rice pudding, and there may be a berry dessert such as cranberry parfait.

A mixture of nuts, raisins and chocolate provides a traditional way to round off the meal and there's lots and lots of coffee. The Finns are said to be the world's greatest coffee drinkers. Sometimes they'll dip some 'oven cheese', such as the deliciously unusual Ilves or Ostrobothnian round cheese, into their coffee and eat it when it's soft and warm. These cheeses are sometimes prepared at home by curdling a mixture of salted beestings (the first milk made by a cow for her calf), cream, eggs and buttermilk. The curd cheese is drained overnight, then baked.

The Finns also drink a large amount of milk and throughout the meal there'll be milk and buttermilk. Mineral water, *kalja* or home-made beer, a lemony mead and hot Swedish *glögg* are available.

On Christmas Day many are up early to attend church at 6 a.m. At the end of each pew a candle burns. The warm glow of candlelight on the early morning worshippers symbolizes the light and hope brought into the world with the birth of Jesus nearly two thousand yours ago. As in many other countries, even those who normally don't go to church try hard to get there.

A FINNISH CHRISTMAS EVE SUPPER

LIPEAKALA *Baked lutefish with white sauce*

KEITETYT PERUNAT *Boiled potatoes with dill*

RIIMISUOLAINEN LOHI *Freshly salted salmon*

GLASSMASTER'S HERRING

ROSOLLI *Herring salad*

BEETROOT SALAD

COLD MEATS

MAKSALAATIKKO *Liver pâté with cranberry jam*

CHEESES

KARJALANPIIRAAT *Karelian pasties*

JOULUKINKKU
Christmas ham with apple, onion and prune stuffing

LANTTULAATIKKO *Swede casserole*

PORKKANALAATIKKO *Carrot pudding*

~

RIISIPURO *Rice pudding*

ICED CRANBERRY PARFAIT

GINGERBREAD HOUSE

JOULUTORTUT *Christmas stars*

SAFFRANSBRÖDET *Saffron pulla*

~

NUTS, RAISINS AND CHOCOLATE

Lipeakala

BAKED LUTEFISH WITH WHITE SAUCE

Sun-dried ling, a fish of the Cod family, is soaked in water for a week, then soaked in a solution of lye for 3–5 days, then soaked in water which is changed every day for a week. The resulting product is known as lutefish or lyefish. Bland and springy in texture, lutefish is eaten as a traditional Christmas dish in Finland. Some households go to the trouble of preparing the lye solution themselves from sifted birch ash (which contains sodium hydroxide or lye) and lime. Outside Finland, dried ling is stocked by some delicatessens, and ready-prepared 1kg vacuum packs of lutefish can be ordered from specialist Scandinavian food shops in October. Lutefish is served with boiled potatoes sprinkled with dill, melted butter, white sauce and mustard and lots of freshly ground black pepper.

lutefish	1kg	2¼ lb	2¼ lb
coarse sea salt	5ml	1tsp	1tsp
butter	25g	1oz	2tbs
white flour	25g	1oz	3tbs
milk, lukewarm	600ml	1 pint	2½ cups
salt to taste			
lemon, cut into wedges	1	1	1

Place the fish on a large piece of cooking foil and sprinkle with salt. Wrap up into a parcel and put into a baking dish. Bake at 200°C (400°F/Gas 6) for 30–40 minutes. Discard the liquid.

Make a roux by melting the butter, adding the flour and mixing well. Slowly add the lukewarm milk, stirring well, and simmer for 5 minutes. Season with salt to taste. Pour the white sauce over the lutefish on a serving dish and garnish with lemon wedges.

Riimisuolainen lohi

FRESHLY SALTED SALMON

This traditional Christmas delicacy is simple to make at home. It takes at least one and preferably three days to reach its full flavour.

piece of fresh salmon	1kg	2¼ lb	2¼ lb
coarse sea salt crystals	50g	2oz	3tbs
caster sugar (US: granulated)	30ml	2tbs	2tbs
white peppercorns, roughly ground	10ml	2tsp	2tsp
dried dill OR a handful of fresh dill, chopped	15ml	1tbs	1tbs

Choose a dish large and deep enough to take the whole piece of fish and sprinkle a little of the salt on to the bottom of the dish. Fillet the piece of salmon, leaving the skin on, and dry the fillets with kitchen paper. Lay the two fillets on a clean surface, skin-side down, and sprinkle with most of the remaining salt and all the sugar and pepper. Lay one fillet skin-side down in the dish, and place the other fillet on top, skin-side up. Sprinkle the dill and the rest of the salt over the fish. Cover with foil. Place several weights over the foil down the length of the salmon. Refrigerate for up to three days.

Before serving remove the salmon from the dish, scrape off any seasoning, and cut each fillet obliquely down to the skin in thin slices.

Glassmaster's herring

These aromatic and spicy herrings are at their best after four to five days in their sweet-and-sour marinade.

malt vinegar	300ml	1/2 pint	1 1/4 cups
sugar	275g	10oz	1 1/4 cups
water	600ml	1 pint	2 1/2 cups
large herrings, filleted and skinned	4	4	4
red onions	3	3	3
carrots	2	2	2
whole allspice seeds	15	15	15
whole white peppercorns	15	15	15
bay leaves	4	4	4

First prepare a sweet-and-sour marinading liquid. Put the vinegar, sugar and water into a large saucepan. Heat gently, stirring, until the sugar is dissolved, then bring to the boil. Remove from the heat and leave to cool at room temperature.

Cut the herring fillets into large pieces. Peel the onions and cut into thin rings. Peel the carrots and cut into rounds. Put a layer of herring pieces into a dish and cover with a layer of onions, carrots, spices and bay leaves. Repeat the layers until everything is used up, then pour the previously prepared and cooled liquid into the dish. Cover and leave to marinade in a cool place of 4–5 days.

Maksalaatikko

LIVER PÂTÉ WITH CRANBERRY JAM

This unusual liver pâté is made with rice, syrup, raisins and ginger as well as the customary pâté ingredients. Eaten with cranberry jam and one of the many sorts of Finnish bread, it is a treat in itself and is frequently served as part of the Christmas Eve feast.

rice	150g	5oz	3/4 cup
salt	10ml	2tsp	2tsp
butter	15g	1/2 oz	1tbs
small onion, chopped	1	1	1
liver, minced twice	350g	12oz	1 1/2 cups
golden (dark corn) syrup	60ml	4tbs	1/4 cup
ground ginger	5ml	1tsp	1tsp
egg, beaten	1	1	1
water	250ml	9fl oz	1 cup
milk	400ml	14fl oz	1 3/4 cups
raisins	75g	3oz	1/3 cup
pinch of white pepper			
fresh marjoram, chopped OR pinch of dried marjoram	5ml	1tsp	1tsp
breadcrumbs	50g	2oz	1/4 cup
butter, cut into pieces	25g	1oz	2tbs

Cook the rice in boiling salted water until tender. Melt the butter and sauté the onion in it until soft and transparent. Mix the rice and onion with all but the last two ingredients and transfer the mixture to a well-greased baking dish. Sprinkle with breadcrumbs and dot with butter. Cover tightly with foil and set the dish in a tin (pan) with enough water to come halfway up the side of the dish. Bake at 180° C (350° F/Gas 4) for 45 minutes, then reduce the temperature to 150° C (300° F/Gas 2) and cook for a further hour.

Serve hot or cold with cranberry jam and melted butter. Cranberry sauce is the nearest equivalent to cranberry jam.

Karjalanpiiraat
KARELIAN PASTIES

These flattened rice-filled pasties (turnovers) are served spread with melted butter and 'egg-butter'. They are eaten with soup or just as part of the *voileipäpöytä* (*smörgåsbord*).

Filling

rice	225g	8oz	1 cup
water	350ml	12fl oz	1½ cups
milk	1 litre	1¾ pts	3½ cups
salt to taste			

Pastry

rye flour	350g	12oz	3 cups
salt	10ml	2tsp	2tsp
water	175ml	6fl oz	¾ cup

Glaze

butter, melted	75g	3oz	6tbs
single cream	50ml	2fl oz	¼ cup

Egg butter

eggs, hard-boiled chopped	4	4	4 and
butter, melted	50g	2oz	½ stick

Cook the rice until soft in the milk and water and cool.

Mix the flour and salt into a stiff dough with the water. Knead and shape into a long roll. Cut the roll into 20 pieces and shape these into balls. On a floured board roll each ball into a paper-thin circle. Stack the circles in a pile with flour sprinkled between each layer to prevent sticking, and cover the top with a damp cloth.

Put a tablespoonful of rice in the middle of each pastry circle and spread evenly, leaving the edges uncovered. Turn the sides to the centre but leave a narrow gap in the centre to show a streak of rice. Pleat the edges of the turned-in pastry and bake in a hot oven at 230°C (450°F/Gas 8) for 15 minutes.

After baking, glaze each pasty with melted butter mixed with cream.

Serve hot with egg butter made from mixing the warm chopped hard-boiled eggs with melted butter.

Joulukinkku
CHRISTMAS HAM WITH APPLE, ONION AND PRUNE STUFFING

Stuffed roast ham makes a delicious change from mustard- or honey-glazed ham on the Christmas table. This is a traditional Finnish recipe which makes enough stuffing for a 1½ kg (3lb) ham.

medium cooking apple peeled, cored and sliced	1	1	1
medium onion, chopped	1	1	1
prunes, cooked and stoned (pitted)	10	10	10
parsley, chopped	15ml	1tbs	1tbs
ham	1½ kg	3lb	3lb

Sauce

pan juice (from the baked ham)	60ml	4tbs	¼ cup
medium cooking apple peeled, sliced, cooked in a little water and puréed	1	1	1
pinch of ground ginger			
mild made (table) mustard	15ml	1tbs	1tbs

Mix all the ingredients together for the stuffing.

Score the fatty surface of the ham into a diamond pattern and then cut a large pocket just under the surface of the ham. Fill this pocket with the stuffing and close the opening with small skewers or with a trussing needle and fine string. Put the ham on a rack in a roasting pan and bake for 2 hours at 180°C (350°F/Gas 4).

When the ham is cooked, mix together the sauce ingredients and serve with the ham.

Lanttulaatikko

SWEDE (RUTABAGA) CASSEROLE

Baked dishes of Swedish turnips or swedes (rutabagas), carrots or potatoes are a must on the Finnish Christmas table and are eaten with the baked ham. Mixed with breadcrumbs, cream, eggs and nutmeg and baked, the swede (rutabaga) is unexpectedly delicious. Make this recipe up a day or two before you need it because its flavour improves with re-heating.

swedes (rutabagas), peeled and diced	575g	1¼ lb	1¼ lb
small onion, finely chopped	1	1	1
knob (pat) of butter			
salt	5ml	1tsp	1tsp
breadcrumbs	30ml	2tbs	2tbs
black treacle (molasses) or golden (dark corn) syrup	15ml	1tbs	1tbs
double cream (US: whipping)	100ml	4fl oz	⅓ cup
large pinch of grated nutmeg			
egg, beaten	1	1	1
butter, melted	15ml	1tbs	1tbs
breadcrumbs	50g	2oz	¼ cup
butter, cut into pieces	25g	1oz	2tbs

Cook the swedes (rutabagas) in boiling water for 20 minutes until soft. Drain, reserving some of the water, and mash. Sauté the onion in a knob of butter until golden. Add the cooked onion, salt, breadcrumbs, treacle (molasses) or syrup, cream, nutmeg, egg and melted butter to the mashed swede and stir well. Add some of the reserved water if necessary to give the mixture a loose, soft consistency. Spoon into a greased casserole dish, sprinkle with breadcrumbs and dot with the pieces of butter. Bake uncovered at 180°C (350°F/Gas 4) for 1 hour, until lightly browned.

Porkkanalaatikko

CARROT PUDDING

This casserole of carrots and pearl barley is a traditional accompaniment to the Christmas ham. Don't forget to allow time to let the barley soak overnight.

pearl barley	100g	4oz	1/2 cup
water	350ml	12fl oz	1 1/2 cups
milk, boiling	350ml	12fl oz	1 1/2 cups
carrots, cleaned and grated	450g	1lb	2 cups
salt to taste			
sugar or golden (dark corn) syrup	10ml	2tsp	2tsp
egg, beaten	1	1	1
breadcrumbs	30ml	2tbs	2tbs
butter, cut into small pieces	25g	1oz	2tbs

Rinse the barley in cold and then in hot water and soak overnight. Drain and put into a thick-bottomed pan with the water and milk. Simmer for about 1 hour until the barley is nearly cooked, then add the carrots, sugar or syrup, salt and egg. Stir well and transfer the mixture to a greased casserole dish, levelling the top and pressing it down with a spoon. Sprinkle the breadcrumbs on top and dot with butter. Bake for about an hour at 200°C (400°F/Gas 6).

Iced cranberry parfait

Berries are made into a light, creamy, frozen dessert for the Christmas period. Either cranberries, cloudberries, lingonberries or blackcurrants can be used.

water	75ml	3fl oz	1/3 cup
caster sugar (US: granulated)	100g	4oz	1/2 cup
egg yolks	6	6	6
whipping cream	450ml	3/4 pint	2 cups
frozen berries 5 cups	1.5 litres	2 1/2 pints	or fresh berries if available
extra berries for decoration			

Bring the water and sugar to the boil. Beat the yolks and add the water and sugar syrup, beating all the time. Pour into the saucepan and continue beating over a low heat until the mixture thickens. Do not boil. Cool, beating occasionally. Whip the cream and fold into the cooled mixture. Thaw the berries, mash them and add to mixture.

Transfer to a cooled bowl or mould and freeze for 4–5 hours.

When ready to serve, dip the mould into hot water for a moment and invert on to a serving dish. Decorate with whole berries.

Gingerbread house

Making gingerbread is an integral part of the Christmas preparations for many Finnish families. A gingerbread house is easier to construct than you might imagine and children of all ages will enjoy decorating and, later, demolishing and eating it. In some homes an entire gingerbread village complete with manger and Christ child, and lit with candles, takes pride of place in the living-room.

golden (dark corn) syrup	450g	1lb	2 cups
granulated sugar	275g	10oz	1 1/4 cups
dried ginger	10ml	2tsp	2tsp
cinnamon	10ml	2tsp	2tsp
cloves, finely ground	10ml	2tsp	2tsp
butter	275g	10oz	2 1/2 sticks
eggs, beaten	2	2	2
bicarbonate of soda	10ml	2tsp	2tsp
water	15ml	1tbs	1tbs
plain flour	1.1kg	2 1/2 lb	10 cups
cardboard for templates			
granulated sugar for building 'glue'	350g	12oz	1 1/2 cups

Icing

icing sugar (confectioner's sugar)	200g	7oz	3/4 cup
egg white	1	1	1

Decorations

small sweets

other decorations such as a chimney, Father Christmas, stars, etc

extra icing (confectioner's) sugar for sifting on roof

cotton wool (cotton) for snow base

Put the syrup, sugar and spices into a very large saucepan and heat gently, stirring, until the sugar has melted. Add the butter and stir until melted. Remove the pan from the heat and leave to cool for 15 minutes. Add the eggs, the bicarbonate (soda) dissolved in the water, and the flour. Mix thoroughly, then put the mixture into a bowl and leave in a cool place for an hour to make it easier to roll out.

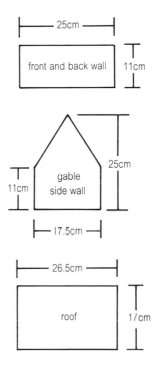

Cut 3 cardboard templates: one for the front and back walls, one for the gabled side walls and one for the two pieces of the roof. Cut a door and window panes out of the template you will use for both front and back walls.

Roll out some of the dough to about 3mm ($1/8$ in.) thick, using flour to keep the rolling pin and work surface dry. Use the templates to cut out 2 roof pieces, 2 side walls, a front wall and a back wall, rolling out more dough as necessary. Put the shapes onto greased baking trays. Cut window panes and a door from the front wall only. Use any left over dough to make biscuits, or freeze it in a polythene bag.

Bake at 220°C (425°F/Gas 7) for about 10–15 minutes or until golden-brown. Carefully loosen the shapes by sliding a palette knife underneath and while still soft use a sharp knife to straighten the edges, which will almost certainly have bulged. Put a wire rack over the shapes and carefully turn the baking tray, shapes and rack upside-down. Remove the tray and leave the shapes to cool and harden on the rack.

It is easier to decorate the shapes before you build the house. Make some icing with the icing (confectioner's) sugar and $^1/_2$ to $^3/_4$ of the egg white. Pipe squiggly line decorations around the front door, windows and all the edges of the shapes, then pipe lots of parallel horizontal lines on the roof, and perhaps also a Christmas greeting. Position the sweets and other small decorations.

Choose a heavy-based frying pan of at least 25cm (10 in.) internal width. Put the granulated sugar for the building 'glue' into the pan and heat gently to melt, then heat till golden. Build the house on a tray—you can remove it afterwards if you wish. It is all too easy to burn your fingers as you construct the house with the sugar glue, so please be extra careful and have a large bowl of cold water standing by to dip your fingers in if necessary.

Take the back of the house and one gable wall and dip the side edges into the melted sugar. Stick together and hold in position on the tray until the sugar cools sufficiently to hold the pieces together. Add the front wall and other gable wall, dipping their side edges into the sugar as before. Finally put the roof into position, again using the sugar as glue.

Put the chimney into place, then sieve some icing sugar over the roof and put the house on a rolled out piece of cotton wool (cotton) or white cloth or paper.

Joulutortut
CHRISTMAS STARS

These prune-filled pastries originated from Sweden and resemble the little plastic windmills on sticks that children run around with in summer. The rich pastry is made with cream and butter and contrasts well with the sweet filling. Christmas stars can be eaten with dollops of whipped cream or simply by themselves, preferably with lots of strong coffee, Finnish-style.

prunes, soaked, cooked and stoned (pitted)	425g	15oz	1$^3/_4$ cups
caster sugar (US: granulated)	150g	5oz	$^1/_2$ cup
plain flour	350g	12oz	3 cups
baking powder	5ml	1tsp	1tsp
double or whipping cream	175ml	6fl oz	$^3/_4$ cup
butter, softened	250g	9oz	2$^1/_4$ sticks
egg, beaten	1	1	1

Mash the cooked prunes and mix with the sugar.

Sift the flour and baking powder into a large bowl and stir in the stiffly beaten cream. Quickly stir in the softened butter and leave in a cool place for half an hour.

Roll the pastry out on a floured board to a thickness of 6 mm ($^1/_4$ in.), then cut into 10cm (4 in.) squares. Put a teaspoonful of filling in the centre of each square. Make a cut from each corner towards the middle about 2.5cm (1 in.) long and fold over every other point to meet in the middle. Glaze by brushing with the beaten egg. Bake in a hot oven at 200°C (400°F/Gas 6) for 15–20 minutes and serve hot or cold.

Saffransbrödet

SAFFRON PULLA

The fragrant scent of saffron and cardamom from a baking *pulla* is a sure sign that Christmas is on its way. The Finns eat sweet spicy *pulla* with their coffee much as Americans eat cookies. At Christmas *pulla* is specially scented and coloured with saffron, the precious golden stamens from a particular type of crocus, *Crocus sativa*. *Pulla* dough is coaxed into a variety of shapes before being baked. Some families use a large knot of *pulla* as a base for a group of tall white candles on their Christmas table.

fresh yeast	50g	2oz	2tbs
strong white flour	850g	1lb 14oz	7$\frac{1}{2}$ cups
caster sugar (US: granulated)	150g	5oz	$\frac{2}{3}$ cup
milk	500ml	17fl oz	2 cups
butter	200g	7oz	1$\frac{3}{4}$ sticks
large pinch of saffron strands, ground to a powder			
cardamom, ground	2ml	$\frac{1}{2}$ tsp	$\frac{1}{2}$ tsp
salt	2ml	$\frac{1}{2}$ tsp	$\frac{1}{2}$ tsp
egg, beaten	1	1	1

Decoration

egg, beaten	1	1	1
raisins	50g	2oz	$\frac{1}{4}$ cup
almonds, whole or chopped	50g	2oz	$\frac{1}{4}$ cup
granulated sugar	50g	2oz	$\frac{1}{4}$ cup
icing sugar (confectioner's sugar)	75g	3oz	$\frac{1}{3}$ cup
a little hot water			

Crumble the yeast into a bowl. Add 50g (2oz/$\frac{1}{4}$ cup) of the flour and 25 g (1oz/2tbs) of the sugar. Heat the milk in a small saucepan until lukewarm (44 C/110 F). Pour over the yeast and stir well. Leave this mixture in a warm place for about 20 minutes or until frothy. Sift the flour and salt into a large bowl and make a well in the middle of the flour. Melt the butter. Pour into the well the melted butter, frothy yeast mixture, ground saffron, cardamom, remaining sugar and beaten egg. Mix together, gradually drawing the flour into the liquid in the well, and then knead for about 10 minutes until the mixture is elastic and leaves the sides of the bowl clean. Add more flour if necessary. Cover the dough in the bowl loosely with a cloth and leave it to rise in a warm, draught-free place for 1–1$\frac{1}{2}$ hours or until doubled in size.

Knead the dough again until smooth and use the dough to make one large shape such as a wreath, a knot, or 'priest's hair', or many small shapes such as animals (birds and snails), people, crosses, S-shapes and plaited hearts. Put the shapes on to a greased baking tray, decorate with raisins and almonds, and brush with beaten egg. Leave to rise again for about 40 minutes. Pre-heat the oven to 190 C (375 F/Gas 6). Bake for about 30–35 minutes. Turn the *pulla* shapes out on to a wire rack to cool.

When cool, decorate with lines of piped white glacé icing, made from the icing (confectioner's) sugar and water. *Pulla* is best eaten warm.

~ EXTRA RECIPE ~

Kalja

NON-ALCOHOLIC BEER

This is the customary drink after the sauna and with the Christmas fare and is made at home.

rye malt	175ml	6fl oz	³/₄ cup
sugar	225g	8oz	1 cup
boiling water	6 litres	10 pints	25 cups
fresh yeast	5ml	1tsp	1tsp

Mix the malt and sugar in a sterilized pail or other large container and pour on the boiling water. When the mixture is hand-hot, add the crumbled yeast. Cover the container with a cloth and leave the *kalja* to ferment overnight. The next day strain and bottle it, then keep in a cool place.

G R E E C E

Greece is a country steeped in religious tradition, and its Christmas celebrations are scarcely touched by the rampant commercialization of the festival so apparent in some countries. Many people use the pre-Christmas period as a time of spiritual preparation by prayer, confession and communion. Strict members of the Greek Orthodox Church fast for forty days, eating only fish, fruit and vegetables and not even fish on Wednesdays and Fridays. Others prefer to fast for only a couple of weeks but most are especially careful in the week before Christmas when, in addition to the ban on meat, eggs and dairy produce, fish and even olive oil are given up.

The Greek Orthodox Church attaches more importance to the 'spiritual birth' of Christ, when he was baptized at the age of thirty, than to his physical birth celebrated on 25 December so, while Christmas is important and schools and offices are closed, it doesn't assume quite the same importance as other religious festivals such as Epiphany and Easter. Many Christmas customs are similar to those at New Year, because 25 December was once the beginning of the New Year, and when it became Christmas Day instead, a number of New Year traditions were absorbed.

The Greeks approach Christmas with careful preparation, and many Greek homes are cleaned and painted ready for Christmas Day. Washed and sparkling, each receives a Christmas tree of pine or fir, decorated with a star on top, tinsel and artificial snow. Christmas cards are sent between family and friends, most depicting religious scenes.

Christmas is a feast day, and some food is prepared in advance. *Kourambiethes*, the melt-in-the-mouth Greek shortbread traditionally made for special occasions, or its cousin *melomakaroma*, the round and scented honey shortbreads specially made at Christmas, scent the air with their sweet smell and are packed away in tins ready for the great day. It's traditional too to bake *moustokouloura*—shortbread flavoured with ouzo (an aniseed-flavoured aperitif), rose-water or vanilla—for Christmas.

Year round it's customary for neighbours—especially in villages—to give each other samples or *mirothia* ('sniffs') of the food they've cooked. Neighbours take special care to visit pregnant women who, it is feared, might miscarry if they are not given a taste of whatever they fancy.

In some rural villages it's still customary to pay to have food cooked in the baker's oven. The family name is scribbled on the container and a collection time arranged before baking. An electric cooker sometimes stands in the kitchen as an unused status symbol, a camping gas stove coping with simple cooking and the baker's oven with the rest. In towns and cities some families take food to be cooked in the oven of the local 'tea-house' (*zaharoplastion*). The bakers' shops and tea-houses tend to be focal points of Greek communities where people meet and all the news is passed on.

Christmas Eve dawns and children everywhere prepare to go round the houses singing *kalenda* ('carols') to the accompaniment of little clay drums and metal triangles. Further back in history, children did exactly the same sort of thing at the time of the Roman festival of Kalends at the New Year, hence the word *kalenda*. Housewives reward the singers with little cakes, nuts and small gifts.

In southern Greece the ovens are lit to bake the flat loaves of sweet, spicy, golden *Christopsomo* (Christ-bread). Glazed with sugar on top, the bread is decorated with nuts, sometimes in the shape of a cross to represent Christ, or perhaps with an emblem representing an aspect of the family's life and profession. Some women outline the shape of their hand on the bread. In some kitchens you'll see a loaf of *Christopsomo* nailed to the wall, a constant reminder of Christ's blessing throughout the year.

At supper time on Christmas Eve the table is laid with the *Christopsomo* and a pot of honey, and dried fruit and nuts as well. The master of the house makes the sign of the cross over the loaf, then greets everyone and cuts the first slice. Some families in Messenia keep this slice to give the first beggar that calls at the house on Christmas Day, and sprinkle crumbs under trees, for pagan legends say that their sacred power will improve the trees' yield! A variety of other dishes is eaten and, when supper is finished, the table-cloth is left on the table, 'in case Christ should come and eat during the night'.

This overlaying of pagan lore with Christian traditions is widespread in Greece. At dawn on Christmas Day, the village girls in Epirus draw water which is believed to have supernatural powers. They use it to mix yeast, then they light a candle and stick it to the edge of their bowl, saying three times 'Christ is born, the light is rising—so that my yeast may be good.' This yeast is used throughout the coming year to make sourdough bread and symbolizes the power of Christ to work in the hearts of people to make their lives fruitful and meaningful.

On Christmas morning, at seven o'clock or thereabouts, there is the Christmas mass. In the past men and women were strictly segregated in the Greek Orthodox Church but today this only happens in some isolated villages. After the service people greet each other with *Hronea bola*, which means 'many happy years' and this is the traditional greeting for each person you meet for the first time after Christmas.

Breakfast after church usually consists of soup, bread and coffee. Because it is now Christmas Day and meat is allowed after the fast, a traditional soup is made with chicken broth thickened and flavoured with *avgolemono*— an egg and lemon sauce—and rice. Few Greeks eat butter with their bread though some dunk their bread in the soup.

Christmas Day in Greece is somewhat unusual in that no presents are exchanged because it is considered first and foremost a religious celebration. Gift-giving is reserved for New Year's Day (St Basil's Day) when St Basil himself brings toys down the chimney for the children. Though St Nicholas is the patron saint of Greece as well as the patron saint of seamen, he doesn't appear as a gift-bringer.

Christmas morning is spent preparing for the feast which will start at lunch time. The house is by now filled with family members from near and far who tend to congregate near the cook and help her or just talk. As many families are large compared with those in other European countries, there is plenty to talk about. Everyone who can afford it has a new outfit bought or made especially for today. The table is laid and is called 'our Lady's table', in honour of Mary, just for this day. In some country areas the hearth is the site for the ancient pagan custom of pouring libations of wine and then oil in front of the fire, which has long been a symbol of the sunshine to come.

While the food is being prepared, drinks are handed round with the toast, '*Kaly orexi*' or 'good appetite'. In Greece no one drinks unless they also eat, and so *mezethes* (appetizers) are circulated. These include nuts, several varieties of olives, tomatoes and cubes of cheese.

Lunch is a long drawn-out affair which

nobody wants to hurry and it may go on throughout the day right up until bedtime. In fact, Greeks consider it impolite to get the meal over and done with when guests are present. Children snooze in the afternoon and awake fighting fit for more fun and food. Grown-ups talk and laugh, eat and drink, and the cook continually brings new delights to the table. It's customary in Greece to make it obvious that you are enjoying your food, to give choice morsels from your plate to your neighbour at the table and to fill up empty glasses.

To begin with there are more *mezethes*. They may include such delicacies as *bourekakia* with *myala*—little triangular pies made from *phyllo* pastry baked a golden-brown and filled with a delicious mixture of poached brains flavoured with cheese and dill. Little fish such as sardines or anchovies are fried as they are or in fritter batter and served with *skorthalia* (garlic sauce). *Keftethes* (meatballs) are fragrant with oregano, 'the joy of the mountains' as it is known in Greece. Greek cheese is fried in butter and served in the pan as *saganaki* with a little lemon juice sprinkled over it. Also popular are home-made pork sausages (*maties a saffathes*) and squid stuffed with onion, rice, herbs, garlic, pine nuts and perhaps blackcurrants or spinach. Some families serve kebabs, or crispy fried rings of squid (*kalamarakia*) or little Greek cuttlefish (*soupies*) with lemon wedges, while others roast quail, sausages or pigs' sweetbreads on skewers in the open fire, or chestnuts in the embers. A dish of giant white beans baked with olive oil and a tomato sauce is traditional for the Christmas table.

After the *mezethes* the usual dish today is roast turkey, stuffed perhaps with chestnuts, rice, pine nuts and bacon, served with *tzatziki*, a refreshing salad of cucumber and rich garlicky live yoghurt garnished with black olives. A white cabbage salad is a well-liked alternative to *tzatziki*. Roast pork, lamb or even a fat capon is still the traditional fare in some country villages. Often a family pig is specially fattened up for Christmas. Sausages, ham and bacon from this Christmas pig last the family throughout the coming year. *Pastichio* is sometimes served with the meat of the main dish. This is made from layers of macaroni moistened with egg yolk, and minced beef flavoured with onion, tomatoes, parsley and wine. The whole is topped with cheese sauce and cooked in the oven.

As the afternoon draws on to dusk, sweet dishes are brought to the table. Some families serve *kolyva*, a mound of cooked wheat grains mixed with sesame seeds, currants, walnuts, sugar and spice, and often decorated with a cross and the initials of a deceased loved one in icing sugar, almonds and silver dragées. *Kolyva* is a dish of remembrance: an acknowledgment of the spiritual presence of the dead. The wheat is a symbol of Jesus' resurrection which brings everlasting life (represented by the sugar) to the deceased. This custom dates back to the time of Athanasius the Great, Archbishop of Alexandria in the fourth century.

Rich, syrupy desserts are served only on special occasions. For Christmas, though, the table bears such pastries as *galatoboureko*—the most delicious custard tart you can imagine, with layers of *phyllo* pastry and rich egg custard made with semolina, all soaked with a syrup of cinnamon-flavoured honey.

Baklava is a well-known Greek pastry, its layers of *phyllo* pastry interspersed with almonds and cinnamon and soaked in syrup. *Kataifi* pastry is made with a nutty dough passed through a fine mincer. Balls of the tiny strands of pastry are filled with almonds, sugar and cinnamon, baked, then sprinkled with rosewater and a lemony syrup. Not to be forgotten are the *diples*, sweet fried 'lovers' knots' of risen dough, and the Christmas shortbreads, *melomakaroma* and *moustokouloura*, each piece with a clove in the middle. These are served with coffee and plenty of fresh fruit, including large Greek oranges.

On into the evening the party continues, with plenty to drink and ample portions of the various sweets on the table. Toasts are frequent and spontaneous during the evening. If the mood of the evening is right, there is singing and dancing amidst the chatter. Later small cups of strong black coffee are served accompanied by glasses of water and spoonfuls of *glyko*—home-made candied fruit such as orange peel, green walnuts (*karithi*) which turn black as they are crystallized, cherries, water melon and slices of quince. Greek coffee is nearly always served ready-sweetened with sugar: those who prefer their coffee without sugar must ask for it served *sketos*.

Christmas festivities continue throughout the next twelve days. New Year's Eve, when gifts are traditionally exchanged, is a carnival day with more pagan customs and superstitions intermingling with Christian symbolism and legend, and New Year's Day is a very important feast day. A New Year's cake (St Basil's cake or *vasilopitta*) is eaten either at midnight on New Year's Eve or at lunchtime on New Year's Day. Whoever finds the gold coin traditionally hidden in the cake is said to be lucky throughout the year. Children wake on New Year's Day to find presents left for them by the chimney by St Basil, a figure who looks remarkably like Father Christmas.

During the twelve days of Christmas you may hear mention of *kallikantzari*—the hideous goblins who are traditionally the terror of the Greek country folk. The legend goes that these goblins try all year round to chop down the tree supporting the earth. Just as they have nearly succeeded, Jesus is born and makes the tree whole again, which causes the *kallikantzari* to surface in rage.

Whether they are connected with werewolves, as in much of European folklore, with the spirits of the departed, or with the very ancient custom of dressing up as part animal associated with the winter festival of Dionysus (supplanted in Roman times by the festival of Kalends) or whether they are simply nightmares caused by overeating, nobody knows. Nevertheless the Greeks protect themselves against the *kallikantzari* by painting their doors with a black cross on Christmas Eve or by burning a large log—the Christmas or 'twelve day' log—with something very strong-smelling such as an old shoe in their hearth. Some believe to this day that children born at Christmas may join the *kallikantzari* unless prevented by being bound with straw or garlic or having their toe-nails singed, because toe-nails are essential for these evil creatures!

Christmas ends with Epiphany on 6 January, In Greece 6 January has lost its connection with the wise men—these are remembered on Christmas Day itself. Epiphany is a church festival recalling the baptism of Jesus as a man, when he began his work of teaching and preaching a message that changed the world.

A GREEK CHRISTMAS LUNCH

BOUREKAKIA WITH MYALA
Tiny brain pies

PSARIA TIYANITA WITH SKORTHALIA
Fried fish with garlic sauce

SAGANAKI *Fried cheese with lemon*

MATIES A SAFFATHES *Greek sausages*

~

ROAST TURKEY WITH CHESTNUT, PINE NUT, RICE AND BACON STUFFING

with
TZATZIKI *Cucumber and yoghurt salad*

~

KOLYVA *Sweet, spicy remembrance wheat*

KOURAMBIETHES *Shortbread*

GALATOBOUREKO OR OTHER PASTRIES

~

GLYKO *(candied fruit peel, pistachio nuts, etc)*

Bourekakia with myala

TINY BRAIN PIES

Sheets of paper—thin *phyllo* (strudel) pastry are used to make little triangular pies baked with a delicious filling of brains lightly flavoured with dill. Brains are considered a great delicacy in Greece and little pies of varying shapes are usually only made for special occasions such as Christmas. All the women in the house join together to wrap the pastry and filling into the many layers of each pie. *Phyllo* means 'leaf' and this pastry can be bought ready-made in many towns, usually frozen but occasionally fresh. If unavailable, it can be made at home or substituted with puff pastry, in which case the pastry is simply rolled out thinly and cut into 8cm (3in.) squares which are filled and then folded over into triangles.

This recipe makes 30–35 pies.

set of brains, really fresh, lamb's, sheep's or calf's	1	1	1
salt	5ml	1tsp	1tsp
white wine vinegar	15ml	1tbs	1tbs
egg, beaten	1	1	1
cheese, grated (kefalotyri, Gruyère or Parmesan)	25g	1oz	2tbs
salt and pepper to taste			
fresh dill, finely chopped OR	5ml	1tsp	1tsp
dried dill	2ml	1/2 tsp	1/2 tsp
unsalted butter	100g	4oz	1 stick
olive oil	60ml	4tbs	1/4 cup
phyllo pastry	225g	8oz	10 sheets

Soak the brains in lukewarm water for 30 minutes then gently wash them under cold running water. Fill a saucepan with water, add the salt and vinegar and bring to the boil, then carefully lower the brains in and simmer for 6–8 minutes (lamb's) or 10–12 minutes (sheep's or calf's). Remove with a perforated spoon and put into a large bowl. Add the egg, cheese, seasoning and dill and mix thoroughly with a fork, breaking the brains up into a relatively smooth mixture suitable for filling the pies.

Melt the butter in a bowl standing in a pan of boiling water and add the oil. Take the *phyllo* pastry and cut the rectangular block of sheets into 4 strips of layers lengthways, each strip measuring about 8cm (3in.) wide. Put one strip in front of you and cover the remaining pastry with a damp cloth to prevent it drying out and becoming brittle.

Brush the top layer of pastry from one strip with the melted butter and oil. This top layer is now progressively folded over teaspoonfuls of brain filling to make one little pie as follows:

Put a heaped teaspoonful of the filling in the centre of one end of the top layer, about 4cm (1 1/2 in.) in from the end. Take one point of the top layer of the pastry and fold it diagonally to form a triangle. Now put another teaspoonful of filling on the pastry 4cm (1 1/2 in.) in front of the triangle. Take the pointed free end of the triangle, fold it down to cover the pile of filling. Put another teaspoonful of filling in front of this now three-layered triangle, then take the free point of the triangle and fold it diagonally across the filling to form a four-layered triangle. Continue until you have finished up the pastry in this top layer: this is one pie.

Repeat the process until you have used up all the layers in each of the four strips. Put the pies on greased baking sheets with the loose end of pastry underneath. Brush the tops of the pies with the remaining butter and oil and bake in a pre-heated oven at 180°C (350°F/ Gas 4) for 30 minutes or until golden-brown.

Skorthalia

GARLIC SAUCE

This garlicky sauce is widely used in Greece as a dip for crisply fried vegetables such as aubergines (eggplant) and courgettes (zucchini) and for tiny fried fish such as sardines or anchovies. It also goes very well with chicken and with boiled potatoes and beetroot. Traditionally it is made with finely ground walnuts but ground almonds can be used instead if you prefer them.

stale white bread, medium slices, crusts removed	4	4	4
large cloves of garlic, peeled and crushed	4	4	4
walnuts or almonds, ground	75g	3oz	1/3 cup
white wine vinegar	30ml	2tbs	2tbs
olive oil	100ml	4fl oz	1/3 cup
salt to taste			

Soak the bread in water then squeeze well. Add the garlic, nuts and vinegar and mix well till smooth. Gradually add the oil, drip by drip at first, then season to taste. If the garlic dip is too thick, add a little cold water and stir it in well.

Saganaki

FRIED CHEESE WITH LEMON

A little Greek frying pan with two black handles lends its name to this traditional dish. Full of hot fried cheese, the pan is brought straight off the hob (stove) to the Christmas table. Fried cheese eaten with lemon and black pepper is a popular *meze*, or appetizer. In Greece they use a hard cheese such as *kefalotyri* (a Parmesan-like cheese made from the milk of sheep or goats) or *kaseri* (a firm, creamy cheese made from sheep's milk), but any hard cheese tastes good. In this recipe this cheese is fried just as it is, but you may like to dip the slices in beaten egg yolk, then in flour or breadcrumbs before frying.

hard cheese	225g	8oz	8oz
butter	50g	2oz	1/2 stick

lemons, cut into wedges	2	2	2
black pepper			

Cut the cheese into slices 12mm (1/2 in.) thick. Heat the butter in a frying pan and put the slices in a single layer in the pan. Cook for 1–2 minutes until the cheese bubbles, then take the pan to the table. Let people help themselves to the cheese and pass round quarters of lemon and black pepper.

If you are making a meal out of the fried cheese, double or triple the quantities in the recipe.

Maties a saffathes

GREEK SAUSAGES

Home-made pork sausages are often served at Christmas as a *meze* (appetizer). Most butchers will supply you with casings to make your own sausages: the natural casings are better than the synthetic ones.

pork, minced	675g	1 1/2 lb	1 1/2 lb
rice, uncooked	50g	2oz	1/4 cup
cloves of garlic, crushed	2	2	2
ground cumin	10ml	2tsp	2tsp
grated orange peel	2ml	1/2 tsp	1/2 tsp
fresh parsley (preferably flat-leaf), chopped OR dried parsley	45ml 10ml	3tbs 2tsp	3tbs 2tsp
egg, beaten	1	1	1
black pepper	2ml	1/2 tsp	1/2 tsp
salt to taste			
casing for 675g (1 1/2 lb) meat			

olive oil for frying

Mix together all the ingredients and knead until smooth. Cut the casings into 38cm (15in.) lengths. Tie a knot in one end of each casing and stuff with the mixture, then tie the open end. Next knot the stuffed casings in 7–10cm (3–4in.) sections. Heat a large pan of water to boiling point, add the sausages and boil for 1–1$^1/_2$ hours. Allow the sausages to cool in the water, then drain and dry with kitchen paper. Heat some olive oil in a frying pan and fry the sausages until golden-brown all over. Serve hot.

Roast turkey with chestnut, pine nut, rice and bacon stuffing

In Greece the Christmas turkey is simply served roasted and stuffed, with a salad to accompany it. This recipe includes chestnuts, which are very popular in Greece at this time of year.

chestnuts	675g	1$^1/_2$ lb	3 cups
butter	225g	8oz	2 sticks
onion, finely chopped	1	1	1
bacon, finely chopped	175g	6oz	$^3/_4$ cup
cooked rice	225g	8oz	1 cup
pine nuts	25g	1oz	2tbs
pinch of nutmeg			
salt and pepper to taste			

Cut a cross into the skin of each chestnut and cook in boiling water for 15 minutes. Remove from the water and take off the skins and inner coverings, then cut each chestnut into quarters. Melt half the butter in a frying pan and fry the onion until golden. Add the remaining ingredients (including the left over butter) and cook for 5–10 minutes, stirring occasionally. Use to stuff the neck end of the turkey, putting any remaining stuffing into the body cavity. Roast the turkey in a pre-heated oven, working out the cooking time from its oven-ready weight (see section on Great Britain).

Tzatziki

CUCUMBER AND YOGHURT SALAD

With cucumbers now available all year round, this has become a popular salad to eat with the roast turkey on Christmas Day. The addition of double cream is optional—Greek yoghurt is rich and, if you can't get it, the cream helps to make average yoghurt more like Greek yoghurt.

Tzatziki can also be used as a dip—in which case make sure the cucumber is particularly finely chopped or even grated. Use crisply fried slices of courgette (zucchini) or aubergine (eggplant) to dip into it.

cucumber, chopped into 5mm ($^1/_4$ in.) cubes	1	1	1
salt or sugar	15ml	1tbs	1tbs
plain yoghurt, Greek if possible	450ml	$^3/_4$ pint	1$^3/_4$ cups
double cream (optional) (US: whipping)	60ml	4tbs	$^1/_4$ cup
cloves of garlic, crushed	3	3	3
fresh mint or dill, chopped **OR**	15ml	1tbs	1tbs
dried mint or dill	5ml	1tsp	1tsp
white wine vinegar	15ml	1tbs	1tbs
salt and pepper to taste			
black olives to garnish			

Sprinkle the salt or sugar over the cucumber in a sieve resting over a bowl and leave for an hour to drain the bitter juices out. If you have used salt, wash the cucumber under running cold water to remove it, then drain well. Mix together the yoghurt, cream, garlic, mint or dill and wine vinegar and add the cucumber. Adjust the seasoning to taste and serve garnished with black olives.

Kolyva

SWEET, SPICY REMEMBRANCE WHEAT

Many old Greek families put a dish of *kolyva* on the table at Christmas time in memory of their dead relatives. This custom dates back to the time of Athanasius the Great, Archbishop of Alexandria in the fourth century. It's usual to take three spoonfuls of *kolyva*, which comes to the table beautifully decorated with icing sugar, almonds and silver balls. The wheat in *kolyva* is a symbol of Jesus's resurrection which brings everlasting life (represented by the sugar) to the deceased.

whole wheat grains, soaked in water overnight	450g	1lb	2 cups
sesame seeds, toasted till golden-brown	225g	8oz	1 cup
currants	50g	2oz	2tbs
walnuts, ground	150g	5oz	3/4 cup
sugar	100g	4oz	1/2 cup
cinnamon	15ml	1tbs	1tbs
seeds from 1 pomegranate, if available			
icing sugar (confectioner's sugar)	275g	10oz	1 1/4 cups
blanched almonds	175g	6oz	3/4 cup
flour, lightly toasted	25g	1oz	2tbs
decorative silver balls	50g	2oz	1/4 cup

Cook the soaked wheat grains in a large pan of salted water until tender, stirring frequently. Drain, rinse in

cold water, drain again and dry by squeezing in a tea cloth. Spread out on kitchen paper to dry for several hours. Put the wheat in a large bowl and add the sesame seeds, currants, walnuts, sugar, cinnamon and pomegranate seeds. Mix well. Shape a rounded mound of the wheat mixture on a serving dish and sift the icing (confectioner's) sugar liberally over it. Decorate with the almonds by making a cross and also putting them round the base of the mound. Sprinkle the toasted flour over the almond cross. Outline the cross with silver balls. Some people like to form the initials of the person they particularly want to remember with more almonds.

Kourambiethes

SHORTBREAD

A s the shortbread is cooking the whole house fills with its sweet smell. Each piece of shortbread has a clove on top as a reminder of the spices brought by the wise men to Jesus. As soon as they are cooked, the pieces are dipped into rose-water, then rolled in icing sugar.

unsalted butter	225g	8oz	2 sticks
egg yolks	2	2	2
caster sugar (US: granulated)	50g	2oz	1/4 cup
brandy	15ml	1tbs	1tbs
blanched almonds, coarsely chopped (optional)	100g	4oz	1/2 cup
plain flour	275g	10oz	2 1/2 cups
cloves	24	24	24
rose-water			
icing sugar (confectioner's sugar)	450g	1lb	2 cups

Cream the butter (with an electric mixer for speed if you have one) until white. Add the egg yolks, caster sugar and brandy and beat well, then stir in the almonds and flour thoroughly. On a floured board, make a long roll about 2cm (1in.) in diameter and cut this diagonally in 24 slices, each about 2cm (1in.) thick. Press a clove into the top of each slice. Put them on to a greased baking tray, leaving them some room to spread. Bake at 180°C (350°F/Gas 4) for 15–20 minutes but check that they do not go brown. Remove from the oven and dip the biscuits one at a time into the rose-water, working quickly and using a pair of kitchen tongs. Next roll each biscuit in a bowl of icing sugar and leave to cool in a tin lined with a layer of icing sugar. Covered tightly, the biscuits will keep well for a week.

Galatoboureko

GREEK CUSTARD TART

R ich desserts are rarely eaten in Greek homes except on special occasions such as Christmas. This typically Greek dish is made from paper-thin sheets of *phyllo* ('leaf' or strudel) pastry layered with a sweet thick semolina egg custard and soaked in cinnamon-flavoured syrup. It is similar to the Middle-Eastern *baklava*.

Filling

milk	600ml	1 pint	2 cups
sugar	75g	3oz	1/3 cup
unsalted butter	50g	2oz	1/2 stick
semolina	50g	2oz	1/4 cup
eggs, beaten until frothy	3	3	3
vanilla essence (extract)	2ml	1/2 tsp	1/2 tsp

Syrup

water	175ml	6fl oz	2/3 cup
honey	75g	3oz	1/4 cup
cinnamon stick	1/2	1/2	1/2
OR			
dried cinnamon	2ml	1/2 tsp	1/2 tsp
orange-blossom water	15ml	1tbs	1tbs
clove	1	1	1

grated peel of 1/2 lemon

Pastry

phyllo pastry	350g	12oz	15 sheets
unsalted butter	75g	3oz	3/4 stick
corn oil	30ml	2tbs	2tbs

Prepare the filling by heating the milk and sugar in a saucepan to boiling point, without letting it actually boil. Add the butter and stir till melted, then slowly pour in the semolina, whisking to prevent lumps from forming. Cook until the mixture begins to thicken. Stir in the beaten eggs and vanilla essence.

Make the syrup by putting all the ingredients except the orange-blossom water into a large pan and bringing to the boil. Cover and simmer for 20 minutes, then add the orange-blossom water and allow to cool. Remove the clove and cinnamon stick, if used.

Take a metal cake tin with high sides—a Swiss roll tin or a roasting pan won't do because the tart rises during cooking—about 23 x 30cm (9 x 12in.) and cut 10 sheets of *phyllo* pastry to fit the base of the tin. Melt the butter and stir in the oil. Brush some of this butter and oil mixture liberally over the pastry. Spread half the filling over the pastry and cover with a further 10 sheets of *phyllo*. Brush with more butter and oil. Spread the remaining filling over, then cover with a final 10 sheets of *phyllo*. Brush with the remaining butter and oil.

Bake at 160°C (325°F/Gas 3) in a pre-heated oven for about 45 minutes until golden-brown.

Let the *galatoboureko* stand for 5 minutes, then pour the syrup over it. Leave for 6 hours and serve cut into diamond-shaped pieces.

~ EXTRA RECIPE ~

Avgolemono soup

This lemony chicken soup with rice is always part of a Greek Christmas breakfast. A less well-known version is made with sour dough noodles instead of rice. A basic chicken stock is slowly added to some avgolemono (egg and lemon sauce). Avgolemono by itself is a good accompaniment to all kinds of meat, fish and vegetables, as long as no garlic or tomatoes have been used in their preparation.

chicken, preferably old for a better flavour	1	1	1
carrots, chopped	2	2	2
onions, sliced	2	2	2
sticks of celery, chopped	2	2	2
bay leaf			
water to cover			
rice	100g	4oz	1/2 cup
eggs, well beaten	2	2	2
juice of 1 large or 2 small lemons			
salt and pepper to taste			

Cover the chicken, vegetables and bay leaf with water and bring to the boil. Cover and simmer for 1 hour or more, until the meat easily comes away from the bone. Strain and put 1.8 litres (3 pints/7$\frac{1}{2}$ cups) of the stock in a large pan. Add the rice and cook until tender—about 25–30 minutes, depending on the type of rice. Meanwhile, slowly add the lemon juice to the beaten eggs, beating constantly as you do so. Take about 300ml ($\frac{1}{2}$ pint/1 cup) of the slightly cooled stock and add a tablespoonful at a time to the eggs, beating constantly to prevent curdling. Add this mixture to the rest of the stock and season to taste with salt and pepper. Serve at once. If the soup has to be reheated, take great care not to boil it as this will cook the eggs and make the soup look unpleasant.

POLAND

Based on an C18ᵗʰ Polish woodcut

Poland has Christmas traditions that are among the richest and most colourful in the world. The country's boundaries have changed many times. Because of this, Poland has absorbed traditions from neighbouring countries which have added further colour to an already fascinating festival.

Favourite traditions vary from one area to another and many have their roots in pre-Christian times, though many Christian overtones have been added.

Advent is heralded by the old custom of eating goose on St Martin's Day (11 November) in preparation for the pre-Christmas fast. Originally Advent lasted for forty days instead of four weeks. During this time of preparation homes are cleaned and polished, glasses and china are washed, rooms are repainted if necessary and the table linen is washed and starched for the Christmas Eve table.

On 6 December, St Nicholas' Day, St Nicholas arrives in some towns on a horse-drawn sleigh and magically produces from his cloak gifts of heart-shaped honey cakes, holy pictures and big red apples, for the children.

Christmas preparations become more urgent as December progresses. Letters to friends and relatives living far away are written in plenty of time to arrive for Christmas Eve. They contain the precious *opłatek*—wafers of bread embossed with nativity scenes which have been blessed by the priest and sent as tokens of love, friendship and peace.

Early in December spiced honey cakes (*pierniki*) are made, for they improve with keeping in an airtight tin. Instead of breaking the eggs for her cakes, a mother may carefully blow them so that her children can use the shells to make birds with paper beaks for the Christmas tree. A dove symbolizes peace but the more popular rooster stands for health, fertility and good luck. The egg itself symbolizes new life and the miracle of Jesus' birth.

The smell of honey wafts through the house as the children busy themselves making these egg ornaments and other decorations. Intricate paper cut-outs are made to decorate the kitchen shelves and *pajaki*, spidery, umbrella-shaped decorations often made from straw, are put aside to be ready for the tree.

With grown-up help the children make a wreath from corn, apples, nuts, feathers and coloured tissue. This is suspended from the ceiling over the dining table ready for the *wilja* supper (the Christmas Eve supper). Straw chains on some wreaths symbolize Poland's long chaining to foreign rule.

During December a bowl of beetroot and water with a piece of rye bread on top is set aside in a warm place to ferment for a week. The resulting alcoholic brew—*kwas*—is later used to make the special Christmas Eve *barszcz* (beetroot soup). A day or two before Christmas Eve a fragrant dish of *bigos* is prepared for lunch on Christmas Day. *Bigos* is made from a mixture of meats and sauerkraut and improves with keeping.

Some time before Christmas Eve the family goes out to buy its tree (*choinka*), although country-dwellers may still take an axe and cut their own. According to ancient belief, Jesus' cross was made from a fir tree. Since then, it is said, branches springing from the trunk of the fir form crosses with each other in memory of that day. The tree is said to have become an evergreen from the time Jesus' blood was spilled on the cross.

The tree is decorated with sweets, gilded walnuts, apples, miniature dolls, blown eggs,

pająki, animals and slippers, paper baskets and angels and more modern commercially produced ornaments too. Stars are favourite Christmas decorations—in fact, the popular name for Christmas Day—*Gwiadzka*—means 'little star', after the star of Bethlehem. Real candles are preferred because they give light and warmth. They are a remnant of pagan belief: long ago fires were lit to avert evil, drive away unclean spirits and spread fertility and goodwill. But for Christians today they are a reminder of what Jesus said about himself: that he is the light of the world. Candles have a lovely fragrance, especially when made from beeswax.

There is great excitement in the air when Christmas Eve dawns. Christmas Eve is the beginning of the twelve days of Christmas, known here as *gody*. This time of celebration stems from the popular ancient Roman midwinter festival of Saturnalia which left so many traces on Christmas customs in Europe, and which symbolized the death of the old year and the beginning of the new. It also echoes the ancient Babylonian festival called *Sacaea*, and the twelve days of chaos, representing the conflict between good and evil, found in ancient Chinese, Vedic and European writings.

Long before dawn the fishermen are busy about their work. Poland's rivers and lakes teem with fish such as carp and pike, and by morning the catch will be on sale at the fishmongers' ready for the shoppers who are out purchasing what they need for the Christmas Eve, or *wilja*, supper. This meal breaks the pre-Christmas fast but is traditionally meatless. *Wilja* or *wigilja* comes from the Latin *vigilare*, 'to watch', and in the evening the children will watch for the first star to appear in the sky. This twinkling light reminds them of the star of Bethlehem which led the wise men to Jesus. Christmas Eve is called the 'Festival of the Star'.

The house must now sparkle and smell

be an even number of people seated at the *wilja* table. An odd number would indicate the death of one person present during the year ahead and having thirteen people present is to be especially avoided. An extra place is laid in case Mary and Jesus should knock at the door of the house ('the inn of Bethlehem') and ask for shelter and food for the night.

Strangers are always welcome at the *wilja* table. A Polish proverb tells us *'Gość w domu, Bóg w domu'*—'A guest in the home is God in the home.' A story goes that long ago a Polish nobleman went astray on Christmas Eve in a snowstorm and entered a house at random. It happened to be the home of his deadly enemy. There was great surprise on both parts, but then the host went to his visitor, offered him an *opłatek* and a greeting, then invited him to share supper. The result was that long years of hatred vanished at once and both men became great friends ever after. On Christmas Eve there is no room for hatred.

Before the meal begins, the father and mother enact the rite of the *opłatek*. They face each other, break their *opłatek*, then exchange and eat a piece. Next they embrace and wish each other a happy new year and the fulfilment of their deepest wishes in the year to come. This is perhaps a reminder that Christmas Eve is the last day of the pagan year. Other wafers are passed around by the father and everyone exchanges greetings of love, good health and happiness or at least an untroubled life. The ceremony reminds the family of their distant relatives who are at this very moment doing the same thing with the *opłatek* they received in the post.

In times past when servants were plentiful, the *wilja* supper—often known as the apostle's supper—consisted of twelve dishes, in memory of the twelve apostles. The meal begins with an

sweet, for no cleaning is allowed on Christmas Day. All morning the children help in the kitchen, cracking nuts for special tortes and preparing poppyseed filling for the poppyseed cake. As the cake rises, they are sent out of the kitchen so there is no disturbance in the air.

Before the table is laid for supper, some country families bring in sheaves or handfuls of the best of the harvest's grains. A sheaf is put in each corner of the room, 'the gold of the wheat, mingling with the silver of the rye', as one poet described it. This custom probably originated with pagan festivities rejoicing at nature's fertility but now it reminds Christians of the birth of Jesus in a stable. Some sweet-smelling hay is laid under the table-cloth too. During supper, if a girl pulls a piece of hay from under the table-cloth, a young green wisp means she will marry a young man and a wrinkled one, an old man!

An old superstition decrees that there must

appetizer such as pickled herring with salad, then continues with soup. *Barszcz* (beetroot soup) is a favourite for Christmas Eve and is similar to the Russian *borshch* but more refined, with a flavour reminiscent of claret. *Uszka* are tiny, ear-shaped stuffed dumplings (similar to ravioli) which are cooked in boiling water just before the meal is served, then added to the *barszcz*. Mushroom soup, made with Poland's delicious forest mushrooms, is also popular, as is almond soup, served after the fish course. Some homes serve a light soup and a dark one. Savoury pancakes may come next, stuffed perhaps with onions and cabbage.

The supper continues with fish, served baked or boiled. A large fish is usually cut up for cooking and reassembled before being served. Polish carp is a fragrant dish with a sauce made from gingerbread, almonds and raisins. Vegetables to go with the fish may include the traditional cabbage—red or white and sometimes pickled—often stuffed with barley; cauliflower topped with breadcrumbs fried in butter, chopped egg white and egg yolk, and parsley; potatoes with sour cream; and 'meatless *bigos*'—a mixture of sauerkraut, mushrooms and yellow peas.

Desserts usually include a fruit compôte—

sometimes made with twelve fruits (again for the twelve apostles); a walnut cake; or a poppyseed cake. *Kutia* is a porridge served on Christmas Eve in families near the Byelorussian or Ukrainian borders in order, some say, to commemorate the dead. It is made from grain, poppyseed and honey. Each ingredient has a symbolic meaning: the grain is a reminder of the times when there were no mills; the poppyseed stands for peaceful dreaming; and the honey for the sweetening or easing of daily toil. There is a particular ritual over the serving of *kutia*. The head of the household stands up, makes the sign of the cross over it, and says a prayer for health and for good crops in the coming year.

After supper, crumbs are put out for the birds; leftover *oplatek* are mixed in with the cattle food by farming families; and sheaves or handfuls of grain are tied to fruit trees in the orchard or garden so they bear plentiful fruit next year. These old customs have died out in many areas, but some families still remember them.

Now is the time for everyone to take their coffee into the living room and to nibble at the crystallized fruit, sweets and nuts. The fire blazes, candles on the tree are lit and the violin is tuned for the *kolendy* (carols), such as Chopin's

hauntingly beautiful *'Lulajże Jezuniu'*, a lullaby to Jesus.

Lullaby, Jesus, O cease from your crying,
Here on Thy Mother's warm breast softly lying.
Lullaby Jesus, O sleep now, my treasure,
Mother is watching with love none can measure.

See how the world lies in sorrow and sadness;
Give us thy blessing, O bring Heaven's gladness!
Lullaby, Jesus, O sleep now my treasure;
Mother is watching with love none can measure.

Before bedtime, the children put a letter on the window-sill for the gift-bringer, Mother Star, hoping she will leave them the presents they want. A few children are still put to bed on a pile of hay, reminding them that Jesus was born in a manger.

At midnight, the time set for Jesus' birth, legend has it that the heavens and the earth are opened. If you are pure in heart, you may see Jacob's ladder stretching upwards, or the earth opened to reveal treasures. For one hour, animals can speak, but only the good can hear them!

Those who wish now go out into the cold air and snow to the midnight shepherds' mass, the *pasterka*. In some places the entire village is lit up for the occasion and the bells ring. The service is a reverent but joyous one. Afterwards, some may go visiting. If a man is the first visitor after the midnight mass, that means success for the house. Traditionally the first visitor goes straight to the hearth to make some sparks fly from a burning log and sprinkles some corn on the floor, saying, 'Christ is born.' Someone in the family replies, 'He is born indeed,' and shakes some corn over him in return.

Christmas Day dawns and the children open their presents with the usual glee of children all over the world. Christmas Day is a quiet family day: both today and tomorrow are public holidays. Some go to mass again—the angels' mass or the mass of the three kings—and admire the beautiful and elaborate *szopka* (nativity scene) in church. Christmas Day lunch is a special meal, though not as special as the *wilja* supper.

On 26 December, St Stephen's Day or the 'second Christmas', everyone is his own master. This tradition dates from the days of servants, when domestic help was hired or rehired for the coming year. It is a day of visiting and perhaps for taking part in the *kulig*. This was once a horse-drawn sleigh ride with bells jingling and the rowdy, costumed occupants of the comfortable, hay-filled sleigh ending up at someone's house for a party. Today the method of transport is likely to be more modern! Fireworks and the sound of the fife lend atmosphere to the occasion.

During the twelve days of Christmas there are colourful customs. Star singers are boys who parade with a large cardboard star on a pole. The star represents the star of Bethlehem and has a transparent centre with a candle inside. One of the boys twirls the star round on a string and they all sing carols or recite verses. The star-carrier sometimes leads a fur-coated creature with a monstrous wooden head—the *turon*—chosen for his skill at making the onlookers laugh. Other boys carry a puppet theatre on four poles and when they stop they enact the nativity story. The whole troupe is rewarded with money or gifts of food for its labours.

In many towns both grown-ups and children enjoy a nativity tableau or play (*jasełko*). The nativity figures are joined by the devil, Herod, Death and ordinary villagers dressed in national costume. This custom dates from the time when monks toured Europe in the middle ages, converting people to Christianity. Although a remnant of a superstitious era, this custom shines with the ring of truth: it is a reminder of the reality of Jesus' birth and his triumph over evil for all time.

A POLISH
CHRISTMAS EVE MEAL

ŚLEDZIE MARYNOWANE *Soused herring*

SALAD

~

BARSZCZ Z USZKAMI
Beetroot soup with stuffed dumpling 'ears'

~

NALEŚNIKI Z CEBULA I KAPUSTA
Pancakes stuffed with onions and cabbage

~

KARP W SZARYM SOSIE *Carp with gingerbread sauce*

~

GROCH Z GRZYBAMI Z KAPUSTA
Sauerkraut with mushrooms and peas

~

ZIEMNIAKI Z KWASNA SMIETANA
Potatoes in sour cream

~

STRUCEL Z MAKEM *Poppyseed cake*

~

KUTIA *Sweet wheat porridge with poppyseeds*

Śledzie marynowane

SOUSED (PICKLED) HERRINGS

Herrings are very popular in Poland. Many families preserve herrings in salt and keep them in a cool place until needed. Salted or fresh herrings can be marinaded in oil, vinegar or sour cream, perhaps with horseradish, mustard, or other spices. Soused herrings are particularly delicious. A recipe for salted herrings is given first, but you can use fresh herrings for Christmas Eve if you can get them. Begin sousing at least 5 days before you want to eat the herrings. The Poles are very partial to eating soused herrings with sour cream mixed with a little of the sousing liquid.

To salt herrings:

fresh herrings	4	4	4
malt vinegar	600ml	1 pint	2½ cups
coarse sea salt	45ml	3tbs	3tbs
allspice berries, crushed	6	6	6

Clean and gut the herrings and remove the head and fins, then put the fish in a large bowl and cover with the vinegar, reserving 60ml (2tbs). Leave overnight and drain. Sprinkle the base of a deep dish with a third of the salt, reserved vinegar and allspice, and place two herrings on top. Sprinkle with another third of the salt, etc., and lay the other herrings over the first two. Sprinkle the remaining salt, vinegar and allspice on top. Cover with foil, place weights on the foil, and leave in a cold place until needed.

To souse herrings

fresh or salted herrings	4	4	4
malt vinegar	350ml	12fl oz	1½ cups
water	60ml	4tbs	¼ cup
onions, sliced	3	3	3
bay leaves	3	3	3
peppercorns	10	10	10
sugar	100g	4oz	½ cup
sour cream (optional)	225ml	8fl oz	1 cup

Soak salted herrings in cold water for 24 hours and drain. Gut fresh herrings and remove their heads and fins. Slit the salted or fresh herrings down their bellies and open them out flat. Skin the fish, then remove their backbones with a sharp knife.

Put the herring fillets into a deep dish. Put the vinegar, water, onions, bay leaves, peppercorns and sugar into a pan and bring to the boil. Cover the pan and simmer for 5 minutes. Leave to cool, then pour over the herrings. Cover and leave in a cold place for 5–7 days.

Drain the herrings before serving them with lettuce or a tomato salad. If you wish to have them with sour cream, reserve 100ml (4fl oz/½ cup) of the sousing liquid, then mix the liquid with the sour cream and pour over the fish.

Barszcz z uszkami

BEETROOT SOUP WITH STUFFED DUMPLING 'EARS'

This clear beetroot soup is traditionally served on Christmas Eve. This recipe from an old Polish cookery book contains *kwas*—a very slightly alcoholic beetroot 'beer', made by fermenting beetroot with rye bread for a week. It is the old-fashioned way of making *barszcz* and is well worth the effort, but if you want to make a simpler recipe, leave out the *kwas* and add 1kg (2lb) of beetroot to the vegetable stock recipe, replacing about a quarter of the water used with light ale.

Uszka are little stuffed 'ears' of boiled dough and the traditional Christmas Eve filling includes fish, onions and mushrooms. They are added to the soup just before serving.

An old custom is to count the number of women and girls expected for supper and then to include enough linked pairs of *uszka* so that there is one pair for each female. If a single girl finds a pair of linked ones, says the tradition, she will soon marry. If a married woman finds a pair, she will soon expect twins!

The preparation of this Christmas Eve *barszcz* takes some organization. Start a whole week before by making the *kwas*. On Christmas Eve morning, prepare the vegetable stock and the *uszka*, but don't cook the *uszka*. Just before you wish to eat, prepare the *barszcz* by combining the *kwas* and the vegetable stock. Cook the *uszka* and add to the soup just before serving.

Kwas (fermented beet juice)

raw beetroot	1kg	2lb	2lb
rye bread	50g	2oz	2tbs
lukewarm water	1.2 litres	2 pints	5 cups

Peel the beetroot and slice into 12mm ($^1/_2$ in.) slices. Put the slices into a bowl and cover with the water. Put the bread on top. Cover with a cloth and leave in a warm place to ferment. During the next week, from time to time remove the scum that rises to the top. On the eighth day, remove the bread and strain the juice. This *kwas* keeps for 2 weeks in a cool place.

Vegetable stock

water	2.25 litre	4 pints	8 cups
carrots	4	4	4
sticks of celery	4	4	4
bay leaf	1	1	1
salt and pepper to taste			
onion	1	1	1
sprigs of parsley	2	2	2
butter	25g	1oz	2tbs

Wash the vegetables but do not peel. Cut into small pieces. Melt the butter in a large pan and add the vegetables. Sauté gently until softened. Add the water and bay leaf and simmer for 30 minutes. Strain.

Uszka with Christmas Eve filling

plain flour	225g	8oz	2 cups
egg	1	1	1
water	100ml	4fl oz	$^1/_2$ cup
pinch of salt			
mashed potato	50g	2oz	$^1/_4$ cup
Christmas Eve filling (see below)			

Put the flour into a large bowl and make a well in the centre. Beat the egg with the water and salt and pour into the well. Draw the flour into the egg gradually. When all the flour is incorporated, add the potato and knead well until elastic. Cover and put in a warm place for about 10 minutes. Divide the dough in half for ease of working. Roll out each piece of dough thinly and cut into 5cm (2in.) squares. Place 2ml ($^1/_2$ tsp) of filling a little to one side on each square. Moisten two sides of each square with water. Fold into triangles and press the edges of each triangle together. Bend the base of each triangle and stick the points at either side of the base together. Drop the filled *uszka* into salted boiling water and cook until they float to the top.

Christmas Eve filling

white fish, cooked and finely chopped	100g	4oz	$^1/_2$ cup
small onion, fincly chopped	1	1	1
butter	10ml	2tsp	2tsp
mushrooms, boiled till tender	100g	4oz	$^1/_2$ cup

salt and pepper to taste

Melt the butter in a pan and sauté the onions gently until softened. Add the finely chopped mushrooms and fish, salt and pepper. Cook for 5 minutes, stirring. Leave to cool before using.

Barszcz

vegetable stock	2.25 litre	4 pints	8 cups
kwas	600ml	1 pint	2 cups
sour cream	225ml	8fl oz	1 cup
flour	50g	2oz	½ cup

uszka

sour cream to decorate OR	50ml	2fl oz	¼ cup
cooked beetroot, cut into strips OR	50g	2oz	¼ cup
croûtons			

Bring the vegetable stock to the boil in a large pan. Blend the cream and flour and add to the pan. Mix well and bring to the boil again. Remove from the heat. Heat the *kwas* in a pan but do not boil. Add to the thickened stock. Put the soup into a serving dish, add the *uszka* and garnish with swirls of sour cream, strips of cooked beetroot or croûtons.

Naleśniki z cebula i kapusta
PANCAKES WITH ONIONS AND CABBAGE

Pancakes have been eaten in Eastern Europe in winter since pre-Christian times and their shape and colour are said to represent the sun and the return of longer days with the forthcoming spring. Polish pancakes are made with lots of eggs and are very light. Don't despair if your first pancake is a disaster—the second one is invariably easier to make.

plain flour	225g	8oz	2 cups
egg	1	1	1
eggs, separated	3	3	3
milk	300ml	½ pint	1¼ cups
water	300ml	½ pint	1¼ cups
oil	15ml	1tbs	1tbs
pinch of nutmeg			
salt	5ml	1tsp	1tsp

butter or lard for frying pancakes

Filling

large onions, sliced	3	3	3
cabbage, finely shredded	350g	12oz	1¼ cups
oil	15ml	1tbs	1tbs

Sift the flour into a bowl and add the egg and egg yolks, milk, water, oil and nutmeg. Whisk the mixture well to make a smooth batter. Whisk the egg whites and salt with a clean whisk until stiff, then fold into the batter. Put a small knob of butter or lard into a frying pan and heat until the pan is very hot, (but don't allow the butter to burn). Coat the bottom of the pan with the butter or lard. Pour enough batter into the pan to spread to the edges when you tilt the pan, and cook until air bubbles appear under the surface of the pancake. Turn carefully and cook the other side until lightly brown, lifting the edge of the pancake with a fish-slice to gauge when it's done. Turn the pancake out on to a plate and cover it with foil. Keep the pancake warm either by putting the plate over a large pan of simmering water, or in the oven. Use the batter to make a stack of pancakes.

To make the filling, heat the oil in a frying pan and fry the onions until softened. Stir in the cabbage and cook for 8–10 minutes. Put a spoonful of the onion and cabbage mixture on each pancake and fold over before serving.

Karp w szarym sosie
CARP WITH GINGERBREAD SAUCE

Carp is available in most large towns to order and is best cooked very fresh. The aromatic sauce of gingerbread, almonds and raisins complements the flavour of the fish perfectly. It's said that if you keep a few scales from the Christmas carp in your purse, you'll have money to see you the whole year through.

carp	1.25kg	2¹/₂ lb	2¹/₂ lb
water	1.2 litres	2 pints	5 cups
carrots, sliced	2	2	2
leek, sliced	1	1	1
onions, sliced	2	2	2
sticks of celery, sliced	4	4	4
sprigs of parsley, chopped	6	6	6
onion, stuck with 2 cloves	1	1	1
slices of lemon	2	2	2
salt to taste			
bay leaf	1	1	1
beer	600ml	1 pint	2 cups
gingerbread or honeycake, crumbled	100g	4oz	¹/₂ cup
almonds, blanched	50g	2oz	¹/₄ cup
seedless raisins	50g	2oz	¹/₄ cup

Cover the carp in salted water for 3 hours to remove any muddy taste. Put the water, vegetables, lemon, salt, parsley and bay leaf into a fish kettle or a large pan. Bring to the boil and simmer for 10 minutes. Cut the fish into as few chunks as possible to fit into your pan, or leave whole if you can. Lower the fish into the simmering liquid and add the beer. Cover and simmer for 30 minutes or until a fin on the head of the fish can easily be pulled out. Remove the fish, keep it warm and strain the stock, reserving 450 ml ($^3/_4$ pint/approx 2 cups) of the liquid. Pour this liquid back into the pan and add the gingerbread or honeycake, almonds and raisins. Cook for 10 minutes. Arrange the fish on a large plate, reforming the shape of the fish if necessary. Spoon the sauce over the fish and serve at once.

Groch z grzybami z kapusta
SAUERKRAUT WITH MUSHROOMS AND PEAS

Sauerkraut is usually bought from large barrels in Polish markets and is available in glass jars in delicatessens in many other countries. Home-made sauerkraut is simple to make and takes a week or so to ferment.

yellow split peas	60ml	4tbs	1/4 cup
Sauerkraut, home-made (see recipe below) or bought	1kg	2lb	3 1/2 cups
water	600ml	1 pint	2 cups
onions, chopped	2	2	2
lard	50g	2oz	1/4 cup
mushrooms, chopped	100g	4oz	1/2 cup
flour	25g	1oz	3tbs
hot water	300ml	1/2 pint	1 cup
pinch of salt			
shake of black pepper			

Soak the split peas overnight in a pan of cold water. Drain and cover with more cold water. Bring to the boil and simmer for 45 minutes, then drain. Rinse the sauerkraut and chop. Put it into a large pan with the water and bring to the boil. Simmer for about 15 minutes, then drain. Fry the onions in the lard in a large pan until softened, then add the mushrooms and cook for 5 minutes more. Remove from the heat and mix in the flour. Add the sauerkraut and cooked peas and about 300ml (1/2 pint/1 cup) of hot water, and heat through. Season and serve.

Sauerkraut

firm white cabbage, finely shredded	1kg	2lb	3 1/2 cups
salt	30ml	2tbs	2tbs
caraway seeds	5ml	1tsp	1tsp
cardamom, ground	2ml	1/2 tsp	1/2 tsp
rye flour	50g	2oz	1/4 cup
warm water	150ml	1/4 pint	1/2 cup

Mix the shredded cabbage, salt, caraway seeds and cardamom. Sprinkle the rye flour into an earthenware, glass or plastic container, add the salted cabbage, and pour in the warm water. Brine will start forming quickly and should be kept at a level above the cabbage to prevent air getting to it. Cover and leave in a warm place (about 21 C–70 F), stirring every couple of days and removing the scum on the surface. The sauerkraut is mature or ready when it has stopped bubbling, usually about 7–10 days, but sometimes several weeks, depending on the temperature.

Ziemniaki z kwasna smietana

POTATOES IN SOUR CREAM

medium potatoes, peeled	6	6	6
medium onions, peeled and chopped	2	2	2
butter	50g	2oz	1/2 stick
sour cream	100ml	4fl oz	1/2 cup
fresh dill, chopped OR	15ml	1tbs	1tbs
dried dill	5ml	1tsp	1tsp
salt and pepper to taste			

Boil the potatoes for 5 minutes. Drain and slice. Sauté the onions gently in the butter until softened. Add the potatoes, sour cream, dill, salt and pepper and cover the pan. Cook slowly for about 20 minutes or until the potatoes are tender. Serve hot.

Strucel z makem

POPPYSEED CAKE

Poppyseeds are an old favourite of Polish cooks and no wonder, because they once used 'maw'— poppyseeds from the opium poppy! Whether or not the poppyseeds you can buy today will make you sleep well, this yeasty roll with its sweet poppyseed filling will make you ask for more. Poppyseed cake is the most traditional Polish Christmas cake.

milk	225ml	8fl oz	1 cup
egg yolks	4	4	4
salt	5ml	1tsp	1tsp
butter	50g	2oz	1/2 stick
sugar	100g	4oz	1/2 cup
vanilla essence (extract)	5ml	1tsp	1tsp
almond essence (extract)	2ml	1/2 tsp	1/2 tsp
dried yeast	15ml	1tbs	1tbs
lukewarm water	50ml	2fl oz	3tbs
plain flour	450g	1lb	4 cups
poppyseed filling (see below)			
icing sugar (confectioner's sugar) to decorate	25g	1oz	2tbs

Bring the milk to the boil in a pan then cool until lukewarm. Beat the egg yolks with the salt until thick. Cream the butter and sugar. Add the essences and the egg yolks to the creamed mixture and stir well. Dissolve the yeast in the lukewarm water and add to the mixture. Sift the flour and add alternately with the cooled milk, beginning and ending with the flour. Knead until the dough leaves the fingers. Cover with a damp cloth and leave to rise in a warm place until double the size. Punch the risen dough down and let it rise again until doubled in size. Divide the dough into two and roll each half on a floured board into a rectangular shape the thickness of a finger. Spread with poppyseed filling. Roll up tightly, beginning with the wide side, much like a Swiss roll. Seal the edges by pinching them together. Place in two greased tins about 33 x 12 x 6cm (13 x 4$\frac{1}{2}$ x 2$\frac{1}{2}$ in.). Cover and let the dough rise until it fills each pan. Bake for 45 minutes at 180°C (350°F/Gas 4). Sprinkle the top with sifted icing (confectioner's) sugar while still hot.

Poppyseed filling

Poppyseed is expensive to buy if you get it in small containers. Large amounts are best bought from specialist grocers or health food stores selling loose poppyseed by weight.

milk	350ml	12fl oz	1$\frac{1}{2}$ cups
ground poppyseed (use a pestle and mortar to grind)	300g	11oz	1$\frac{1}{4}$ cups

sugar	225g	8oz	1 cup
eggs, beaten	2	2	2
vanilla essence (extract)	5ml	1tsp	1tsp
almond essence (extract)	2ml	$1/2$ tsp	$1/2$ tsp
sultanas (golden raisins)	75g	3oz	$1/3$ cup

Bring the milk to boiling point and add the poppyseed. Cook until the milk is absorbed, stirring constantly (about 5 minutes). Add the sugar and cook for a further I minute. Add the beaten eggs and stir over the heat without boiling until thick. Add the sultanas (golden raisins). Remove from the heat. When cooler, stir in the essences. Use the filling when cold.

Kutia

SWEET WHEAT PORRIDGE WITH POPPYSEEDS

Dishes of cooked, sweetened grain are eaten throughout much of Europe. In some countries they are traditionally associated with Christmas, funerals, or the anniversary of the death of a loved one. Greek *kolyva*, Scandinavian rice pudding, Russian *kasha*, and Russian and Polish *kutia* are some examples, and even the British Christmas pudding can trace its origins back to a much plainer grain recipe.

Today, Poles use honey to sweeten and poppyseeds to flavour their delicious wheaten *kutia* just as their ancestors did for centuries at Christmas. Soak the wheat grains the day before Christmas Eve, and cook them the next morning, as the custom is to eat *kutia* cold for Christmas Eve supper.

You can cook this recipe with whole wheat grains, but many people prefer the texture of 'pearled' wheat grains. These are wheat grains (kernels/groats/berries) without their outer husks. If you can't buy them ready pearled, find whole-wheat grains instead and remove the husks. You do this by soaking the grains overnight, then putting them between the layers of a clean, folded linen tea cloth on a work surface, and rolling them repeatedly with a rolling pin. Rinse the pearled grains in a sieve with boiling water to wash the husks away.

(Russians often cook their wheat grains in 'almond milk', made by putting 100g (4oz/$1/2$ cup) of almonds in a pan of water, bringing to the boil, allowing to cool, then draining and reserving the 'milk'. Chopped, toasted almonds replace the walnuts in the following Polish recipe.)

pearled wheat	300g	11oz	$1 1/4$ cups
poppyseeds	250g	9oz	1 cup
runny honey	400g	14oz	$1 3/4$ cups
cherry conserve (preserves)	150g	5oz	$3/4$ cup
walnuts, broken into large pieces	150g	5oz	$3/4$ cup
raisins	15ml	1tbs	1tbs

Put the pearled grains into a pan, cover with plenty of cold water, and soak overnight. Add enough cold water to cover the soaked grains, bring to the boil and simmer until the water has been absorbed and the grains are tender but still intact, stirring occasionally to prevent the grain sticking to the bottom of the pan. Put the poppyseeds in a bowl and cover with boiling water. Leave for two minutes and drain, then repeat with more boiling water. Grind in a pestle and mortar or an electric blender. Mix the cooked wheat, poppyseeds, honey, cherry conserve, walnuts and raisins and put into a serving dish. Serve the *kutia* cold.

~ EXTRA RECIPES ~

Bigos
HUNTER'S STEW

Rich, fragrant *bigos* is Poland's national dish and has a long history. It is said that it was originally made with the game left over from banquets. Today it is often served at Christmas and is usually prepared several days ahead because it tastes better when re-heated. *Bigos* contains a variety of vegetables and meats, apples and sometimes prunes. This is one of the simpler of the many recipes and is enough to serve ten people.

salt pork or bacon, diced	100g	4oz	4–6 slices
cooking oil	15ml	1tbs	1tbs
large onions, peeled and sliced	2	2	2
mushrooms	100g	4oz	1/2 cup
cooking apples, cored, peeled and sliced	2	2	2
tomatoes, chopped	3	3	3
mixed cooked meats: (beef, lamb, pork, ham, game, poultry) cut into small bite-sized chunks	1.5kg	3lb	3lb
sauerkraut, washed and drained	1kg	2lb	4 cups
Polish sausage(kiełbasa), cut into 12mm (1/2 in.) slices	225g	8oz	1 cup
sugar, salt and pepper to taste			
Madeira wine	100ml	4fl oz	1/2 cup
water to cover			
single cream (half and half)	100ml	4fl oz	1/2 cup

Fry the salt pork in a large saucepan in the cooking oil, stirring until browned. Add the onions and cook until softened. Add the mushrooms, apples, tomatoes, sauerkraut, meats, sausage, sugar, salt and pepper. Add the wine and enough water to cover the ingredients. Bring to the boil, cover the pan and cook slowly for 1 hour. Add the cream just before serving.

Mazurek
CHRISTMAS FRUIT BARS

There are several different recipes for *mazurek*, some using ground almonds or other nuts instead of flour. This recipe has a topping rich in dried and glacé fruit and nuts.

sugar	350g	12oz	1 1/2 cups
plain flour	225g	8oz	2 cups
butter	100g	4oz	1 stick
eggs	3	3	3
double cream (US: whipping)	45ml	3tbs	3tbs
sultanas (golden raisins)	200g	7oz	3/4 cup
pitted dates, cut into small pieces	225g	8oz	1 cup
chopped nuts	175g	6oz	3/4 cup
juice of 1 orange			
juice of 1 lemon			
glacé fruit: a mixture of cherries, pineapple, orange and lemon peel, chopped	450g	1lb	2 cups
rum	50ml	2fl oz	1/4 cup

Mix 225g (8oz/1 cup) of the sugar with the flour and rub in the butter. Beat 1 egg and add to the mixture with the cream. Mix well. Spread in a greased tin about

38 x 25cm (15 x 10in.). Bake at 180°C (350°F/Gas 4) for 20 minutes. Beat the other 2 eggs and mix with the remaining sugar, raisins, dates, nuts, orange and lemon juice and glacé fruit. Spread over the cooked base and bake for a further 20 minutes. Cut into bars when cold.

Makes 48 small bars.

Piernik

HONEYCAKE

Spiced cakes sweetened with honey have been made in Eastern Europe ever since the crusaders brought spices back from the orient in the fourteenth century. Honeycakes without the spice date back at least to the ninth century, when they were made with rye flour, berry juice and honey. Nowadays the honey is sometimes replaced or supplemented with sugar. A variety of spices can be used, and sometimes nuts and sultanas (golden raisins) are added. The older recipes were fat-free—some say because butter and other animal fats were avoided during the pre-Christmas fast, while others say it was done out of deference to the cows in Jesus' stable. Oil or butter are usually included nowadays. This recipe tastes good with a light frosting of glacé icing.

runny honey	250g	9oz	1 cup
eggs, beaten	4	4	4
caster sugar (US: granulated)	225g	8oz	1 cup
corn oil	90ml	6tbs	6tbs
self-raising flour	500g	18oz	4 1/2 cups
milk	225ml	8fl oz	1 cup
allspice	2ml	1/2 tsp	1/2 tsp
cloves, ground	2ml	1/2 tsp	1/2 tsp
cinnamon	2ml	1/2 tsp	1/2 tsp
nutmeg	2ml	1/2 tsp	1/2 tsp
ginger	2ml	1/2 tsp	1/2 tsp
icing sugar (confectioner's sugar), sifted	225g	8oz	1 cup
hot water	30ml	2tbs	2tbs

Grease and line a baking tin, then grease the lining paper. Put the sugar in a large bowl and mix in the beaten eggs. Warm the honey in a pan and stir into the mixture. Stir the flour and spices together, then gradually fold into the mixture. Add the oil and milk and mix thoroughly but gently. Pour the mixture into the prepared tin and bake at 180°C (350°F/Gas 4) for one hour. Test with a skewer to see if it is done.

Let the cake cool on a wire rack and, when it is cold, frost it with an icing made by mixing the icing sugar with sufficient hot water to allow it to run smoothly.

Tort orzechowy

WALNUT CAKE

Nuts are plentiful and popular in Poland at Christmas time and walnuts give a wonderful flavour to this light, cream-filled sponge cake. This recipe is adapted from the one in Mary Pininska's book 'The Polish Kitchen' (published by Macmillan in 1990), and is the best we have tried.

large eggs, separated	4	4	4
caster sugar (US: granulated)	100g	4oz	1/2 cup
ground walnuts	100g	4oz	1/2 cup
dried breadcrumbs	45ml	3tbs	3tbs
Drambuie or brandy	45ml	3tbs	3tbs
double cream (US: whipping)	300ml	1/2 pint	2 1/2 cups

Beat the egg yolks with the sugar until thick and pale. If you haven't an electric beater, this is quicker if you do it in a bowl over a pan of simmering water. Whisk the egg whites until very stiff. Mix the ground nuts with 30ml (2tbs) of the breadcrumbs, then fold the yolks alternately with the whites into this mixture.

Oil a 20cm (8in.) cake tin, then line it with greaseproof (waxed) paper and brush the paper with more oil. Sprinkle the base of the tin with the remaining breadcrumbs to help prevent sticking. Pour in the cake mixture and put into an oven pre-heated to 200°C (400°F/Gas 6). Turn the oven down at once to 180°C (350°F/Gas 4) and bake for about 45 minutes. Carefully turn the cake out on to a wire rack to cool, then cut into two layers and sprinkle the cut surfaces with 30ml (2tbs) of the Drambuie.

Whip the cream and remaining Drambuie until thick and spread over the bottom layer of the cake. Sandwich the layers together and serve.

Kompt z suszonych owoców

DRIED FRUIT COMPÔTE

A compôte of dried (and sometimes fresh) fruit is a favourite on the Christmas Eve table in parts of Poland, as well as in southern Russia and the Ukraine, and is often eaten with the *kutia*. If you wish to put twelve fruits in the compôte in memory of the twelve apostles, add three other types of fruit, such as a sliced banana, two halved and stoned (pitted) fresh plums, and some pitted canned or bottled cherries to the cooked compôte.

dried pears	50g	2oz	1/4 cup
dried apples	50g	2oz	1/4 cup
dried figs	75g	3oz	1/3 cup
lemon, sliced	1/2	1/2	1/2
pinch of mixed (pumpkin) spice			
cinnamon stick	1	1	1
water	900ml	1 1/2 pints	3 cups

prunes	50g	2oz	1/4 cup
dried peaches	50g	2oz	1/4 cup
dried apricots	50g	2oz	1/4 cup
seedless raisins	50g	2oz	1/4 cup
grated rind of 1 orange			
brandy	45ml	3tbs	3tbs

Put the pears, apples, figs, lemon, mixed spice and cinnamon stick into a large pan and add the water. Bring to the boil, cover and simmer for 10 minutes. Add the prunes and peaches and simmer for 10 minutes. Lastly add the apricots, raisins and grated orange rind and simmer for another 15 minutes or until all the fruit is just tender. Remove from the heat and discard the cinnamon stick and lemon slices. Stir in the brandy. Cover the pan and leave to cool.

SWEDEN

Detail from Swedish painted furniture

Sweden has changed dramatically in the last century. A mere hundred years ago it was a nation of farmers. Today 83 per cent of the people live in cities and urban areas, and only 4 per cent earn their living from farming. Despite this mass migration the Swedish calendar is littered with rural festivals and many deeply rooted customs and traditions are kept alive. Some, such as St Lucia's Day, have even benefited from the modern influence of the mass media.

St Lucia Day, 13 December, was once only celebrated in isolated parts of Sweden. At that time it was dedicated to St Lucia of Syracuse, who was martyred because she preferred the love of Christ to the love of a young man. That is until the 1920s, when a Stockholm newspaper arranged a competition to choose a Lucia bride to represent the city. The idea caught on like wildfire and today nearly every home, school, office and club selects a Lucia bride.

According to the medieval calendar, 13 December marked the longest night of the year and was a time when people and animals needed extra nourishment. Originally it was only men who celebrated the festival with much eating and drinking, attended by young girls dressed in long white robes with crowns of evergreens and candles in their hair. Today on St Lucia morning the oldest daughter of the family dresses in the same way and serves her family a breakfast of coffee, ginger biscuits and *lussekatter*, which are sweet buns delicately flavoured and coloured with saffron. Sometimes a retinue of similarly dressed attendants accompanies her and they all sing a hauntingly beautiful Lucia song and Christmas carols.

Lucia comes from *lux* meaning light and this festival, although devoid of any religious meaning, brings light and gaiety to the Swedish mid-winter. Nobel prize winners, arriving in Stockholm to collect their prizes at this time of year, often take home unforgettable memories of these radiant young girls and their Christmas songs.

Another source of light in the long cold winter is the lighting of the first of four Advent candles on the fourth Sunday before Christmas. Advent means 'coming' and it is a time of preparation for the coming Christmas season. Stars made of straw, paper or metal are hung in the windows. Even those who generally don't bake like to make cakes and biscuits for Christmas. Little fingers help to shape the *pepparkakor* (gingerbread biscuits) into hearts, stars, men and goats. *Mandelmusslor* (almond tarts) are made and stored in an airtight tin to be sandwiched together at the last moment with redcurrant jelly and cream. *Klenäter*, like the Norwegian *fattigman*, are delicious twists of dough deep fried and sprinkled with icing (confectioner's) sugar.

Straw is the stuff of Christmas in Sweden, and straw is plaited, twisted, tied and bent into elaborate shapes which are strung from the ceiling and hung on the tree as decorations. Every home has a *Julbock*, a straw goat, or two. These are sometimes used as table decorations, but the larger ones are put under the tree. The significance of straw is now generally forgotten but in their forebears' day the Swedes believed that the Yule straw, especially saved from the last harvest, contained the corn spirit. Many of the shapes of today's decorations are in fact ancient fertility symbols. Before Father Christmas became popular in Sweden the gift-bearer was dressed as a goat.

On Christmas Eve the preparations come to a climax. Shops and offices close in time for everyone to go home to the traditional lunch-

time *Julbord*, a huge smörgåsbord which will have been planned and prepared for days.

To say that a *smörgåsbord* is a large buffet would not do it justice, for it is a feast of sumptuous foods chosen for their harmonious flavours, cleverly and colourfully presented. The word literally means bread-and-butter table, because you eat bread and butter with the various dishes. The idea is said to have originated many years ago when guests would bring their own dishes to country parties to augment those of their hostess. Although all the dishes, hot or cold, are put on one table there is a particular order in which they should be eaten.

Before anything is eaten, however, there is a customary Christmas toast wishing all the family a happy Christmas and a good appetite.

Songs are sung and there is much good-natured banter.

The meal begins with the herring dishes. There can be up to half a dozen different sorts: marinated and served on a block of ice; *sillsallad* (a herring salad in a sour cream sauce); smoked herring pieces; or pickled herring. Each one has a slightly different flavour, sweet/sour or salty, but all are delicious, served with tiny boiled new potatoes to balance the flavours.

After a change of plate the family tries the other fish dishes. Traditionally there is *lax* (salmon) either as *gravlax*, a marinated salmon, or hot smoked salmon with a spicy butter. Perhaps some halves of hard-boiled egg topped with red cod roe and a cucumber salad are chosen as well.

Yet another change of plate takes place, this time to accommodate the selection of cold meats, brawn and Swedish cheeses. A centre-piece of the Christmas table is the *Julskinka*, the succulent Christmas ham which is first boiled and then baked. In many homes there is still the traditional *dopp-i-grytan* when the family dips pieces of sweet, dark *vörtbröd* (wortbread) into the stock in which the ham was boiled, before eating them. A spoonful of potato salad or red cabbage is eaten with the cold meats. A selection of breads—hard, thin crispbread, soft rye bread and a dark malted loaf—is always on hand.

Finally after yet another change of plate the hot dishes are eaten. Amongst these there will invariably be *små köttbullar* (tiny tasty meatballs). If the family members haven't already tried some of *Jansson's frestelse* they have a helping of these creamy potato slices layered with onions and anchovies and baked in cream.

In between the visits to the *smörgåsbord*, the toasting and singing gets more frequent as the warmth of the company and the aquavit and Christmas beer take effect.

After the meal it is time for a visit from the *tomte*, or Christmas gnome. He is credited with looking after the family and the farm and has gradually assumed the role of Santa Claus. An uncle or friend usually dresses up in traditional red robes and white beard and distributes gifts to the children from his sack. On each present it is customary to write a little verse giving a clue to the contents of the package. His work done for the evening, the *Jul-tomte* will slip out, but not before he has had a glass of something fortifying and tasted a few of the Christmas biscuits now on the coffee table.

Dinner on Christmas Eve is a plain fish dish *lutfisk*. Dried ling, a fish of the cod family, is soaked in a lye solution, and then boiled and served with a white sauce, boiled potatoes and peas. Tradition requires that the fish should be put to soak on Lucia Day.

Just as in Denmark, a thick creamy rice porridge dessert, *risgrynsgröt*, is served hot with a sprinkling of cinnamon sugar. Hidden in the porridge is a single almond, and the person to find it, it is said, will be the next person to marry. Some families prefer a set cold rice pudding with pieces of orange in it and decorated on top with orange slices soaked in Cointreau or served with a hot fruit sauce. As in the rest of Scandinavia it is still customary to put a bowl of rice porridge out to keep the *tomte* (Christmas gnome) happy.

As early as 5 o'clock on Christmas morning sleepy Swedes go to church and welcome the dawning Christmas Day. It is pitch black out-side, with the church glowing with the light of candles. Special songs sung only on Christmas morning express the rejoicing at the arrival of the Christ child.

There was a time when it was customary to race sleds or sleighs home from the services believing that the winner would have the best harvest in the coming year. On coming home, a mug of *glögg* (mulled wine) with a 'treasure' of almonds and raisins in the bottom of the glass, is a warming welcome and warming drink. The day is spent quietly within the family circle, visiting friends, skiing, walking and eating.

In Sweden the Christmas season doesn't end until *Tjugondag Knut*, Knut's day, which is a week after Epiphany. *Tjugo* literally means twenty days. The Swedes have a name attached to each day and the name for 20th day happens to be Knut. This is when people finally part with their Christmas tree. The children hold a party when friends and family plunder the tree of any edibles and care-fully store precious decorations for next year.

The tree then is tossed out to a little rhyme: 'Christmas has come to an end, and the tree must go. But next year once again we shall see our dear old friend, for he has promised us so.'

For Swedish Christians, however, and for Christians all over the world, the joy of the Christmas message lasts throughout the year.

A SWEDISH CHRISTMAS EVE LUNCH

JULBORD (SMÖRGÅSBORD)

consisting of

SILLSALLAD *Herring salad with potatoes, apple and beetroot*

VARM RÖKT LAX MED SMÖR
Warmed smoked salmon with savoury butter

POTATISSALLAD *Potato salad*

GURKASALLAD *Cucumber salad*

SYLTA *Veal brawn*

LEVERPASTEJ *Liver pâté*

OST, VÄSTERBOTTEN, SVECIA, KRYDDOST
Assorted Swedish cheeses

JULSKINKA *Christmas ham*

BRÖD *Assorted breads*

JANSSON'S FRESTELSE
Jansson's temptation (anchovy/potato bake)

SMÅ KÖTTBULLAR *Tiny meatballs*

KORV *Assorted Swedish sausages*

Sillsallad

HERRING SALAD WITH POTATOES, APPLE
AND BEETROOT

A feature of the Swedish *Julbord*, or Christmas *smörgåsbord*, is the variety of herring dishes. This is just one way of serving this versatile fish.

filleted salted herring or pickled herring	450g	1lb	1lb
cold boiled potatoes	2	2	2
apple (Granny Smith), peeled and cored	1	1	1
pickled cucumber	1	1	1
onion, preferably red	1	1	1
whole pickled baby beetroot	3	3	3
freshly ground black pepper to taste			
capers			
soured cream	45ml	3tbs	3tbs
hard-boiled eggs	2	2	2

Soak the salted herring fillets overnight in plenty of water. Alternatively use pickled herrings which do not need to be soaked. Cube the herring, potatoes, apple, cucumber and beetroot. Gently mix these together with the onion sliced into rings. Season with black pepper and arrange in a glass salad bowl. Refrigerate for 4–6 hours. Before serving mix in the sour cream, and garnish with chopped hard-boiled eggs.

Varm rökt lax med smör

HOT SMOKED SALMON WITH
SAVOURY BUTTER

It may be a surprise to find that smoked salmon is equally delicious warm. The piquant butter adds additional flavour.

smoked salmon	1kg	2–2¼ lb	2–2¼ lb
butter	75g	3oz	¾ stick
juice of ½ lemon			
fresh dill, finely chopped	30ml	2tbs	2tbs
capers, finely chopped	30ml	2tbs	2tbs
grated lemon rind	5ml	1tsp	1tsp
pinch of lemon pepper or white pepper			

Cream the butter with the lemon juice, dill, capers and seasonings. Shape into a roll and wrap in foil. Refrigerate until required.

Pre-heat the oven to 220°C (425°F/Gas 7). Wrap the smoked salmon in foil. Place on a baking sheet and heat in the oven for 15–20 minutes. Remove the foil and place on a warm platter. Garnish with dill and serve slices of the savoury butter separately.

Gurkasallad

CUCUMBER SALAD

See Norway for recipe.

Julskinka
CHRISTMAS HAM

The stock made from cooking the Christmas ham is used for *doppa i grytan* (dip in the pot), a Christmas Eve ritual of dipping rye bread into the stock and eating it with the fingers.

bacon (or ham) joint (gammon collar or forehock)	1.75kg	4lb	4lb
small onion	1	1	1
peppercorns	6	6	6
carrot	1	1	1
bay leaf	1	1	1
allspice	10ml	2tsp	2tsp
rosemary	10ml	2tsp	2tsp
marjoram	10ml	2tsp	2tsp
cloves	10ml	2tsp	2tsp
bay leaves	6	6	6
sweet Madeira wine	100ml	4fl oz	1/2 cup

Soak the ham in plenty of cold water for about 12 hours. Drain and weigh the joint to calculate cooking time. Allow 20 minutes per 450g (1lb) plus 20 minutes at the end. Return the joint to the pot adding the small onion, peppercorns, carrot, and a bay leaf plus sufficient cold water to cover. Bring to the boil and then lower the heat and simmer for half the cooking time. Meanwhile crush the allspice, rosemary, marjoram, cloves and bay leaves in a mortar. Pre-heat the oven to 160°C (325°F/Gas 3). Drain the ham, remove the rind, pat dry and rub the spice mixture on all sides. Wrap foil around the joint, making a well-sealed package. Bake for the remainder of the cooking time. About half an hour before the end of the cooking time open out the foil and increase the heat to 200°C (400°F/Gas 6) to allow the fat to crisp up. Baste frequently with the Madeira wine.

Slice the joint before serving hot or cold as a centrepiece to the *smörgåsbord*.

Jansson's frestelse
JANSSON'S TEMPTATION

Whoever Jansson was, one can quite easily understand why he was tempted!

old (floury) potatoes, medium-sized	6–8	6–8	6–8
onions, thinly sliced	2	2	2
can of anchovy fillets	125g	4 1/2 oz	4 1/2 oz
butter	25g	1oz	2tbs
vegetable oil	15ml	1tbs	1tbs
dry white breadcrumbs	30g	2tbs	2tbs
single cream (half and half)	150ml	5fl oz	1/2 cup
white pepper to taste			

Peel the potatoes and slice into julienne strips. Heat the oil and butter in a frying pan and gently fry the onion slices until soft but not brown. Butter an ovenproof dish well. Alternate layers of potatoes, onions and anchovies, beginning and ending with a layer of potatoes. As you go, season each layer with a little pepper. Pour the cream over. Top with the breadcrumbs and a few dots of butter and bake at 190°C (375°F/Gas 5) for about 40 minutes until the liquid is absorbed and the potatoes are tender.

Små Köttbullar

SMALL MEATBALLS

These little meatballs are traditionally eaten towards the end of a *smörgåsbord*. The mixture of beef and pork is lightened with egg and breadcrumbs and the meatballs are served without a sauce.

The quantities given are sufficient for 4 as part of a *smörgåsbord*. Make double the amount if you are serving them on their own.

fresh white breadcrumbs	25g	1oz	2tbs
double cream (US: whipping)	75ml	3fl oz	1/4 cup
minced lean pork	100g	4oz	1/3 lb
minced beef	100g	4oz	1/4 lb
small onion, grated	1	1	1
salt	2ml	1/2 tsp	1/2 tsp
freshly ground black pepper to taste			
allspice	2ml	1/2 tsp	1/2 tsp
small potato, cooked and mashed	1	1	1
egg, beaten	1	1	1
flour	30ml	2tbs	2tbs
butter	30ml	2tbs	2tbs
oil	15ml	1tbs	1tbs

sides. Keep shaking the pan to cook them on all sides, which will take 8–10 minutes. Transfer to an oven-proof dish and keep them warm in the oven until ready to serve.

Soak the breadcrumbs in the cream for about 10 minutes. In a large bowl mix the meats, onion, spices, mashed potato and then add the soaked breadcrumbs and the beaten egg. Beat well with a wooden spoon until the mixture is smooth. Form into little balls about 2.5cm (1 in.) diameter and chill for an hour or so before frying.

In a frying pan melt the butter and oil over a high heat. Toss the meatballs in a little flour before frying. Reduce the heat once the meatballs are browned on all

~ EXTRA RECIPES ~

Glögg
PUNCH

A heady and warming punch—ideal after a Christmas walk.

red wine	1 litre	1³/₄ pints	4¹/₃ cups
schnapps, aquavit or vodka	100ml	4fl oz	¹/₂ cup
muscatel	500ml	17fl oz	2 cups
ginger root, whole	50g	2oz	¹/₄ cup
cinnamon sticks	2	2	2
cardamon seed	2ml	¹/₂ tsp	¹/₂ tsp
cloves	6–8	6–8	6–8
caster sugar (US: granulated) to taste	100g	4oz	¹/₂ cup
peel of 1 orange			
seedless raisins	175g	6oz	²/₃ cup
whole blanched almonds	100g	4oz	¹/₂ cup

Mix all the ingredients in a large pot except the aquavit, sugar, almonds and raisins. Leave the mixture overnight for the spices to blend. When required add the aquavit and sugar to taste. Heat thoroughly but do not boil. Stir in the raisins and almonds and serve piping hot in mugs with a spoon to fish out the almonds and raisins.

Saffransbröd og lussekatter
LUCIA BUNS AND SAFFRON BREAD

Sweet buns are always served by the eldest daughter to the rest of the family on St Lucia's day, 13 December.

milk	300ml	¹/₂ pint	1¹/₄ cups
caster sugar (US: granulated)	100g	4oz	¹/₂ cup
dried yeast	30ml	2tbs	2tbs
saffron powder	2ml	¹/₂ tsp	¹/₂ tsp
brandy	15ml	1tbs	1tbs
butter, melted	100g	4oz	1 stick
salt	2ml	¹/₂ tsp	¹/₂ tsp
large egg, lightly beaten	1	1	1
ground almonds	50g	2oz	¹/₄ cup
plain strong bread flour, white	450g	1lb	4 cups
raisins	100g	4oz	¹/₂ cup
egg	1	1	1
water	15ml	1tbs	1tbs
sugar	15ml	1tbs	1tbs

extra raisins to decorate

Warm the milk until it is lukewarm. Add 5ml (1tsp) of the caster (US: granulated) sugar and the yeast to half the milk. Whisk and leave to froth for 15 minutes. Dissolve the saffron in the brandy. In a large bowl mix the saffron brandy, melted butter, salt, lightly beaten egg, ground almonds and the remaining milk with half the sifted flour. Add the yeast liquid, remaining flour and the sugar, beating all the time until you have a firm smooth dough. Knead in the raisins and place in a lightly oiled bowl. Cover with plastic wrap and leave to rise in a warm place until double its size, about 2 hours.

On a floured surface knead the dough for about 10 minutes until smooth and elastic. To make *lussekatter*, the buns eaten on St Lucia's Day, roll small pieces of dough into strips about 20cm (8in.) long. Shape into a simple S-shape, coiling each end loosely. Decorate with a raisin in the centre of each coil. To make the buns larger simply cross two S-shapes into a simple star formation.

If you prefer a single loaf, shape into a large bun or plait the dough.

Place on to a well buttered baking tray and leave to rise in a warm place for a further 30 minutes. Brush the buns with a glaze of beaten egg, water and sugar. Bake in a pre-heated oven 200°C (400°F/Gas 6) until golden-brown. The buns will take 10–15 minutes to cook, the loaf about 25 minutes.

ITALY

Inspired by Italian frescoes at Pompeii.

Italy greets the festival of Jesus' birth with joyful enthusiasm. *This country is the home of the Roman Catholic Church and at noon on Christmas Day the Pope delivers his Urbi et Orbi Christmas blessing to the teeming throngs in front of the Vatican. In the vast colonnaded square people weep, shout for joy and hug each other as their spiritual leader speaks to the people of the city and of the world.*

The pattern of the Italian Christmas reflects this Catholic heritage. On St Lucia's Day—13 December—the fairs in many of the large towns sell Christmas gifts as well as plaster or wooden figurines for the *presepio* or crèche which is seen in churches, banks, railway stations, grocers' shops and chain stores as well as in people's homes. Some of these *presepi* are dramatically beautiful and a few are life-sized. In the church of the *Ara Coeli* (the altar of heaven) in Rome there is a life-sized figure of Jesus decorated with jewels and swaddled in gold and silver cloth and in silk. This *Bambino* is reputed to have miraculous healing powers and is closely guarded. Each Christmas, children are brought to the *Bambino*. They stand on a wooden platform in front of him and quite unselfconsciously make their speeches of praise.

The *presepio* takes pride of place in the Italian home at Christmas and nearby, in a corner of the living-room, stands the Christmas tree, which is usually brought in about a week before Christmas. Trees were popularized in Italy by American soldiers after the Second World War. Ribbons, greetings posters and holly help make the house look festive.

Just before Christmas, children may dress up as shepherds and go from house to house singing, reciting and playing pipes in return for money. In Rome, real shepherds from Abruzzi still come down from the hills with their bagpipes. These pipers or *pifferai* are dressed in sheepskins, red vests and hats with red tassels and white peacock feathers. They go round the town playing in front of each shrine to Jesus in return for gifts of food or money. The chestnut sellers ply their trade and, as the pipers play, the aroma of roasting chestnuts wafts through the air, the evocative scent bringing with it memories of Christmases past.

Before the *cenone* or great supper on Christmas Eve, the family kneels round its *presepio* and prays and sings carols. This used to be a day of fasting, when no meat was eaten and there was only one meal, in the evening. Fasting is no longer required of Roman Catholics, but fish is still the customary food in many homes today.

Eels are a particular favourite, especially near Italy's long coastline. *Capitoni*—the large eels—are the most popular. They are bought smoked or pickled or—more likely—fresh that day to be fried or simmered in a fragrant sauce. Artichokes cooked with eggs are often served to accompany eel. Octopus, carp, clams and squid are other Christmas delicacies and the meal includes pasta in some shape or form, perhaps accompanied by red peppers, garlic and Parmesan cheese, and maybe a Christmas Eve salad of cauliflower cooked *al dente* and served cold and dressed with a garlicky sauce, olives, tomatoes and anchovies.

As midnight Christmas bells ring, the churches fill with people. December 24 is the last day of the Christmas *novena*—the nine days of special singing and prayers which usher in the festival. The churches are packed service after service throughout Italy and the aisles ring with excitement and noise as children run around, banging their Christmas drums, and parents and grandparents greet their friends and neighbours.

On their return home, the adults exchange gifts before going to bed. If the children are still awake, the figure of Jesus is placed in his crib in the *presepio* but this is delayed until Christmas morning if they've fallen asleep.

The great Christmas candle—the *ceppo*—is lit tonight and will burn right through to the New Year. The children go to bed excitedly looking forward to their Christmas presents. St Nicholas—the legendary bringer of gifts to children throughout much of northern Europe on 6 December—was Bishop of Myra in Turkey in the fourth century. His remains are housed in the beautiful Basilica of St Nicholas in Bari in south-east Italy. In Italy, however, it is not St Nicholas as such but good old Father Christmas (*Babbo Natale*), his descendant, who climbs down the chimney on Christmas Eve to fill the stockings. In other homes he leaves presents in front of the *presepio* or under the tree.

But Father Christmas isn't the only gift bringer in Italy. Until 1861 Italy was divided into different states, each with its own traditions and life-style. Although it is now united under one government, many regional differences still exist, not the least to do with Christmas presents. In some northern parts, Santa Lucia brings presents on 13 December. In Sicily the children may be given gifts on behalf of their dead relatives on All Souls' Eve. The gift-bringer in Italy is also called *la Vecchia di Natale* (the old woman of Christmas) who comes on Christmas Eve; *Strina* (the old woman) who comes at the New Year; and *la Befana* who comes at Epiphany.

La Befana, her name derived from *Epifania* (Epiphany), comes down the chimney in her long skirt and woollen shawl on the Eve of Epiphany all over Italy and fills the children's shoes, socks, pillow cases or baskets with gifts and sweets if they've been good and with coal or charcoal if they haven't. A kindly but sharp-eyed old lady, *la Befana* also carries a cane and naughty children are warned that if they don't behave themselves she may eat them up. It's said that she was directed to Bethlehem by a shepherd but delayed setting out to see Jesus and so missed him.

Ever since she has gone from house to house on her donkey at Epiphany leaving presents in case the Christ child is there. The legend must have the same origin as that of the Russian *Baboushka*.

Christmas Day is the warmest and most intimate of Italian holy days. It is a family time, and the meal is at the heart of family life in Italy. The Italians have been called a nation of epicures and they have a saying: '*A tavola non s'invecchia*'—'At the table you never grow old.' Food is important and meals are savoured with delight. Many Italian women spend long hours shopping and cooking for their families and it's been said that love is an essential ingredient in their cooking.

The day starts with a light breakfast or *prima colazione* of coffee and rolls, perhaps with some preserves, and hot chocolate for the children. The children spend the morning playing with their toys and going to church with their fathers while busy mothers find time to prepare Christmas lunch. This is a rich meal—five or more courses in many homes.

A typical family meal starts off with an *antipasto* such as *crostini neri*—chicken livers flavoured with rosemary, onion and wine and served on *croûtes* of fried bread. Delicately cured ham or sausage are other popular starters.

Next comes the pasta, once known only in southern Italy but now popular throughout the country. At Christmas the pasta may be home-made. Ribbons of *tagliatelle*, plain or flavoured with spinach, are accompanied by ricotta cheese or by a cream or Bolognese sauce. *Tortellini*—the small brothers of *tortelloni*—are a favourite form of pasta and can be made at home, though busy Italians buy theirs freshly made or even dried. *Tortellini* are little triangular envelopes of pasta containing a filling of perhaps pork or chicken and sausage and curled round so that the two base corners are joined together like fortune cookies. They are often cooked in chicken broth and served as *tortellini in brodo*. There's a close resemblance between *tortellini* and the *uszka* of Poland. Less rich than *tortellini* are *cappelletti*, little hat-shaped pieces of pasta, also served in chicken broth.

After the pasta a roast turkey may be served, perhaps stuffed with prunes, chestnuts and pears, or roast goose, veal or guinea fowl. Italians often eat their meat course by itself, or with a single vegetable dish of artichokes or beans. In Sicily, however, a favourite main dish on Christmas day is *falsomagro*—tender beef surrounding a fragrant, garlicky stuffing of eggs, breadcrumbs, mild cheese, bacon and parsley, all moistened with red wine.

A salad is a likely follow-on and a crisp refreshing salad of fennel, with its slight taste of aniseed, and tomatoes clears the palate well for the next course of 'honeyed things'.

Italians often complete their everyday meals with fresh fruit and one of the glorious regional cheeses but at Christmas the table is laden with sweet biscuits, cakes and other delights. Today's love of special sweet foods at Christmas may well stem from an old custom. Way back in the days of ancient Rome, Emperor Caligula issued an edict that high-ranking officials must give him presents of money at the new year festival of Kalends. The habit of present-giving became popular among private citizens. Originally, branches from the grove of the goddess Strena (hence the old term *strenae* for these gifts) were given but later people gave 'honeyed things, that the year of the recipient might be full of sweetness, lamps that it might be full of light, copper and silver or gold that wealth might flow in'.

Present-day Italians often give each other bell-shaped, beribboned boxes of fruity *panettone* at Christmas. This sweet brioche, sometimes stuffed with a creamy chocolate or other filling, is a favourite on the Christmas table, as are *struffoli*. These little balls of sweet dough are deep-fried, then sprinkled with coloured sugar to look festive. Warmed golden bread or *pandoro* and *panforte*—a rich slice containing nuts, dried and glacé fruit (including glacé melon rind and glacé pumpkin) and figs, cocoa and spices— may also grace the table.

A delicious Sicilian dessert, *cassata Siciliana*, is not, as you might think, an ice-cream, but a sponge cake moistened with Marsala and filled and covered with sweetened ricotta cheese laden with mixed peel and decorated with chocolate and cherries.

Biscuits are made in abundance at Christmas, such as *pinoccate* (pine nut 'macaroons' no larger than walnuts), *ricciarelli* (long almond macaroons) and *cavallucci* in Siena; *pizzicati* in Messina; *cicerchiata* in Abruzzi; and *bicciolani* in Vercelli. Taking pride of place is the *torrone* or nutty nougat also popular in Spain.

Other desserts may include cheesecake, fruit flan, fresh fruit salad laced with liqueur, *zabaglione* and perhaps *monte bianco*—a 'white mountain' of sweetened chestnut purée flavoured with chocolate and rum or Marsala and decorated with *marrons glacés*. A *tronco di Natale*, or Christmas log, made from sponge cake, cream and coffee cream, is often bought for this special meal.

Italy is the world's leading wine producer and, of its two billion gallons of wine each year, only 25 per cent is exported. There is no trouble in selecting exactly the right wine to complement each part of the Christmas meal!

The long drawn-out meal ends with small cups of strong coffee, clementines (or tangerines), figs and walnuts, and perhaps a glass of Italian liqueur.

The Italians continue their celebrations through the New Year and on to Epiphany, when the figures of the wise men join the holy family in the *presepio*. In this symbolic gesture they remember not only that Jesus came into the world, but also that people must come to him.

AN ITALIAN
CHRISTMAS DAY MEAL

CROSTINI NERI
Chicken livers on toast

~

TORTELLINI IN BRODO
Tortellini in chicken broth

~

TACCHINO ARROSTO RIPIENO
Roast turkey with prune, chestnut and pear stuffing

or

FALSOMAGRO *Garlicky stuffed beef*

~

INSALATA DI FINOCCHIO POMODORI
Fennel and tomato salad

~

PANETTONE DI MILANO FARCITO
Sweet fruity brioche

or

CASSATA SICILIANA
Marsala sponge cake with citrus/cream cheese topping

~

STRUFFOLI *Honey-fried pastry balls*

~

FRESH FRUIT AND CHEESE;
DRIED FIGS AND WALNUTS

Crostini neri
CHICKEN LIVERS ON TOAST

F amiliar on the Italian Christmas table are little circles of fried bread, or croûtes, topped with mounds of chicken livers sautéed in butter and flavoured with rosemary or sage, and tomato. Quick and easy to prepare, they make an excellent antipasto. Turkey liver could be used instead of chicken livers but would taste rather strong and is better used in a turkey stuffing instead. Sage makes a good alternative to rosemary: use 3 leaves of fresh sage or 2ml ($^1/_2$ tsp) dried sage.

butter	50g	2oz	$^1/_2$ stick
small onion	1	1	1
chicken livers, chopped finely	225g	8oz	1 cup
sprig of fresh rosemary, the leaves chopped **OR**	1	1	1
dried rosemary, chopped	5ml	1tsp	1tsp
tomato purée	15ml	1tbs	1tbs
stick celery, chopped finely	$^1/_2$	$^1/_2$	$^1/_2$
white wine	15ml	1tbs	1tbs
pinch of salt			
pinch of black pepper			
small slices of bread	6	6	6
butter	40g	$1^1/_2$ oz	3tbs
olive oil	15ml	1tbs	1tbs
parsley, chopped	15ml	1tbs	1tbs

Melt 50g (2oz/4tbs) butter in a frying pan and add the onion. Fry gently until soft and golden. Add the liver, rosemary (or sage), tomato purée, celery, wine and seasoning, and cook for 10 minutes, stirring frequently. Remove from the heat and keep warm. Cut the slices of bread into large circles. In another frying pan heat 40g ($1^1/_2$ oz/3tbs) butter and the olive oil, then fry the bread until golden brown on both sides. Spread the chicken liver mixture on to the croûtes and sprinkle with parsley before serving.

Tortellini in brodo
TORTELLINI IN CHICKEN BROTH

T hese little stuffed pasta rings floating in a well-flavoured chicken broth are made at home as a treat for Christmas Day in much of northern Italy, where pasta is particularly popular. Busy people may be able to buy fresh ready-made *tortellini*.

Chicken broth

small chicken	1	1	1
water			
onion, quartered	1	1	1
carrot, cut into chunks	1	1	1
stick celery, diced	1	1	1
bay leaf	1	1	1
salt to taste			
pinch of black pepper			

Meat filling

butter	50g	2oz	$^1/_2$ stick
raw veal, minced	175g	6oz	$^3/_4$ cup
ham, minced	75g	3oz	$^1/_3$ cup
Italian sausage, such as Mortadella, chopped	75g	3oz	$^1/_3$ cup

Parmesan cheese, finely grated	45ml	3tbs	3tbs
eggs, beaten	2	2	2
pinch of salt			
pinch of black pepper			
Pasta			
plain flour	225g	8oz	2 cups
eggs, beaten	2	2	2
oil	10ml	2tsp	2tsp
salt	2ml	1/2 tsp	1/2 tsp
water			
fresh parsley, chopped to garnish	45ml	3tbs	3tbs
Parmesan cheese, finely grated	45ml	3tbs	3tbs

Put the chicken into a large pan and cover with water. Add the remaining ingredients. Bring to the boil, cover the pan, and simmer for 1 1/2 hours, topping up with water if necessary. Remove the cooked chicken and chill or freeze until needed for another meal. Strain the broth and add more salt if needed.

Melt the butter in a large frying pan, add the veal, and cook, stirring frequently, for 10–15 minutes. Add the remaining ingredients and stir well. Keep in a cool place until needed.

Sift the flour on to a clean work surface and make a well in the centre. Put the eggs, oil and salt into the well, gradually draw in the flour with your fingertips, and mix into a dough. Knead for about 10 minutes, adding a few drops of water if the dough seems too dry, until it is smooth, firm and elastic. Put into an air-tight bag and chill for an hour.

Put the dough on to a floured surface and roll it out into a paper-thin square, dusting with flour as necessary. Leave it for 15 minutes so that it becomes drier and easier to work with.

Cut the rolled-out pasta into about 40 small

(3.5cm/1 1/2 in.) squares. Put a little meat filling (about 2ml/1 1/2 tsp) in the middle of each square. Fold the square into a triangle to enclose the filling and press the edges well together with your fingers. The edges of the pasta should stick as you press them together but, if they don't, moisten them with a tiny bit of water to help seal them. Bend the long base of the triangle round your little finger and stick the points together.

Put 1.2 litres (2 pints/4 cups) of the chicken broth into a pan, bring to the boil, and drop in the tortellini. Simmer, stirring occasionally, for 5 minutes. Turn off the heat, cover and leave to stand for 30 minutes. Serve in bowls with a little of the broth and sprinkle some parsley into each bowl. Serve the Parmesan cheese separately.

Tacchino arresto ripieno

ROAST TURKEY WITH PRUNE, CHESTNUT AND PEAR STUFFING

Roast turkey together with this unusual and fragrant stuffing needs no accompaniment, but some families like to serve a hot vegetable with it. To save time you could use a can of puréed chestnuts instead of cooking and chopping the chestnuts yourself, but if you do the texture of the stuffing will be a little different even though the flavour is similar.

Stuffing			
chestnuts in shells	450g	1lb	2 cups
OR			
tinned chestnut purée	450g	1lb	2 cups
butter	50g	2oz	1/2 stick
turkey liver, chopped	1	1	1
veal, minced	450g	1lb	1lb
large prunes, cooked, stoned (pitted) and chopped	12	12	12

ripe pears, cored and chopped	3	3	3
dry white wine	100ml	3fl oz	1/3 cup
pinch of salt			
pinch of black pepper			
pinch of grated nutmeg			

Make a small cut in the skin of each chestnut at the pointed end. Put the chestnuts into a pan of boiling water and boil for 30 minutes. Drain and peel off the shells and inner skins. Return the chestnuts to the pan, cover with water, bring to the boil and simmer until tender, then drain, chop and put to one side.

Heat the butter in a large frying pan and add the liver and the veal. Fry, stirring frequently, for 10 minutes. Remove from the heat and stir in the chopped chestnuts or canned chestnut purée, prunes, pears, wine, salt, pepper and nutmeg. Use this mixture to stuff the turkey.

Cook the stuffed turkey in a pre-heated oven and calculate the cooking time according to its oven-ready weight (see page 208).

Falsomagro

GARLICKY STUFFED BEEF

An Italian friend tells me that the name of this popular Sicilian Christmas dish means 'pretend (*falso*) lean (*magro*)'—the rather plain exterior hides a surprisingly delicious and unusual stuffing. Ask your butcher for tender, well-hung beef cut in one large slice 1cm (1/2 in.) thick. Creamy mashed potatoes and fried mushrooms go very well with *falsomagro* and any left-overs make a fine cold meal.

slice of topside beef	700g	1lb 9oz	1lb 9oz

Stuffing			
white breadcrumbs	75g	3oz	1/3 cup
milk	50ml	2fl oz	3tbs
garlic cloves, crushed	5	5	5
handful of fresh parsley, chopped			
lean minced beef	175g	6oz	6oz
pork shoulder, minced	175g	6oz	6oz
egg, beaten	1	1	1
Parmesan cheese, finely grated	30ml	2tbs	2tbs
pinch of salt			
pinch of black pepper			
unsmoked streaky (regular) bacon rashers (slices)	4	4	4
eggs, hard boiled and shelled	3	3	3
Fontina or Edam cheese, cut in strips	75g	3oz	3oz
spring onions, cleaned	4	4	4
olive oil	30ml	2tbs	2tbs
onion, chopped	1	1	1
red wine	75ml	6fl oz	2/3 cup

Sauce			
flour	25g	1oz	2tbs
red wine	100ml	4fl oz	1/3 cup
beef stock cube	1	1	1

Garnish

handful of fresh parsley

egg, hard boiled, shelled and sliced	1	1	1

Lay the slice of beef out on a clean surface and beat or roll it firmly with a rolling pin to flatten it. Ideally the meat should end up as a rectangle of about 25 x 35cm (10 x 14in.).

Into a large bowl put the breadcrumbs, milk, garlic, parsley, minced beef, minced pork, beaten egg, Parmesan cheese, salt and pepper, and mix well. Position the slice of beef with a short side towards you. Spread the stuffing over the beef, leaving a rim of about 2.5cm (1in.) clear round the edges. Lay the uncooked bacon rashers (slices) lengthways (away from you) in two pairs and also arrange the 3 whole hard-boiled eggs in a row lengthways. Cut the spring onions in half lengthways and lay them in two pairs lengthways. Arrange the strips of cheese over the stuffing.

Roll up the slice of beef with its stuffing, working away from you, and tie it in several places with string to secure the roll. Heat the olive oil in a heavy-based casserole dish and gently sauté the onion till softened. Put the beef roll into the dish and carefully brown all over. Add the red wine, cover tightly and cook in a pre-heated oven at 180°C (350°F/Gas 4) for 1 1/2 hours. Check every half hour and add a little hot water to the dish if all the liquid has evaporated.

Put the rolled beef on to a serving dish and garnish it with slices of egg and parsley. Make a sauce by stirring the flour into any remaining pan juices in the casserole dish and adding the red wine and stock cube. Bring to the boil, stirring, and simmer for 2 minutes, then pour over the beef.

Panettone di Milano farcito
SWEET FRUITY MILANESE BRIOCHE

This is a must for the Christmas table. Its name comes from a baker called Toni who is said to have first baked it by mistake. Customers used to go into the shop and specifically ask for Toni's bread rather than for the original variety. Most Italians buy their *panettone* nowadays, but some still make their own. Choose a tall cylindrical *panettone* mould about 15cm (6in.) in diameter and about 18cm (7in.) high. In Italy you can buy special paper *panettone* moulds called *pirottino*. *Panettone* is traditionally served warm. Sometimes it is stuffed with ice-cream (*cassata*, vanilla, coffee, rum or chocolate), or with a chocolate and chestnut filling, or with ricotta cheese.

fresh yeast	25g	1oz	1tbs
caster sugar (US: granulated)	75g	3oz	1/3 cup
lukewarm water	150ml	5fl oz	1/2 cup
strong white plain flour	400g	14oz	3 1/2 cups
salt	5ml	1tsp	1tsp
butter, softened	100g	4oz	1 stick
egg yolks, beaten	3	3	3
glacé citron or citrus peel, chopped	50g	2oz	1/4 cup
sultanas (golden raisins)	50g	2oz	1/4 cup
raisins	50g	2oz	1/4 cup
grated rind of 1 lemon			
butter, melted	25g	1oz	1/4 stick
icing sugar, sifted (confectioner's sugar)	25g	1oz	2tbs

Crumble the yeast into a small bowl and cream with 5ml (1tsp) of sugar. Add the water and beat with a fork. Leave in a warm place for 10–15 minutes until frothy. Sift the flour and salt into a bowl, make a well in the centre and pour in the yeast mixture and remaining sugar. Draw in the flour from the sides of the bowl and mix until a ball of dough forms. Turn the dough on to a floured board and knead for 10 minutes until it is firm, elastic and smooth. Put the dough into a plastic bag and leave it in a warm place for about 2 hours, until it has doubled in size.

Put the dough into a bowl, make a well in the centre, add the softened butter, egg yolks, glacé citron peel, sultanas (golden raisins), raisins and lemon rind, and knead until incorporated. Put the dough into a buttered mould or tin and brush the surface of the dough with half the melted butter. Cover with a cloth or plastic food wrap and leave in a warm place for about 30 minutes to let the dough rise a little. Bake in a pre-heated oven at 200°C (400°F/Gas 6) for 30 minutes, then turn the heat down to 180°C (350°F/Gas 4) and continue baking for another 30 minutes. Leave it to cool in the mould for 20–30 minutes, then turn it out on to a wire rack. Dredge with sifted icing (confectioner's) sugar.

The *panettone* may be served warm or, alternatively, cold with one of the fillings suggested above.

Creamy chocolate and chestnut filling for panettone

Try filling a hollowed-out home-made or shop-bought *panettone* with this wonderfully rich and smooth filling to delight your family and friends.

Panettone,	1kg	2¼ lb	2¼ lb
dark rum (optional)	30ml	2tbs	2tbs

Filling

plain chocolate (or semi-sweet)	150g	5oz	5oz
instant coffee	15ml	1tbs	1tbs
hot water	15ml	1tbs	1tbs
butter, melted	25g	1oz	¼ stick
dark rum	30ml	2tbs	2tbs
egg, separated	1	1	1
caster sugar (US: granulated), or more to taste	50g	2oz	¼ cup
marrons glacés, finely chopped	8	8	8
whipping cream, whipped	200ml	7fl oz	¾ cup

Cut the top off the *panettone* and scoop out the centre with a spoon, leaving a rim of *panettone* of 3cm (1¼ in.). Moisten the inside by sprinkling it with rum if you wish.

Carefully melt the chocolate with the coffee and hot water in the top of a double saucepan. Remove from the heat. Stir in the melted butter, rum, egg yolk, sugar and marrons glacés. Fold in the whipped cream. Whisk the egg white till stiff and fold that in too. Spoon the chocolate mixture into the *panettone*, then cover and chill for 10 hours.

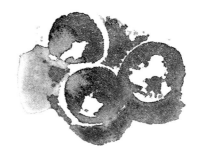

Cassata Siciliana

MARSALA SPONGE CAKE WITH CITRUS/ CREAM CHEESE TOPPING

This creamy dessert is not ice-cream but an unusual Marsala-flavoured sponge cake (which actually preceded the well known ice-cream), covered and filled with a sweetened ricotta-cheese frosting. Use half the recipe (not the sponge cake, of course!) to fill a *panettone* for Christmas Day, or serve the sponge cake instead.

Victoria sponge (basic yellow sponge cake) 25cm (10in.) in diameter and about 5cm (2in.) thick	1	1	1
ricotta cheese	800g	1¾lb	3 cups
caster sugar (US: granulated)	100g	4oz	½ cup
dry Marsala or medium sherry	75ml	3fl oz	¼ cup
cold water	25ml	1fl oz	1½ tbs
pinch of cinnamon			
mixed glacé citrus peel, finely chopped	100g	4oz	½ cup
plain chocolate (semi-sweet) OR	100g	4oz	4oz
plain chocolate (semi-sweet) AND	50g	2oz	2oz
chocolate flakes	50g	2oz	¼ cup
glacé cherries, halved	6	6	6

Mix the ricotta cheese, half the sugar and 10ml (2tsp) of Marsala until smooth. Add the cinnamon and peel. Cut 50g (2oz) of the chocolate into tiny pieces, about the size of currants, and add to the cheese mixture. Mix well and taste for sweetness. Add more sugar to your taste.

Cut the sponge in half acrossways. Mix the remaining Marsala with the cold water and sprinkle this over both cut surfaces of the sponge and round the sides. The sponge should be moist but not too wet.

Spread just under half the ricotta mixture on to the top of the bottom layer of sponge cake, then put the top half of sponge cake over it. Cover the top and sides of the cake with the remaining mixture.

Using a sharp knife, make little curls with the remaining chocolate, or use chocolate flakes, and decorate the top of the cake with them. Put the cherries in a pattern on top.

Struffoli

HONEY-FRIED PASTRY BALLS

Struffoli are little balls of sweet citrus-flavoured pastry deep-fried then served with in honey. They are eaten along with other 'honeyed things' at the end of the Christmas meal. They are reminiscent of similar confections eaten in Mexico, Russia and northern Europe at this time.

plain flour	275g	10oz	2½ cups
sugar	10ml	2tsp	2tsp
grated rind of ½ lemon			
pinch of salt			
eggs, beaten	4	4	4
egg yolks	2	2	2
lard	50g	2oz	¼ cup
cooking oil			
honey	100g	4oz	½ cup
grated rind of 1 orange			
glacé orange peel, finely chopped	50g	2oz	¼ cup
glacé citron peel, finely chopped	50g	2oz	¼ cup

coloured sugar crystals

In a large bowl mix the flour with the sugar, lemon rind and salt, then add the beaten eggs, yolks and the lard cut into little pieces. Knead till smooth then shape into rolls the size of your finger. On a floured board, slice the rolls at an angle into pieces about 12mm ($^1/_2$ in.) wide. Heat the oil, then lower the *struffoli* in, a few at a time, and fry until golden-brown. Remove from the oil with a perforated spoon and drain on kitchen paper.

Heat the honey gently in a large pan until runny, then remove from the heat. Stir in the grated orange rind, glacé orange peel and glacé citron peel and lastly the *struffoli*. Wait for 3–5 minutes then pour the *struffoli* on to a serving dish. Sprinkle with coloured sugar while still warm and serve when cool.

~ EXTRA RECIPES ~

Insalata di rinforz di Napoli
NEAPOLITAN CHRISTMAS EVE SALAD

This fresh cauliflower salad is served around Naples on Christmas Eve along with eels or other fish. The firm white florets, mixed with black olives, anchovies, capers and a lemony dressing, not only look appetizing but complement the fish perfectly.

large, firm cauliflower	1	1	1
cloves of garlic, peeled and crushed	2	2	2
mild mustard	5ml	1tsp	1tsp
fresh tarragon or mint OR pinch of dried tarragon or mint	2ml	$^1/_2$ tsp	$^1/_2$ tsp
juice of $^1/_2$ lemon			
olive oil	30ml	2tbs	2tbs
salt and freshly ground black pepper to taste			
caster sugar (US: granulated)	2ml	$^1/_2$ tsp	$^1/_2$ tsp
anchovy fillets, chopped	6	6	6
capers	15ml	1tbs	1tbs
small black olives	50g	2oz	$^1/_4$ cup
fresh parsley or mint, chopped	15ml	1tbs	1tbs

Wash the cauliflower and soak head-down in cold salted water for 30 minutes. Break the cauliflower into florets and drop them into plenty of boiling water. Simmer for 5 minutes or until just tender. Drain and rinse under cold water. Mix together in the serving bowl the garlic, mustard, herbs, lemon juice, olive oil, seasoning and sugar, then toss the cauliflower in this dressing. Scatter the anchovies, capers and olives over the top, then decorate with the parsley or mint.

Anguilla in umido al vino bianco
EELS IN WHITE WINE

Eels are considered a great delicacy in Italy and near the coast are traditionally eaten on Christmas Eve. In this recipe the eels are fragrant with garlic, onion, tomato, lemon and sage, not to mention the white wine in which they are cooked. A medium-sized eel is enough for four.

fresh eel, skinned	675g	1¹/₂ lb	1¹/₂ lb
olive oil	60ml	4tbs	¹/₄ cup
small onion, finely chopped	1	1	1
clove garlic, peeled and crushed	1	1	1
strip of lemon peel	5cm	2in.	2in.
fresh sage, chopped OR large pinch of dried sage	5ml	1tsp	1tsp
bay leaves	2	2	2
tomato purée	15ml	1tbs	1tbs
warm water	60ml	4tbs	¹/₄ cup
dry white wine	150ml	¹/₄ pint	¹/₂ cup
salt and freshly ground black pepper to taste			
fresh parsley to garnish			

Cut the skinned eel into pieces about 2.5cm (1in.) long. Wash, then dry with kitchen paper. Heat the olive oil in a large pan then gently fry the onion and

garlic until pale gold. Add the pieces of eel and fry until golden. Add the remaining ingredients and bring to the boil. Simmer gently for 20 minutes in an uncovered pan, stirring occasionally, until the eel is tender and most of the liquid has evaporated. Put into a serving dish and garnish with parsley.

Monte bianco
CHESTNUT PURÉE WITH CREAM AND CHOCOLATE

Chestnuts are a great Italian favourite and in this recipe they are puréed, sweetened, piled into a 'mountain', and topped with a 'snow' of rum-flavoured cream sprinkled with grated chocolate. If you are going to use dried chestnuts, remember that they need to be soaked overnight before being cooked.

dried chestnuts/ canned chestnut purée/boiled fresh chestnuts	350g	12oz	1¹/₂ cups
caster sugar (US: granulated)	175g	6oz	³/₄ cup
vanilla essence (extract)	2ml	¹/₂ tsp	¹/₂ tsp
pinch of salt			
rum/brandy	20ml	4tsp	4tsp
double cream (US: whipping)	150ml	¹/₄ pint	¹/₂ cup
milk	15ml	1tbs	1tbs
icing sugar, sifted (confectioner's sugar)	25g	1oz	2tbs
plain chocolate, grated (or semi-sweet)	30ml	2tbs	2tbs
marrons glacés	10	10	10

Soak the dried chestnuts overnight then cook in boiling water for 45 minutes or until very soft. Fresh chestnuts must first be skinned. Make a cut in each chestnut at the pointed end, then boil in water for about 15 minutes. Drain and remove the shells and inner skins, then cover with water, bring to the boil and simmer for 45 minutes, until very soft. Purée the cooked chestnuts by blending them in an electric blender or pressing them through a coarse sieve.

Add the caster sugar, vanilla essence, salt and half the rum or brandy to the chestnut purée, stir well, and pile in a mound on a serving dish.

Put the cream and milk in a bowl and whisk until stiff. Stir in the remaining rum or brandy and add icing (confectioner's) sugar to your taste. Pipe the flavoured, sweetened cream over the mound of chestnut purée. Decorate with the marrons glacés and sprinkle the top with grated chocolate.

N O R W A Y

Norway is a country steeped in ancient mythology. On the surface Christmas in Oslo doesn't appear to be very different from that in any other large European city. There are colourful window and street displays, garlanded Christmas trees in public squares and throngs of shoppers in the streets and stores. Probe a little deeper, however, or move out of the city and into the country, and you find many ancient Viking Yule customs woven into the celebrations.

In Norwegian celebrations there are many fascinating examples of the positive and creative role mythology plays in expressing the Christian experience.

'Joulu' or 'Jol', better known as Yule, was a pagan feast enjoyed all over Northern Europe in the Viking age. It was in celebration of the return of the sun after the darkest days of the northern winter.

The name of the feast appears to come from that of the Norse god 'Jolnir', better known as Odin or Wodin, who, it is said, lived in Valhalla, a place for the souls of the dead. It was believed that during Yule the spirits of the dead were unleashed to haunt the living. To placate the ghostly hordes, food and drink were left out for them.

Odin was also the god of intoxicating drink and ecstasy, so invariably these feasts involved excesses of food, drink and behaviour. Dark, strong *Juleøl* (Yule beer) was brewed and served freely. When Christianity was brought to Norway, these ancient celebrations were so entrenched that it was a felt necessary to give the old customs new meanings. Today a special Christmas beer is brewed commercially.

In a primitive agricultural society there was a natural preoccupation with the cycle of nature, the seasons, the need for fertility and the fear of death and the unknown. Yule not only welcomed the sun's return but also involved sacrificial rites that called upon the gods to prosper the people, their land and their animals in the coming year. A sheaf of oats, the *julenek*, would be hung out as a fertility sacrifice. This is still done, but now is for the enjoyment of the birds. Many of the customs are common to Scandinavia as a whole, such as putting out a bowl of porridge for the *Julenisse*. This bearded leprechaun, cousin to the Danish *Nisser*, brings Norwegian children their gifts. Although much of Norway lies above the Arctic Circle, well into Santa Claus territory, this jovial figure with his reindeer is not well known. Reindeer steaks are in fact considered a delicacy.

To prepare for the Yule feast households were cleaned from top to bottom. The custom of cleaning the house and polishing silver is still followed today in Norway, and the last Sunday before Christmas is frequently referred to as 'Dirty Sunday'.

Yule candles were essential throughout the days when the sun never rose above the horizon and today people still place candles in windows, on graves in cemeteries and on the Christmas tree in celebration of the birth of Jesus and the coming of a new light to the world.

Despite all the natural spruce forests, it is only in the last century that Christmas trees have become popular. During World War II, when Norway was occupied by Germany, free Norwegian forces would slip through the patrols each Christmas to cut down a Norwegian spruce as a gift for the exiled king. The practice of sending a gift of a tree to England has continued each Christmas since the war, and the tree is given a special place in London's Trafalgar Square. Norwegian spruces are taken even further afield to distant ports under tropical

skies, strapped to the mast-tops of Norwegian ships at Christmas. Like their Viking ancestors in their longboats, the Norsemen celebrate even at sea.

But for a thousand years Yuletide has become the time of a great Christian festival and it is the church bells that ring in the Christmas season at 5 o'clock on Christmas Eve. Whether in the city or the country, as the bells ring out, people hurry off the streets, snow creaking underfoot, to the beckoning glow of their homes.

The family Christmas celebration begins with the reading of the nativity story, and a welcoming toast. Everyone then tucks into a Christmas meal which in its simplicity is a striking contrast to that of some other countries. This may stem from pre-Reformation times when Christmas Eve was a day of fasting. In the 1530s, when Norway was part of Denmark, it adopted the Lutheran religion.

After independence this remained the state religion and today 95 per cent of Norwegians are Lutheran.

The Christmas meal varies from region to region and the more affluent the family the more elaborate it becomes, with the addition of such delicacies as suckling pig, *fårelår* (dried smoked lamb) and game birds. Yet the traditional foods remain as the centre of the meal.

Norway has 2,600 kilometres (over 1,600 miles) of coastline and fish is eaten at nearly every meal. At Christmas, fillets of sweet sea-fresh cod are plunged into salted boiling water for a few minutes and then served firm and flavourful with melted butter and boiled potatoes sprinkled with chopped parsley. A tart cucumber salad contrasts well. In the absence of fresh fish a similar dish is eaten, made from dried cod soaked in a lye solution (*Lutefisk*). It is served with a white sauce or mustard sauce and crispy bacon and peas, but has none of the sea succulence of fresh fish. Strangely contrary to custom elsewhere, red wine is always served with cod in Norway.

The pagan custom of sacrificing a Yuletide boar lingers on as a traditional pork roast called *Ribbe*. This is likely to be served in the central part of Norway and Oslo. These salty spare ribs are traditionally served with *medisterkaker* (meat patties) or *medisterpølser* (sausages), boiled potatoes, and a caraway-flavoured sauerkraut called *surkål* stirred in pan drippings.

Along the west coast *pinnekjøtt* (salted dried lamb ribs) are steamed over a rack of juniper or birch twigs, and served with mashed swede (rutabaga).

To conclude the meal *riskrem*, a thick rice pudding topped with a berry sauce, is served. A simpler boiled rice pudding, *julegrøt* is sometimes preferred. As in Denmark it is customary to hide an almond in the pudding—the finder receives a small gift, often a marzipan pig, and is supposed to have good luck in the coming year.

In the old days Yule biscuits were baked as gifts and there were some peculiar rules governing their consumption. One biscuit was made in the shape of a goat and the person eating it was supposed to bleat like one. Crumbs from these biscuits were thought to have magical curative powers and often the entire household joined in the baking. The custom of baking up to twenty different kinds of biscuit has been modified to the present day minimum of seven kinds. These include *pepperkaker, sandkaker, berlinerkranser* (just like the Danish vanilla rings), *brunekaker* and *fattigmann*. The last are deep-fried brandy and cardamom flavoured twists of dough sprinkled with icing sugar similar to those eaten over much of Europe at Christmas time. *Krumkaker* are cigar-shaped biscuits cooked in special irons engraved with religious and festive patterns.

Sometimes they are served as a dessert with a bowl of *multekrem* (crushed cloudberries and cream). Wafer-thin *goro*, also delicately patterned, are special to Christmas.

A mouthwatering selection of these biscuits is put out on the coffee table to tempt the family when, after dinner, they sing and dance around the Christmas tree and open their gifts. Often the celebration goes on so long that everyone is hungry again and a table is set with *nattmat* (night food). They tuck into herring, salads, cheeses, smoked eel and *sylte* (brawn), and chase the aquavit down with *Juleøl* (Christmas beer) before finally retiring to bed.

To a visitor's eyes, breakfast on Christmas morning is a banquet of cheeses, cold meats, eggs, herring, a variety of breads including *lefser* and *knekkebrød*, a wafer-thin bread, and jams. At Christmas, in addition to this *koldtbord* there is *Julekake* a round sweet bread spiced with cardamom and rich with cherries, raisins and citron peel.

After breakfast those who didn't go to church on Christmas Eve go to morning service. The decorated churches are filled to capacity. Some of the rural churches are the original eleventh-century wooden stave churches, living mementos of Norway's introduction to Christianity. The new religion did not completely erase the memory of the old Norse myths and these churches, among the world's oldest wooden structures, are a curious mixture of pagan and Christian images. The first impression is of an interior elaborately carved with appropriately Christian scenes; but climb into the roof and you find yourself face to face with an assembly of pagan gods. Perhaps they were regarded as evil spirits forced into the service of the church but a more likely explanation is that, despite the new religion, eleventh-century builders didn't dare do without them.

The rest of Christmas Day is spent visiting friends, eating, and perhaps skiing or skating. Sometimes the children and adults dress up in masks, usually as Yule goats, and go *Julebukk*: they go from house to house and are given sweets, biscuits or fruit, with drinks for the adults. Christmas Eve and Christmas Day are only the first days of a season of socializing that continues in Norway often until 13 January — St Canute's Day.

Much about the Norwegian Christmas celebration reveals its pagan origins. But while the builders of the middle ages were slow to relinquish their awe of pagan gods, Norwegian Christians today focus their joy on the birth of Jesus and revel in the light and laughter Christmas brings to their dark mid-winter.

A NOREGIAN CHRISTMAS EVE DINNER

AVKOKT TORSK MED SMELTET SMOR
Baked cod with melted butter

or

LUTEFISK MED BACON
Lye fish with bacon

AGURKSALAT *Cucumber salad*

KOKTE POTETER MED PERSILLE
Boiled potatoes with parsley

or

RIBBE *Roast pork spare ribs*

with

MEDISTERKAKER *Meat patties*

and

MEDISTERPØLSER *Sausages*

SURKÅL *Caraway sauerkraut*

KÅLRABI *Mashed swede*

~

RISKREM MED RØDSAUS
Cold creamy rice pudding with hot fruit sauce

or

MULTEKREM I SANDKAKER
Cloudberry cream in sandcake cases

Agurksalat
CUCUMBER SALAD

This salad is very easy to make and it has a refreshing tartness. The 'salting' process gets rid of the bitterness which many people find indigestible.

large cucumber	1	1	1
salt	25g	1oz	2tbs
cooled, boiled water	100ml	4fl oz	1/3 cup
pinch of salt			
pinch of white pepper			
white wine vinegar	100ml	4fl oz	1/3 cup
sugar	30ml	2tbs	2tbs
chopped parsley or dill	15ml	1tbs	1tbs

Wash the cucumber and slice it very finely into transparently thin slices. Place in a bowl and sprinkle with the salt. Cover with a plate and weight it so that the juices are pressed out of the cucumber. Leave to stand for a couple of hours. Season the boiled water with salt and pepper and add the sugar and vinegar. Rinse the cucumber and squeeze out as much moisture as you can. Pour the dressing over the cucumber and chill thoroughly before serving with the chopped parsley or dill on top.

Serve as an accompaniment to baked cod.

Ribbe
ROAST PORK SPARE RIBS

The sweetness of the prune juice and the long slow cooking makes these spare ribs tender and juicy. It is the most popular Norwegian Christmas Eve dish.

pork spare ribs, all in one piece	2kg	4 1/2 lb	4 1/2 lb
salt	15ml	1tbs	1tbs
black pepper	5ml	1tsp	1tsp
pinch of ginger			
water	150ml	1/4 pint	1/2 cup
prune juice	300ml	1/2 pint	1 1/4 cups

Ask your butcher to cut between each rib but not all the way through so that you still have one piece of meat. Rub the meat well with the seasoning and refrigerate overnight if possible. Pour the water into a roasting tin (pan) and roast the ribs (bone side down) in a moderate oven at 180°C (350°F/Gas 4). After half an hour lift the roast on to a rack and roast for a further hour, basting whenever you remember with the prune juice until done. Serve with *medisterkaker* (patties) and *surkål* (sauerkraut).

Medisterkaker

MEAT PATTIES

These are tasty meat patties which are tradition-ally served with *ribbe* on Christmas Eve. They can be made with either minced beef or minced pork.

minced beef or lean pork	675g	1½ lb	1½ lb
salt	15ml	1tbs	1tbs
white pepper	5ml	1tsp	1tsp
potato flour or cornflour (cornstarch)	30ml	2tbs	2tbs
ground cloves	2ml	½ tsp	½ tsp
boiled, cooled milk	250ml	9fl oz	1 cup
a little oil or butter for cooking			

Mix the potato flour and the seasonings with the minced meat. Gradually stir in the milk. Shape into hamburger-sized patties and brown in a little butter. Add the patties to the *ribbe* roast for the last twenty minutes of roasting.

Surkål

CARAWAY SAUERKRAUT

For extra flavour this sauerkraut is sometimes stirred in the pan juices from the *ribbe* roast.

red or white cabbage	675g	1½ lb	3 cups
cooking apple	1	1	1
butter	50g	2oz	½ stick
salt	5ml	1tsp	1tsp
caraway seed	10ml	2tsp	2tsp
water or stock	500ml	17fl oz	2 cups
white wine vinegar	15ml	1tbs	1tbs
sugar	15ml	1tbs	1tbs

Finely shred the cabbage, removing any thick white pieces. Slice the apple into thin wedges. Melt the butter in a large pot and layer the apple, cabbage and seasoning in it. Add the water or stock, and cover with a tightly fitting lid. Simmer for 30–35 minutes until tender, checking frequently that the cabbage isn't sticking. Stir in the vinegar and sugar and cook for a further 15 minutes. Serve hot with *ribbe*.

Riskrem med rødsaus

COLD CREAM RICE PUDDING WITH HOT FRUIT SAUCE

R ice pudding fans will love this cold creamy version served with a hot fruit sauce.

Make the rice pudding as for the Danish ris à l'amande.
   Pour into a ring mould. When set, turn out and spoon the following sauce over it:

Fruit sauce

frozen raspberries or canned cherries, thawed	225g	8oz	1 cup
redcurrant jelly	45ml	3tbs	3tbs
cornflour (cornstarch)	15ml	1tbs	1tbs
cold water/can juices OR	60ml	4tbs	4tbs
cold water/can juices AND	45ml	3tbs	3tbs
berry liqueur such as Kijafa	15ml	1tbs	1tbs

Over a gentle heat melt the redcurrant jelly. Mix the cornflour with the cold water or juice from the canned cherries and add to the melted jelly with the optional liqueur. Bring to the boil, stirring constantly. Add the raspberries or cherries. Remove when the sauce is thick and glossy, about I minute. Serve the warm sauce over the cold pudding.

Multekrem i sandkaker

CLOUDBERRIES IN SANDCAKES

cloudberries (any soft fruit is good)	225g	8oz	1 cup
caster sugar (US: granulated)	30ml	2tbs	2tbs
double cream (US: whipping)	300ml	1/2 pint	1 1/4 cups
vanilla essence (extract)	5ml	1tsp	1tsp
sandcakes	12	12	12

Sandcakes

T his is a generous recipe and makes about 36 cakes but they are so useful to have over Christmas that it is worthwhile baking extras.

butter or margarine	225g	8oz	2 sticks
icing sugar, (confectioner's sugar) sifted	200g	7oz	3/4 cup
egg	1	1	1
ground almonds	75g	3oz	1/3 cup
plain flour	350g	12oz	3 cups

Cream butter and sugar well. Add egg, flour and ground almonds and mix well. Allow to chill for a day. Press into fluted patty tins, not too thinly or the sides will crumble. Bake at 180°C (350°F/Gas 4) for 12–15 minutes until pale gold. Gently ease from tin once cool and serve filled with cloudberry cream. Whip the cream until stiff. Add the vanilla essence and sugar to the cloudberries. Gently mix into the whipped cream. Spoon into the sandcake cases just before serving.

~ EXTRA RECIPES ~

Fattigmann
DEEP-FRIED CHRISTMAS BISCUITS

The dough for these mouthwatering biscuits is best made the day before and left to rest in a cool place.

egg yolks	2	2	2
sugar	50g	2oz	1/4 cup
double cream (US: whipping)	50ml	2fl oz	4tbs
butter	50g	2oz	1/4 cup
cognac	15ml	1tbs	1tbs
ground cardamom	5ml	1tsp	1tsp
grated lemon rind	5ml	1tsp	1tsp
plain flour, sifted	200g	7oz	1 3/4 cups
vegetable fat or lard for deep frying			
icing (confectioner's) sugar to decorate			

Beat the egg yolks with the sugar until pale and fluffy. Add the cream, the cognac, the cardamom and lemon rind. Rub the butter into the flour. Add the egg mixture to the flour to make a soft dough. Leave to rest overnight in a cool place.

The following day roll out to 5mm (1/4 in. thickness on a lightly floured board. Cut into strips 4 x 10cm (1 1/2 x 4in.). Cut a 2.5cm (1in.) long slit lengthwise in the centre of each rectangle. Pull one end of the strip through this slit to make a half bow. Heat the lard or fat to 190°C (375°F) and deep-fry the biscuits a few at a time until golden brown. Remove with a slotted spoon and drain on absorbent paper. When cold, dredge with icing sugar. These are best eaten on the day of baking. (They are so delicious that there are unlikely to be any left to store anyway!)

Julekake
CHRISTMAS BREAD

In Norway this fruit-filled loaf is eaten for breakfast on Christmas morning. For those who don't like the heavy English Christmas cake this recipe would be an excellent alternative.

sachet (packet) yeast	1	1	1 of dried
sugar	5ml	1tsp	1tsp
half milk/half water	100ml	4fl oz	1/3 cup
plain flour	450g	1lb	4 cups
egg	1	1	1
salt	5ml	1tsp	1tsp
butter	100g	4oz	1 stick
sugar	100g	4oz	1/2 cup
ground cardamom	7ml	1 tsp heaped	1 tsp heaped
raisins	100g	4oz	1/2 cup
red and green cherries, chopped OR	100g	4oz	1/2 cup
mixed candied fruit	100g	4oz	1/2 cup
chopped almonds	100g	4oz	1/2 cup
icing (confectioner's) sugar and glacé fruit to decorate			

Warm the milk and water until hand hot. Whisk in the 5ml (1tsp) of sugar followed by the yeast and leave in a warm place to froth for about 15 minutes. Sift the flour and salt into a large mixing bowl. Stir in the sugar. Rub in the butter until the mixture resembles fine breadcrumbs. Add the cardamom. Stir in the egg and finally the frothy yeast liquid and mix into a dough.

On a floured surface knead the dough until smooth and elastic. Return to the bowl, cover with plastic wrap and leave to rise until it has doubled in size.

Turn out the dough, knock it down and gradually add the raisins, nuts and chopped fruit. Pat into a nice round loaf and put it on a greased baking sheet. Cover with an oiled plastic bag and leave to rise for about 30 minutes until well risen. Remove the bag and bake in a pre-heated oven at 190°C (375°F/Gas 5) for 40–45 minutes. When the loaf is cool, decorate with white glacé icing and glacé cherries.

GERMANY

Based on a stained glass window from Ulm Cathedral, Germany.

Germany seems to have withstood the commercialization of Christmas so evident in many other countries. It remains a holy time celebrated with awe and reverence.

The first Sunday in Advent (four weeks before Christmas) not only marks the accepted beginning of the Christmas season but more importantly it is also the start of the church year. On this Sunday, in homes all over Germany, families sit around the coffee table to light the first of the four Advent candles on the Advent wreath. This wreath is made of fir branches and is decorated with red ribbons and berries. The green of the evergreen fir branches symbolizes the faithfulness of Christ, the red berries and ribbons symbolize the blood he shed on the cross, and the candles represent the light he brings into the world. It was customary for families with relatives and friends in East Germany to remember them by putting a candle at the window. Thankfully, with German unification, that is a thing of the past.

To celebrate Christmas in a traditional German way involves an enormous amount of preparation. The next four weeks see the household preoccupied with making ready for Christmas and the amount of cooking, baking and decorating that is done would be daunting to most of us!

The baking is divided into *grossesgebäck* (big baking), when the *Stollen* (Christmas cake) and *Torte* and other large items are baked, and *Weihnachtskleingebäck* (small Christmas baking), when numerous biscuits (cookies) of all shapes and sizes are baked. The enticing smell of spices wafting through the house during these baking days evokes memories of Christmases past.

There is a long tradition and much symbolism connected with some of these biscuits baked for Christmas. The gingerbread cakes and biscuits, *Lebkuchen*, for instance, originated in Nuremberg monasteries in the middle ages. Honey from the beehives kept in these monasteries was used to sweeten these cakes. The word '*leb*' actually means 'healing' and it appears that these *Lebkuchen* were distributed to the village folk by the monks for their supposed medicinal properties.

Springerle (aniseed biscuits) originated in the district of Swabia. These 'picture-biscuits' are made in wooden moulds and in the nineteenth century it became fashionable to tint them and use them as tree decorations. The little *Pfeffernuss* (peppernut) is said to symbolize the sponge used to moisten Christ's lips as he hung on the cross.

Most famous of all is the *Christstollen* (Christmas loaf) with its oval shape and the dough folded over to represent the swaddling clothes of the Christ child.

As in Holland, St Nicholas' Day is celebrated on 6 December. It is the one occasion when children willingly polish their shoes! These gleaming shoes are left outside the door on St Nicholas' Eve, perhaps with a carrot for St Nicholas' horse, and in the morning the 'good' children find them filled with sweets, clementines, apples, biscuits and nuts. The 'naughty' children are supposed just to get a bundle of birch twigs, but as children's behaviour improves amazingly just before St Nicholas' Day this rarely happens.

St Nicholas' companion is given a different name in different districts of the country. In some places it is Knecht Ruprecht, in others Krampus or Klausmänneken. Whatever his name, it's his role to mete out punishment to the naughty children.

Christmas markets are held in nearly every town and at these markets the family can buy marzipan sweets, biscuits, Christmas decorations, trees and toys. A favourite market delicacy amongst children is a prune-man, a little figure made of prunes threaded on to cocktail sticks and decorated with raisins and nuts. The most famous of the markets is the *Christkindlmarkt* in Nuremberg where the famous golden angels, *Rauschgold Engel* are bought to put on top of the Christmas tree.

Medieval German mystery plays often featured the 'Paradise Tree' or 'Tree of knowledge' mentioned in Genesis in the Bible. Originally hung with apples to represent the good fruit, the decorations became more elaborate with time. The first decorated Christmas tree to be recorded was seen in Strasbourg, Alsace, in 1605. However it was not until the nineteenth century that decorating a Christmas tree became a popular custom throughout Germany and most of Europe. Today the Christmas tree is an intrinsic part of a German Christmas.

Parents or grandparents decorate the tree on Christmas Eve. Keyholes are papered over and great care is taken that no one else sees the tree until it is ready.

Christmas decorations are brought out each year to be used again and again and some of them are generations old. The tree is decorated with straw stars, little wooden figures, paper angels and hearts, as well as biscuits strung on ribbons and nuts spray-painted gold. These golden nuts are said to represent the two aspects of life: the known golden outside and the hidden dark inside.

There is a delightful folk tale about a German Christmas tree first written by Robert Haven Schauffler. It tells of how all the domestic animals, even the mice, were allowed to take a peek at the decorated tree. Only the spiders were excluded because they were literally 'cleaned out' when the house was swept for Christmas. They complained to the Christ child, and when no one was looking he let them in. 'They came creepy, creepy, down the attic stairs, creepy, creepy, up the cellar stairs, creepy, creepy, along the halls—and into the beautiful room. The fat mother spiders and the old papa spiders, and all the little teeny, tonty, curly spiders, the baby ones. And then they looked! Round and round the tree they crawled, and looked and looked and looked. Oh, what a good time they had! They thought it was perfectly beautiful. And when they looked at everything they could see from the floor, they started up the tree to see some more. All over the tree they ran, creepy, crawly, looking at every single thing. Up and down, in and out, over every branch and twig the little spiders ran, and saw every one of the pretty things right up close.'

In doing so they left their cobwebs everywhere so the Christ child, knowing the housewife's dislike of cobwebs, turned them into gold, hence the golden 'angels' hair' on the Christmas tree!

Children leave *Bunteteller* (painted plates made of papier maché) under the tree. A window in the room is also left ajar for the *Christkindl* (a mysterious angel-like figure) to enter and leave some gifts. In some areas the *Weihnachtsmann* (Father Christmas) is the gift bringer.

It is customary to have a nativity scene in many homes and churches in Southern Germany. The children love to help set it up and vie with each other to be the one to put the babe in the manger on Christmas Eve.

Shops and offices close at midday on Christmas Eve and the streets are deserted as families go home to prepare for the evening's celebrations. Many people dress up and children often get new outfits for *Heiliger Abend*—Holy Night.

At 5 o'clock many families go to the carol service at their local church. On coming home the parents light the candles on the tree while the children wait in the dining-room. The anticipation is agonizing but well worth it when, summoned by a bell, they enter the *Weihnachtszimmer* (Christmas room) to find that the *Christkindl* has been there and left the *Bunteteller* overflowing with sweets, nuts and cookies, and lots of parcels under the tree.

The family gathers round while someone reads the Christmas story and the children recite poems or stories which they have secretly been rehearsing to surprise the adults. Then everyone joins in the carol singing. There is a quiet reverence about this intimate family celebration that is treasured by the Germans. (It is exclusively a family celebration, shared only by grandparents; friends are rarely invited). Gifts are exchanged and then the family goes through to the dining-room for dinner.

Because the emphasis is on the religious side of the evening, the Christmas Eve meal is not usually an elaborate one. A family favourite like *Wiener Schnitzel* with asparagus might be served. More often than not it is a cold meal consisting of a selection of herring, cold meats and salads such as Waldorf salad (celery, nuts, cabbage and mayonnaise) or celeriac salad. Dessert is often missed in favour of returning to the Christmas room for coffee and biscuits.

Later in the evening those who wish to do so go to a midnight service. They return to the beautiful sound of all the local church bells ringing in Christmas morning. A glass of warming punch is customary before going to bed.

On Christmas morning the family may again go to church. Today there is a wider family gathering, relatives often travelling long distances to be together. After attending the morning service the family has coffee and their first slice of the *Stollen*.

Lunch is a highlight on Christmas Day. A starched damask tablecloth or one embroidered with Christmas motifs is used on the table. Naturally the best crockery and crystal is used and the hostess will have made a centrepiece of evergreens and candles.

Although there is no traditional meal, there are definite Christmas favourites. A soup is often chosen as a first course, the Germans

have a particular liking for thin clear soups such as *Markklösschensuppe* (marrowbone soup) served with suitably festive heart-shaped dumplings. The main course favourites remain pork, goose and venison in hunting regions. Often the goose is stuffed with whole apples and served with redcurrant jelly. A typical festive pork dish is a roll of pork stuffed with plums. Braised red cabbage is an excellent accompaniment to either of these dishes. In Bavaria *Kartoffelknödel* (potato dumplings) are a must with any celebratory meal. Otherwise rice with apricots and onions can be served, or simply boiled potatoes tossed in butter and strewn with sesame seeds.

Dessert is usually light, more often than not a fruit salad made with the fruit of the season with the addition of perhaps a kiwi fruit, fresh pineapple and a dash of port just to make it special. *Rumtopf*—a heady fruit preserve—is also sometimes served over ice-cream.

After lunch the family goes for a long walk and the children play with their new toys. Later they have coffee and either a slice of *Torte* or more *Stollen* and biscuits. In the evening the candles on the Christmas tree are lit again and there is more singing, everyone wanting the day to linger and storing up memories to last till next time.

A GERMAN CHRISTMAS DAY LUNCH

MARKKLÖSSCHENSUPPE
Marrowbone soup

~

WEIHNACHTSGANS
Christmas goose with pork and apple stuffing

or

SCHWEINEROLLBRATEN MIT PFLAUMEN
Rolled pork with plums

ROSENKOHL *Red cabbage*

LEIPZIGER ALLERLEI
Mixed vegetables: petit pois, carrots and asparagus tips

SESAM KARTOFFELN
Potatoes with sesame seeds

~

OBSTSALAT *Fruit salad*

Markklösschensuppe

MARROWBONE SOUP

cold water	2.25 litres	4 pints	8 cups
beef marrowbones, in pieces	1kg	2lb	2lb
kidney, finely chopped	1	1	1
carrots, cut into chunks	2	2	2
a few stalks of celery, cut into chunks			
onions, cut into chunks	2	2	2
whole black peppercorns	6	6	6
salt	4ml	3/4 tsp	3/4 tsp
pinch of dried thyme			
few sprigs of parsley			
bay leaf	1	1	1

Put all the ingredients in a very large pan with sufficient water to cover. Bring to the boil and remove the scum. Cover and simmer gently for 3$^{1}/_{2}$ hours. Strain and allow to cool completely so that all the fat can be removed and the soup underneath is clear.

Dumplings

marrow from the soup bones			
egg	1	1	1
white breadcrumbs	100g	4oz	1/2 cup
fresh parsley, chopped	15ml	1tbs	1tbs
freshly grated nutmeg to taste			
salt and pepper			

Remove the marrow from the bones, melt it and, when cooled, beat in the egg, breadcrumbs, parsley, grated nutmeg, salt and pepper. Add a little milk if necessary but don't make them too soft. Leave to stand for 20 minutes. Form into marble-sized balls and cook gently in slightly salted water for 10–15 minutes. Alternatively shape the dumplings into star or heart shapes for a festive finish to the soup.

Add the dumplings to the soup just before serving and heat through thoroughly.

Weihnachtsgans

CHRISTMAS GOOSE

fresh goose	5–6kg	10–12lb	

Pork and Apple Stuffing

minced pork	350g	12oz	12oz
cooking apples	350g	12oz	1½ cups
slices of bread, slightly stale	3	3	3
a little milk			
liver of the goose, finely chopped			
egg	1	1	1
egg yolk	1	1	1
dried marjoram	10ml	2tsp	2tsp
grated nutmeg			
salt and pepper			

Peel and core the apples, and chop roughly. Break up the bread and soak in the milk for about 5–10 minutes. Squeeze out well. Place the bread, meat, liver, apples, eggs, marjoram and seasonings into a bowl and mix thoroughly. Set aside until needed.

Using a 5–6kg (10–12lb) goose cut off the large pieces of fat you find mainly just round the inside of the body cavity. This fat can be rendered down and stored in the fridge. It is lovely for frying meat.

Using thick darning needle, prick the goose all over, especially round the legs. This helps reduce the fattiness.

Spoon the prepared stuffing into the body cavity and sew up with fine string. Rub the goose all over with salt and place breast-side up on a rack over a large roasting tin (pan). Place in a pre-heated oven. Cook for 15 minutes at 200°C (400°F/Gas 6) then turn breast side down. Turn oven down to 160°C (325°F/Gas 3) for most of the roasting time until the last 30 minutes when you raise the temperature again, to 200°C (400°F/Gas 6), turn the bird breast-side up and

sprinkle with cold water and roast. Take the goose out of the oven, wrap it in foil and leave in a warm place for 15–20 minutes to rest before carving.

Calculate the roasting time: 25 minutes per 500g (1lb). (You will need approximately 4–4½ hours for a 5–6kg (10–12lb) goose.) No basting is necessary.

Sauce

goosefat	30ml	2tbs	2tbs
chopped onion	15ml	1tbs	1tbs
plain flour	25g	1oz	2tbs
goose stock (made from giblets)	450ml	15fl oz	1½ cups
carrot, chopped	1	1	1
stick celery, chopped	1	1	1
mushrooms, chopped	50g	2oz	¼ cup
small can of tomatoes, drained	200g	7oz	1 cup
salt and pepper			
bouquet garni			
red or white wine	45ml	3tbs	3tbs
a little single cream (half and half)			

Make the sauce while the goose is roasting. Fry the onions in the goose fat until transparent. Stir in the flour and cook over a very low heat to make a brown roux. This takes about 15–20 minutes. Stir occasionally to brown evenly. Add the stock and bring to the boil and stir until smooth. Add the carrot, celery, mushrooms, drained and chopped tomatoes, salt, pepper and bouquet garni. Bring to the boil, cover and simmer for 30–40 minutes. Pour through a strainer into a clean saucepan. Check seasoning and consistency. Stir in wine and simmer for about 10 minutes. Just before serving stir in a little cream.

Schweinerollbraten mit Pflaumen

ROLLED PORK WITH PLUMS

pork, unrolled	1kg	2lb	2lb
salt and pepper to taste			
pinch of marjoram			
apples, peeled, cored and sliced	2	2	2
plums, pitted and roughly chopped	15–20	15–20	15–20
pinch of cinnamon			
sugar	2ml	1/2 tsp	1/2 tsp
breadcrumbs	75g	3oz	1/3 cup
oil	30ml	2tbs	2tbs
onion, cut in two	1	1	1
bunch of mixed herbs OR dried herbs	10ml	2tsp	2tsp
parsley or watercress, to garnish			

Gravy

flour	15ml	1tbs	1tbs
sour cream	75ml	3fl oz	1/4 cup

Season the pork with the salt, pepper and marjoram. Mix the apple slices, plums, cinnamon, sugar and breadcrumbs, and spread over the meat. Roll up the meat then tie with string to form a neat roll. Heat the oil in a casserole and add the meat roll, the onion and the bunch of mixed herbs. Pot roast at 180°C (350°F/ Gas 4) for about 2 hours, adding 300ml (1/2 pint) boiling water every half hour, starting half an hour after you begin the roasting.

When cooked, strain the juices from the casserole, pour into a pan and thicken with the flour and sour cream.

Place the pork on a platter, garnish with parsley or watercress and serve the gravy separately. Serve with a mixture of petit pois (tiny peas), baby carrots and asparagus tips, known as 'Leipziger Allerlei'.

Rosenkohl

RED CABBAGE

red cabbage	1–1 1/2 kg		2–3lb
butter	25g	1oz	2tbs
small onion, finely chopped	1	1	1
brown sugar	30ml	2tbs	2tbs
wine vinegar	60ml	4tbs	4tb
salt, freshly ground black pepper and nutmeg, to taste			
redcurrant jelly	30ml	2tbs	2tbs
apple, grated	1	1	1

Discard the tough outer leaves of the cabbage and shred it finely, avoiding the hard white core. Place the cabbage in a colander and rinse in cold water. Melt the butter in a saucepan and add the onion. Sauté gently until transparent. Add the sugar, vinegar and cabbage. Season to taste with salt, pepper and nutmeg. Mix well, then cover with a tightly fitting lid and allow to cook over a low heat for about 1 1/2 hours. During this time check the liquid level and give the occasional stir, adding water if necessary. Finally, add the redcurrant jelly and the apple, adjust the seasoning once more and cook for a further 15 minutes.

This piquant dish complements roast pork very well. From experience there is never too much of it as it improves with re-heating and is equally delicious served cold on Boxing Day (26 December).

Obstsalat

FRUIT SALAD

small bunch black (purple) grapes			
dessert apple	1	1	1
pear	1	1	1
piece of fresh pineapple OR can of pineapple	225g	8oz	8oz
oranges	2	2	2
small bananas	2	2	2
juice of 1/2 lemon			
juice of 1 orange			
clear honey	15–30ml	1–2tbs	1–2tbs
pinch of ground ginger			
brandy	30ml	2tbs	2tbs
flaked almonds, lightly toasted	30g	1oz	2tbs

Place the juice of the lemon and orange into a small saucepan, add the honey and stir over a low heat until the honey has dissolved. Mix in the ground ginger.

Take off the heat and while this is cooling prepare the fruit. Cut the grapes in half and remove the pips (seeds). Peel the pear but leave the skin on the apple. Core both and cut into small chunks. Prepare the pineapple and cut into small pieces. Segment the oranges and cut into pieces. Peel and slice the bananas.

Place all the fruit into a large bowl. Check the syrup for sweetness and stir in the brandy. Pour over the fruit and mix thoroughly. Cover and leave in a cool place.

Just before serving, sprinkle the almonds over it. Serve with lightly whipped cream and a selection of Christmas biscuits.

~ EXTRA RECIPES ~

Christstollen

This Christmas cake is quite unlike the heavy fruit cake popular in the United Kingdom. The sweet yeasty dough is shaped to resemble the Christ child in swaddling clothes, hence the name *Christstollen*.

strong plain flour	450g	1lb	4 cups
pinch of salt			
ground cardamon	2ml	1/2 tsp	1/2 tsp
ground nutmeg	2ml	1/2 tsp	1/2 tsp
fresh yeast	50g	2oz	2tbs
sugar	100g	4oz	1/2 cup
milk, lukewarm	250ml	9fl oz	1 cup
unsalted butter, softened	225g	8oz	2 sticks
egg, beaten	1	1	1
rind of 1 lemon			

Filling

rum	45–60ml	3–4tbs	3–4tbs
sultanas (golden raisins)	225g	8oz	1 cup
currants	150g	5oz	2/3 cup
citrus peel, finely chopped	100g	4oz	1/2 cup
blanched almonds, chopped	75g	3oz	1/3 cup
marzipan	175g	6oz	3/4 cup

Topping

butter, melted	100g	4oz	1 stick
icing sugar (confectioner's sugar)	75g	3oz	1/3 cup
vanilla sugar	25g	1oz	2tbs

The day before making the *Stollen*, set out all the ingredients at room temperature and soak the sultanas, currants and citrus peel in the rum overnight. The next day, Sift the flour with the salt and spices and make a well in the centre of the flour. Cream the yeast with half of the lukewarm milk plus 5ml (1tsp) of the sugar. Pour into the well. Sprinkle some flour over the top and leave in a warm place for 20–30 minutes until the yeast mixture has gone frothy. Add the softened butter, beaten egg, sugar and lemon rind and enough milk to make a fairly soft yeast dough. Knead well on a floured surface until smooth (about 10 minutes). Drain the rum-soaked fruit and add to the mixture. Knead until evenly mixed. Place the dough in a greased bowl, cover, and leave to rise until doubled in size.

Punch down the dough and shape into an oval about 3–4cm (1 1/2 in.) thick. Shape the marzipan into a roll the same length as the dough and place on top. On the long side fold one third of the dough to the centre and do the same with the other side, overlapping a little at the centre. The loaf now resembles a child wrapped in swaddling clothes.

Transfer the *Stollen* on to a greased baking tray. Loosely wrap a long strip of foil around the *Stollen* and leave to prove (rise) in a warm place for 20 minutes. Bake in a pre-heated oven at 200°C (400°F/Gas 6) for 20 minutes, then turn the oven down to 180°C (350°F/Gas 4) for 40–50 minutes.

While still hot, brush with melted butter and dust thickly with icing (confectioner's) sugar and vanilla sugar which have been sifted together. When cold, wrap in foil and store in a dry and cool place. Leave for at least a week before eating.

Lebkuchen

It seems that every family has its favourite *Lebkuchen* recipe. This one comes from a family in southern Germany.

egg whites	3	3	3
caster sugar (US: granulated)	100g	4oz	1/2 cup
vanilla sugar	5ml	1tsp	1tsp
pinch of ground cloves			
pinch of nutmeg			
pinch of baking powder			
cinnamon	2ml	1/2 tsp	1/2 tsp
rum	5ml	1tsp	1tsp
rind of 1 lemon			
citrus peel, finely chopped	40g	1 1/2 oz	3tbs
ground almonds	60g	2 1/2 oz	5tbs
ground hazelnuts	60g	2 1/2 oz	5tbs
rice paper			
slab of covering chocolate	225g	8oz	8oz
almond halves			

Whisk the egg whites, adding the vanilla sugar and caster sugar a spoonful at a time. Add the rest of the ingredients. Mix well with a wooden spoon. Line the baking sheet with rice paper (or bakewell paper). Spoon the mixture on to the baking sheet, one tablespoonful at a time. Bake for 25–30 minutes at 180°C (350°F/Gas 4). When cold, cover with the melted chocolate and decorate with almond halves.

Another way of making these biscuits using honey is perhaps closer to the original recipe and also very delicious.

Honey Lebkuchen

eggs	2	2	2
caster sugar (US: granulated)	100g	4oz	1/2 cup
honey	15ml	3tbs	3tbs
vanilla sugar	15ml	3tbs	3tbs
lemon, rind only	1/2	1/2	1/2
plain flour	100g	4oz	1 cup
ground almonds	75g	3oz	1/2 cup
baking powder	5ml	1tsp	1tsp
citrus peel	40g	1 1/2 oz	3tbs

generous pinch of each of the following:
ground nutmeg, cardamom, aniseed, clove, cinnamon

split almonds to decorate

Beat together eggs, sugars and honey until creamy. Stir in the lemon zest, citrus peel, spices and ground almonds. Sieve the flour and baking powder and add to the mixture.
Spoon onto baking parchment or a greased baking tray. A heaped teaspoonful makes a generous biscuit. Bake at 160°C (325°F) for 15 minutes. Decorate while warm with almond slivers.

Pignolikipferl
PINE NUT CRESCENTS

These are another Christmas favourite.

egg whites	4	4	4
sugar	200g	7oz	3/4 cup
finely ground almonds	225g	8oz	1 cup
a little lemon rind			
vanilla sugar	5ml	1tsp	1tsp
pine nuts	60g	2 1/2 oz	1/4 cup

Beat the egg whites until stiff, adding the sugar a tablespoon at a time. Stir in the ground almonds, lemon rind and vanilla sugar. Fry this mixture at a low heat until warmed through. Alarming as this may seem, it gives the finished biscuits a deliciously nutty flavour and makes the mixture easier to handle. Sprinkle chopped pine nuts on to a greased baking tray. Roll small strips of the dough in the pine nuts until covered. Shape into crescents (*kipferl*) and place on a buttered baking tray. Bake for 10 minutes at 180°C (350°F/Gas 4).

Schwarz-weissgebäck
BLACK-AND-WHITE BISCUITS

The contrasting swirls of these chocolate and vanilla biscuits look very attractive.

plain flour	300g	12oz	3 cups
butter	200g	7oz	1³/₄ sticks
caster sugar (US: granulated)	100g	4oz	¹/₂ cup
vanilla sugar	10ml	2tsp	2tsp
egg, beaten	1	1	1
egg yolk	1	1	1
cocoa	15ml	1tbs	1tbs
sugar	10ml	2tsp	2tsp

Sift the flour, rub in the butter and then add the caster sugar and vanilla sugar. Whisk the egg and the extra egg yolk and stir into the flour. Gather the pastry with your hands and form into a ball. Divide the dough in two. Into one half knead the cocoa and the extra sugar. Chill well. Roll out each half, place the darker half on top of the light and roll up, swiss roll (jellyroll) fashion. Chill well. When required, slice the biscuits on to a greased baking tray and bake at 180°C (350°F/Gas 4) for 15 minutes.

Grossmutters Punsch
GRANDMOTHER'S PUNCH

This warming drink is often served at midnight on Christmas Eve.

water	250ml	9fl oz	1 cup
brown sugar	100g	4oz	¹/₂ cup
cloves	2	2	2
fresh ginger, finely chopped	25g	1oz	2tbs
bottle red wine	1	1	1
lemon	1	1	1
strong tea	500ml	18fl oz	1³/₄ cups
rum	175ml	6fl oz	³/₄ cup

Place the water, sugar, cloves and chopped ginger in a saucepan and bring to the boil to dissolve the sugar. Boil for 5 minutes. Strain and return to the pan with the red wine. Pare the lemon rind and add it and the juice of the lemon to the wine. Add the tea and the rum and heat gently but do not boil. Serve in punch glasses.

DENMARK

SPLITFLAG — Based on an early 15th seal.

Denmark *celebrates Christmas in a memorable way. The Danes are warm, hospitable people and excellent cooks and Christmas affords a welcome opportunity to enjoy good food and convivial company.*

It is essentially an old fashioned way of celebrating. Not for the majority the pre-packed supermarket fare; instead a good deal of the food and even some of the decorations are home-made. Although time consuming, these preparations have a charm of their own and have become as much part of the celebration as the feast itself.

As Christmas approaches, the kitchen is decorated with red paper garlands and paper cut-outs of gnomes and goblins cooking and baking are pasted on to walls and windows to inspire the cook.

The lighting of the first of the four candles on the Advent wreath four weeks before Christmas is the signal for the baking of *pebernødder* ('pepper' or ginger 'nuts' or biscuits), *brune kager* and *vanille kranse* to begin in earnest. Often the recipes for these delicious biscuits are handed down from generation to generation, sometimes still in great-grandmother's handwriting on the original scrap of paper she used in her kitchen. These biscuits will be produced and eaten at any occasion such as the 'paste and paper' sessions, when friends and family get together one afternoon to make decorations. They will most certainly make the unique woven paper hearts which will be filled with the little *pebernødder* and hung on the tree. Often a narrow red ribbon is tied through the *vanille kranse* and these circlets of biscuit are hung on the tree or in the windows.

Choosing the tree is a highlight when the whole family goes to the nearest plantation to

fell its own or selects a tree from the forestry offices. It is decorated on Christmas Eve, often secretly by the parents and not seen by the children until after dinner. A festive wreath of pine cones is hung on the door. Sheaves of wheat are sold by charities to raise funds and it is customary to hang them out for the birds. In ancient times this was done not only out of kindness to the birds but also as a farmer's signal to his labourers and neighbours that his Christmas preparations were complete and that he was ready to begin the celebrations.

Nowadays, particularly in Jutland, the celebrations begin as early as lunch-time on Christmas Eve when a traditional meal of *grønlangkål* (stewed kale in a cream sauce) is eaten, together with *medisterpølse* (pork sausages), potatoes, glazed carrots, mustard and beetroot.

The climax of all the preparation comes on Christmas Eve, the most important evening of the year, when friends and family go to church. A white Christmas is almost guaranteed in Denmark and there is a particular delight in coming home in the cold from the church service to a warm and festive home and the smell of Christmas dinner.

Having gone to so much trouble in preparing the food, equal care is given to its presentation. The table is beautifully set with the best linen, sometimes heirloom pieces embroidered with Christmas motifs and handed down from mother to daughter. At each place there is a candle and usually there is a centre piece with perhaps a glass or china ornament such as an angel holding a candle.

Surprisingly the meal begins with rice pudding. In the early 1800s rice was imported into Denmark but was so expensive that it was reserved for special occasions such as the Christmas meal. The idea took hold and has

remained ever since. The present-day version of the pudding is rich and creamy, sprinkled with cinnamon sugar and has a blanched almond ceremoniously stirred into it. The lucky person who gets the almond wins a prize of a marzipan pig. In days gone by, instead of a prize you were allowed a wish which would be granted whatever it was, for example to kiss the person of your choice at the table. You became for the evening a privileged person whose every whim had to be catered for. This quaint tradition would appear to have been adapted from a similar one common in France as early as 1500.

One could be forgiven for thinking that *ris à l'amande*, a cold rice and almond pudding, also came from France, but it is totally unknown there. It is a modern adaptation of the traditional rice pudding and in some homes is served as a dessert.

Whether the rice pudding is hot or cold, tradition demands that a bowl of it be put outside in the farmyard or garden to appease the Christmas *Nisser*. These *Nisser* are gnarled, bearded, gnome-like men dressed in red hats, smocks and clogs. They are as old as the Norse festival of Yule itself, stories of them first appearing some 4000 years ago, originally as somewhat sinister sprites associated with ancient solstice celebrations. Legends depict the *Nisser* as ancestral spirits controlling domestic fortunes. These distinctly pagan legends are reminders that Yule existed before Christmas. Today *Nisser* have been commercialized and are more benevolent fellows depicted on Christmas cards and decorations.

The meal continues with a main course of roast duck or goose or perhaps pork. A little Danish flag is tucked into the roast and the decoratively garnished platter is carried through to the dining room to the applause of the guests.

Red cabbage, redcurrant jelly and caramelized potatoes are usually served with this course. During the meal frequent toasts are made to absent friends, the hosts, the guests, and countless other excuses are found to refill the wine glasses.

Those with large appetites will finish their meal with a helping of *æblekage* (apple cake). This is made with layers of toasted breadcrumbs and apple topped with whipped cream. Another favourite is *Hindbærdessert* (raspberry dessert) or some families will have cold, creamy *ris à l'amande* with a hot fruit sauce.

While the table is being cleared the parents sneak out to light the candles on the tree. Real candles are used and the tree is festooned with garlands of little Danish flags made of paper, lametta, paper angels and hearts, and tree ornaments, some of which will have been passed from generation to generation.

The room lights are switched off and the family are ushered in to see the tree in its candlelit glory. Hans Christian Andersen aptly described the scene as 'magnificent, quite unforgettably magnificent'. For Danish Christians, the twin symbols of evergreen, for everlasting life, and light, for the light of the world, are deeply evocative.

The family joins hands and dances round the tree, singing carols, the children eyeing the parcels beneath and hoping that the *Julemand* (Father Christmas) will have crept in during dinner and left a parcel for them. Coffee is served, chocolates and biscuits passed around and then the gifts are opened. Favourite Christmas records play in the background while the family members sit admiring the tree and their gifts and perhaps play some games, until finally sleepiness overcomes everyone.

Christmas Day and 26 December are sociable

days when family and friends gather over lunch. These are huge buffets of herring, pâté, meat balls, salads and cheese washed down with aquavit and beer. The lengthy and relaxed lunches are often followed by a long walk in the snow.

The nibbling of leftovers continues for days. Before New Year's Eve the remaining candles on the tree are burnt right down to the stump, signalling the end of another Christmas.

A DANISH
CHRISTMAS EVE MEAL

RISENGRØD
Rice pudding

~

STEGT AND
Roast duck

RØDKÅL
Red cabbage

BRUNEDE KARTOFLER
Caramelized new potatoes

~

ÆBLEKAGE
Apple cake

or

HINDBÆRDESSERT
Raspberry dessert

or

RIS À L'AMANDE
Cold rice and almond pudding
with hot fruit sauce

Risengrød
RICE PUDDING

milk	900ml	1½ pints	3¾ cups
pudding rice	175g	6oz	¾ cup
generous pinch of salt			
vanilla essence (extract)	5ml	1tsp	1tsp
double cream (US: whipping)	100ml	4fl oz	½ cup
knob of butter			

Cinnamon sugar

granulated sugar	50g	2oz	¼ cup
ground cinnamon	10ml	2tsp	2tsp
whole blanched almond	1	1	1

Put a little cold water into a saucepan, add the milk and bring to the boil, stirring well. Add the rice, salt and vanilla. Cover the pan, lower the heat and simmer for about 35 minutes, checking periodically that the rice isn't sticking. It should have a creamy, porridge-like consistency when cooked. Just before serving stir in the cream. Serve piping hot accompanied by butter, cinnamon sugar and a fruit juice such as blackcurrant to drink.

Don't forget to stir in the almond at the table and have a prize ready.

Rødkål
RED CABBAGE

red cabbage	1–1½ kg	2–3lb	2–3lb
butter	25g	1oz	2tbs
small onion, finely chopped	1	1	1
brown sugar	30ml	2tbs	2tbs
wine vinegar	60ml	4tbs	4tbs
salt, freshly ground black pepper and nutmeg, to taste			
redcurrant jelly	30ml	2tbs	2tbs
apple, grated	1	1	1

Discard the tough outer leaves of the cabbage and shred it finely, avoiding the hard white core. Place the cabbage in a colander and rinse in cold water. Melt the butter in a saucepan and add the onion. Sauté gently until transparent. Add the sugar, vinegar and cabbage. Season to taste with salt, pepper and nutmeg. Mix well, then cover with a tightly fitting lid and allow to cook over a low heat for about 1½ hours. During this time check the liquid level and give the occasional stir, adding water if necessary. Finally, add the redcurrant jelly and the apple, adjust the seasoning once more and cook for a further 15 minutes.

This piquant dish complements the roast very well. From experience there is never too much of it as it improves with re-heating and is equally delicious served cold on Boxing Day (26 December).

Brunede kartofler
CARAMELIZED NEW POTATOES

granulated sugar	75g	3oz	1/3 cup
butter, melted	75g	3oz	3/4 stick
small new potatoes (tinned ones will do)	16–18	16–18	16–18

These delicious potatoes are a favourite accompaniment to the Christmas roast and are easily made by melting the sugar in a pan over a low heat until it caramelizes. This can take some time and needs constant stirring and watching as sugar burns very easily. Add the melted butter and the peeled boiled potatoes. Toss until all the potatoes are well glazed.

Æblekage
APPLE CAKE

white breadcrumbs	225g	8oz	1 cup
sugar	25g	1oz	2tbs
butter	25g	1oz	2tbs
large cooking apples	4	4	4
sugar	50g	2oz	1/4 cup
vanilla pod	1	1	1
whipping cream	150ml	1/4 pint	1/2 cup
redcurrant jelly			

Melt the butter over a low heat and add the first quantity of sugar and the breadcrumbs. Toast until golden brown, taking care to stir them as they burn easily. Peel, core and cook the apples with the second quantity of sugar and the vanilla pod until the apples are mushy. In a round, greased pie dish alternate layers of breadcrumbs with the apple purée, beginning and finishing with a layer of breadcrumbs. Top with whipped cream and decorate with blobs of redcurrant jelly. This dessert is best served slightly warm.

~ EXTRA RECIPES ~

Grønlangkål
KALE IN A CREAM SAUCE

kale	450g	1lb	2 cups
butter	50g	2oz	1/2 stick
plain white flour	50g	2oz	1/2 cup
milk	150ml	1/4 pint	1/2 cup
double cream (US: whipping)	150ml	1/4 pint	1/2 cup
salt and freshly ground black pepper			

Pluck the tender green leaves from the stalks and wash carefully under cold running water. Tear the leaves into large pieces and place them in a large saucepan with just enough salted boiling water to cover. Cook until tender (10–12 minutes). Drain in a colander and extract as much moisture as possible by leaving to stand with a heavy weight pressing down on the kale.

In the meantime prepare the sauce by melting the butter in a saucepan. Remove from the heat and stir in the flour. Add the milk and cream, whisking well. Return the pan to a low heat and cook, whisking constantly, until the sauce comes to the boil and is glossy and thick. Season with salt and pepper.

Chop the kale finely and add to the sauce. Cook gently for a minute or two and serve. It is traditionally eaten with sausages and beetroot for lunch on Christmas Eve.

Ris à l'amande

COLD RICE AND ALMOND PUDDING

milk	600ml	1 pint	2½ cups
long grain rice	100g	4oz	½ cup
vanilla essence (extract)	10ml	2tsp	2tsp
caster sugar (US: granulated)	50g	2oz	¼ cup
double cream (US: whipping)	150ml	¼ pint	½ cup
chopped blanched almonds	50g	2oz	¼ cup

Bring the milk to the boil, add the rice and stir well. Lower the heat and simmer for 20 minutes until the milk is absorbed. Remove from the heat, stir in the sugar and vanilla essence (extract) and cool. Whip the cream, then fold the whipped cream and the almonds into the rice. Chill well before serving.

A spoonful of cherry liqueur on top of the pudding gives it a good flavour, or it can be served with a hot fruit sauce (see Norway).

Hindbærdessert

RASPBERRY DESSERT

There is an abundance of soft fruits in Denmark, so many households freeze some of the berries to use on special occasions during the winter months.

liqueur such as *Kijafa* (cherry liqueur) or *Solbær Rom* (blackcurrant liqueur), or sweet sherry	60ml	4tbs	4tbs
caster sugar (US: granulated)	75g	3oz	⅓ cup
frozen raspberries	225g	8oz	1 cup
macaroons, amaretti or ratafia biscuits	100g	4oz	½ cup
whipping cream	150ml	¼ pint	½ cup

Mix 30ml (2tbs) of the liqueur and the sugar and pour over the raspberries, reserving some for decoration. Allow to soak for a couple of hours. Crush the macaroons, amaretti or ratafias and put in a glass serving dish or in individual glasses. Spoon the raspberries and a little of the liqueur over the biscuits. Whip the cream until thick and gently stir in the remaining 30ml (2 tbs) of liqueur. Pour the cream over the raspberries and decorate with the reserved raspberries. Chill well before serving.

Brune kager

SPICY BROWN BISCUITS

A selection of Danish Christmas biscuits (cookies) always includes *brune kager* and an irresistible spicy aroma will pervade your house when you bake them. The mixture is best made up at least a day before needed.

butter or margarine	225g	8oz	2 sticks
soft dark brown sugar	225g	8oz	1 cup
golden (dark corn) syrup	100g	4oz	½ cup
split blanched almonds	50g	2oz	¼ cup
ground cloves	5ml	1tsp	1tsp
ground cinnamon	10ml	2tsp	2tsp
pinch of ginger			
bicarbonate of soda (baking soda)	5ml	1tsp	1tsp
mixed candied peel	50g	2oz	¼ cup
plain flour	450g	1lb	4 cups

Heat the butter, brown sugar and syrup in a large saucepan but do not allow to boil. Remove from the heat and when slightly cooled stir in the nuts, spices and mixed peel. Dissolve the bicarbonate of soda in a tablespoon of cold water and add to the syrup. Allow the mixture to cool a little more before adding the sifted flour a quarter at a time, kneading well after each addition. It is hard work adding the last quarter of flour, but persevere until you have a soft and shiny dough. It's easier to work this dough on a floured board. Divide the dough into two and form into sausages of about 5cm (2in.) diameter. When completely cold wrap in grease-proof paper or foil and refrigerate at least one day before baking. The dough will keep for at least a week in the fridge and it also freezes well. When required, simply slice thinly with a very sharp knife (a breadcutter is excellent for this) and place the rounds on a greased and floured baking sheet. Bake at 190°C (375°F/Gas 5) for 8 minutes on the top shelf of the oven.

Cream the butter and sugar and add the egg. Sift the flour and mix all the dry ingredients except the hartshorn together. Dissolve the hartshorn in the water and add this to the creamed mixture together with the dry ingredients. Mix well until everything is incorporated, then knead until smooth. Rest the dough for an hour or so then roll it into a long snake and cut the snake into pieces about the size of a hazelnut. Put the 'nuts' on a greased and floured baking sheet and bake in a pre-heated oven at 180°C (350°F/Gas 4).

* Hartshorn may be an unfamiliar ingredient to some cooks. Originally made from powdered deer's horn, it is used as a raising agent to give a particularly pleasant, light and crumbly texture to biscuits. Sodium bicarbonate does not produce the same results. Hartshorn is available from specialist grocer's shops and from pharmacies: ask for ammonium carbonate.

Pebernødder
PEPPERNUTS

C hildren love to help with making the dough for these biscuits (cookies). The dough is rolled into long thin snakes and then chopped into hazelnut-sized pieces. They are used to fill the little paper hearts made to hang on the Christmas tree.

butter or margarine	100g	4oz	1 stick
sugar	100g	4oz	1/2 cup
egg, beaten	1	1	1
flour	250g	9oz	2 1/4 cups
ammonium carbonate (hartshorn)* **AND**	5ml	1tsp	1tsp
water	15ml	1tbs	1tbs
powdered dried ginger	2ml	1/2 tsp	1/2 tsp
ground cardamom	4ml	3/4 tsp	3/4 tsp
pinch of white pepper			

Vanille kranse

VANILLA RINGS

These are both decorative and tasty. This recipe has been handed down for generations.

butter	225g	8oz	2 sticks
plain white flour	350g	12oz	3 cups
sugar	225g	8oz	1 cup
seeds of one vanilla pod			
ground almonds	75g	3oz	1/3 cup
small egg	1	1	1

Lightly rub the butter into the flour until it resembles breadcrumbs. Add the sugar, vanilla and ground almonds and bind with the egg. Knead until all the ingredients are well incorporated. The dough will benefit from being refrigerated for an hour before piping through the star shape of a biscuit maker (cookie press). A piping bag and a star-shaped nozzle for piping potatoes will do as well. Pipe long ribbons of dough, then cut into 10cm (4in.) strips. Join the ends of each strip together to form a circlet and bake on a well greased baking sheet for 8–10 minutes at 200°C (400°F/Gas 6).

Threaded with a red ribbon, these look lovely hanging on the Christmas tree.

NETHERLANDS

17th Dutch Tile.

The Netherlands *are chill and grey in the darkening days of November. In much the same way as their ancestors looked forward to the solstice celebrations to relieve the tedium of the long winter months, the Dutch look forward to the gaiety of St Nicholas' Day.*

The people really go to town, literally and figuratively, over *Sinterklaas*. On a Saturday in late November they line the streets of Amsterdam to see him arrive by steamship, ostensibly from Spain. He is dressed in red and white bishop's vestments with gold embroidery on his cope and mitre and he holds a staff. Riding a snow-white horse he is accompanied by his Moorish servant, Zwarte Piet (Black Peter). After processing through the streets of the city they are officially welcomed in from the city hall by the Lord Mayor, an event televised live to the nation.

Simultaneously many St Nicholases and their helpers appear all over the country. They spend the next few weeks visiting hospitals, classrooms, department stores, offices and countless homes. It is a very exciting time for children because St Nicholas has spent the greater part of the year recording their behaviour in his big red book and there is always that element of doubt as to whether he will see fit to leave a basketful of goodies at the door. Heaven forbid that they have been so naughty that Zwarte Piet will pop them into his big black bag and carry them off to Spain. Some will get the chance to justify their behaviour to St Nicholas in person. Others might just catch a glimpse of Zwarte Piet's black hand scattering sweets and *pepernoten* (tiny spicy biscuits) through the door.

Apart from being a kindly man St Nicholas is also the patron saint of children and so usually takes their side!

The Christmas legend of St Nicholas is based on reality. He was the archbishop of Myra in Asia Minor in AD 300, a wealthy man who distributed his money amongst the poor. The fame of his saintly deeds spread across the Mediterranean and, as often happens, the stories grew more and more fanciful until several legends about him came into being.

One of these tells of how he created some storms and stilled others on the Mediterranean. He is now the patron saint of sailors. Another legend tells of how he secretly provided dowries for the three daughters of an impoverished nobleman. Some of the gold he dropped down the chimney is said to have landed in a shoe. This gave rise to the custom of each child putting a shoe next to the fireplace from the time St Nicholas arrives in Holland in late November until St Nicholas' Day, 6 December. Occasionally children can expect to find a handful of sweets and biscuits or perhaps a little package in their shoe.

St Nicholas' Eve, or Sinterklaas, on 5 December is a time of good-natured fun. Gifts are bought and ingeniously wrapped to disguise their contents. It is also customary to enclose a *Sinterklaas* rhyme with each present revealing some (often embarrassing) incident in the recipient's life. Every poem is signed *Sinterklaas* and the real giver tries to remain anonymous.

Sinterklaas calls for festive food and the Dutch, not usually known for their cuisine, produce some particularly delicious biscuits and pastries especially for this occasion.

The most famous of these is *speculaas*—a crisp, dark brown, aromatic gingerbread. The word *speculaas* is derived from the Latin word *speculum*, meaning 'mirror'. This is because the dough is pressed into carved wooden moulds and turned out on to a baking sheet thus producing a mirror image of the carving. The images are of Dutch domestic scenes, St Nicholas, Zwarte Piet and so on. Sometimes they are seven-to eight-inch-tall carvings of men and women and are known as *speculaaspoppen* (dolls).

In the early 1600s ships of the Dutch East India Company returned from their spice voyages with exotic spices such as cinnamon and ginger. They were very costly and any food containing them was considered a great treat. This is why *speculaas* are made especially for times of celebration such as Christmas.

The Dutch have a notoriously sweet tooth and *borstplaat* (fondants) flavoured with coffee, maraschino or lemon are a favourite. *Banketletter*, pastry initials filled with almond paste, are often used as place cards when the table is set for St Nicholas' Eve. These could also be made of plain dark chocolate.

As St Nicholas' Eve is not a public holiday friends and family gather in the evening after dinner and then the fun begins. Each person has to open his package and read the poem aloud amidst general hilarity. The recipient then says a loud 'thank-you' to *Sinterklaas*, whether he knows the identity of the giver or not. Some children and those with time and imagination will hide their gifts and the recipients have to follow a treasure hunt trail to find them. To fortify the party a mulled wine called *Bisschopswijn* is served. The children drink hot chocolate and everyone enjoys the plates of sweets and biscuits on the table.

Before going to bed the children put out their shoes for the final time, perhaps with a little straw and a carrot for the white horse, anticipating that during the night St Nicholas will come and leave the gifts they have asked him for.

While *Sinterklaas* is a time of gaiety and gift giving, *Kerstmis* (Christmas) is by contrast a much smaller, more serene and intimate family time. As gifts have already been exchanged there

is little of the frantic shopping seen in some other countries just before Christmas. There is however little rest for the cook because Christmas also has its traditional foods. There is *kerstbrood* (Christmas bread) to be made and perhaps the *spekulaas* tin needs to be replenished. Few homes are without a cake known as *kerstkrans* (Christmas wreath) made from the same pastry as *banketletter* and decorated with glacé cherries and angelica leaves.

The tree is decorated on Christmas Eve, usually in silver and white. Real candles are still used and glass decorations are very popular. The house is decorated with greenery tied with red ribbons, and flowering spring bulbs, forced for Christmas, cram every window-sill. Christ-mas Eve is spent quietly at home. Some families attend a midnight church service but most prefer to wait until Christmas day.

It is lovely to wake up on Christmas morning to the sound and smells of breakfast being prepared. Typically there will be coffee, rolls with slices of mature Gouda cheese or slivers of cold ham, followed by the first slice of *kerstbrood*, very like the German *stollen*.

The family will usually go to the local church service. Christmas Day services are always well attended. On returning home the family have coffee with some *kerstkrans* and *spekulaas*.

Those who are able lend a hand in the kitchen to prepare the Christmas meal and, just as when Bruegel painted his famous winter

scenes, the children meet at the nearest pond to 'skate up' an appetite for the Christmas dinner.

The special Dutch Christmas Day meal takes place in the early evening. The table is set with the best white damask cloth. Perhaps there will be a centre-piece of red ribbons and greenery or a vase of freesias, and certainly there will be white candles on the table. There is no traditional meal as such, most families serving their favourite dishes.

Tomato soup is a likely starter. Tomatoes are grown in abundance in Holland and a home-made tomato soup, perhaps laced with *Jenever* (gin) and decorated with a swirl of cream, not only looks suitably festive but is liked by all,

young and old. Holland now raises turkeys on a large scale so turkey is commonly served as a main course. An almond stuffing for the turkey and a selection of vegetables are the usual accompaniments.

Kerstpudding literally means Christmas pudding but this light mousse is far removed from the English type of Christmas pudding. Made with oranges and festively coloured red, it is an attractive way to end the meal.

After coffee and liqueurs, the family retires to the living-room to light the candles on the tree. A few small gifts may be exchanged but the emphasis is on family togetherness, a time to quietly reflect on the message of Christmas.

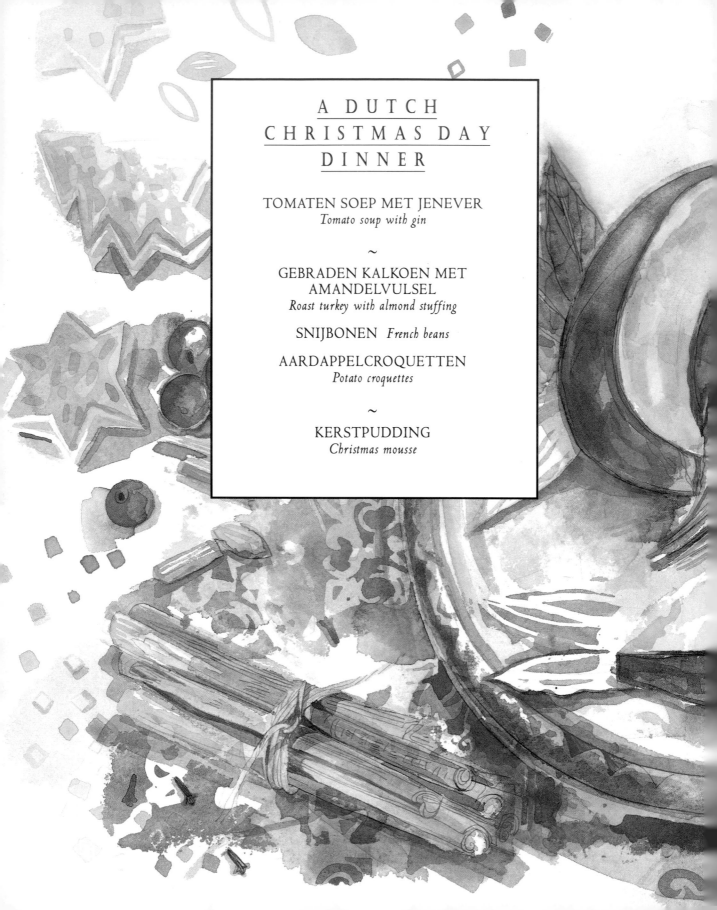

A DUTCH
CHRISTMAS DAY
DINNER

TOMATEN SOEP MET JENEVER
Tomato soup with gin

~

GEBRADEN KALKOEN MET
AMANDELVULSEL
Roast turkey with almond stuffing

SNIJBONEN *French beans*

AARDAPPELCROQUETTEN
Potato croquettes

~

KERSTPUDDING
Christmas mousse

Tomaten soep
TOMATO SOUP

This is a rich, creamy version of tomato soup, spiked with gin, and not at all like the usual canned fare.

bouillon or salted water	1 litre	1³/₄ pints	4 cups
large tomatoes	8	8	8
tomato purée	15ml	1tbs	1tbs
large onion, finely chopped	1	1	1
olive oil	15ml	1tbs	1tbs
white peppercorns	8	8	8
bay leaf	1	1	1
small bunch of parsley			
pinch of basil			
butter	25g	1oz	2tbs
flour	25g	1oz	2tbs
freshly ground black pepper, to taste			
single cream (half and half)	30ml	2tbs	2tbs
gin	15–30ml	1–2tbs	1–2tbs

Quarter the tomatoes and sauté lightly in the oil with the chopped onion. Add the bouillon or salted water, the peppercorns, bay leaf, parsley and basil. Simmer for 20 minutes. Remove from the heat and sieve the soup, pressing out as much of the tomato as possible. Melt the butter in the pan, add the flour and very slowly, stirring constantly, add the tomato soup. Stir in the tomato purée. Cook for a further 5 minutes. Just before serving, add the gin and serve with a swirl of cream, a dash of black pepper and a garnish of parsley.

Gebraden kalkoen met amandelvulsel
ROAST TURKEY WITH ALMOND STUFFING

If this is the only stuffing to be used in the turkey, double the amount.

butter	100g	4oz	1 stick
white breadcrumbs	100g	4oz	½ cup
raisins	50g	2oz	¼ cup
blanched bitter almonds (geschaafde), ground	10	10	10
salt and pepper, to taste			
nutmeg, to taste			

Cream the butter and add the breadcrumbs, raisins and almonds. Season with salt, pepper and nutmeg to taste. Refrigerate in a covered bowl. This is best made the day before you intend to stuff the bird.

Cooking instructions for turkey can be found on page 208.

Kerstpudding
CHRISTMAS MOUSSE

Being a nation of dairy farmers the Dutch tend to be lavish with cream. Their desserts are not for anyone keeping an eye on their waistline! Although made with oranges, *Kerstpudding* should by tradition be red. In Holland you would make it using red gelatine, generally difficult to obtain elsewhere, but a few drops of red food colouring gives the same festive effect.

Mould

juice from 5 oranges
PLUS
the grated rind of one of them

sachet of gelatine (packet)	1	1	1/2 oz
hot water	45ml	3tbs	3tbs
sugar	50g	2oz	1/4 cup
whipping cream	200ml	7fl oz	3/4 cup
egg whites	2	2	2
red food colouring			

Orange garnish

oranges	2	2	2
lemon	1	1	1
sachet of gelatine (packet)	1/2	1/2	1/4 oz
whipping cream	150ml	1/4 pint	1/2 cup
sugar	25g	1oz	2tbs

Decoration

whipping cream	50ml	2fl oz	4tbs
sugar	25g	1oz	2tbs

Oil a plain, unfluted ring mould sparingly. Mix the gelatine with the hot water and stir well until dissolved. Squeeze the oranges, remembering to reserve the grated rind of one of them. Heat the orange juice until lukewarm, then stir in the gelatine and the sugar. Allow to cool.

Beat the egg whites until stiff and similarly beat the cream until thick. Add enough red food colouring to the cooled orange syrup to give an appetizing colour. Add the grated rind of the orange to the syrup and fold in the egg whites. Add the whipped cream and gently fold the mixture together. Spoon into the mould and chill well.

To make the garnish, carefully cut the oranges in half. Proceed as above to make a mousse, adding the

juice and grated rind of a lemon instead of the grated orange rind, and squeezing the juice carefully out of the orange halves. Remove any white pith remaining in the empty orange halves.

Carefully spoon the mousse into the orange halves. Chill until set. Trim the edges of the shells level with the mousse if necessary and then with a sharp knife cut each half into quarters.

Turn the ring mould out on to a serving platter and arrange the orange slices around it. Whip the cream and sugar together and use it to decorate the mousse.

~ EXTRA RECIPES ~

Amandelpers

ALMOND PASTE

This is used in the recipes for *kerstkrans* and *gevuld spekulaas*.

whole blanched almonds	225g	8oz	1 cup
caster sugar (US: granulated)	225g	8oz	1 cup
grated rind and juice of 1 lemon OR rose water	60ml	4tbs	4tbs

Soak the almonds in boiling water for 5 minutes. Drain and put them into a blender with the sugar and grated lemon rind. Blend until the nuts are finely chopped. Add the lemon juice and knead to form a paste. Keep in an airtight container—preferably for 2–3 weeks before using, as this almond paste definitely improves with keeping.

Kerstkrans

CHRISTMAS WREATH

puff pastry	350g	12oz	12oz
almond paste	350g	12oz	1¹/₂ cups
egg, beaten	1	1	1
apricot jam	30ml	2tbs	2tbs
a few glacé cherries			
strips of angelica			

Roll out the puff pastry into a single strip 9cm (3¹/₂ in.) wide and 3mm (¹/₈ in) thick. Roll out the almond paste and shape into a sausage long enough to fit on to the strip of pastry. Place the almond paste sausage on the pastry and fold the pastry over it. Seal the edges with water. Shape the roll into a circle and seal the edges of the join with water. Brush with beaten egg and place on a well greased and floured baking sheet. Bake at 190°C (375°F/Gas 5) for 25–30 minutes until golden-brown.

To decorate, warm the apricot jam in a small pan and brush it over the top of the wreath. Arrange the glacé cherries and angelica to look like holly.

Spekulaas

SPICY ALMOND BISCUITS

Make the dough for these biscuits at least two days before baking to allow the spices to penetrate. This recipe makes 20 biscuits.

plain flour	350g	12oz	3 cups
pinch of salt			
baking powder	2ml	¹/₂ tsp	¹/₂ tsp
ground cloves	5ml	1tsp	1tsp
cinnamon	5ml	1tsp	1tsp
nutmeg	2ml	¹/₂ tsp	¹/₂ tsp
ginger (optional)	2ml	¹/₂ tsp	¹/₂ tsp
pinch of cardamon			
ground almonds	25g	1oz	2tbs
citrus peel, finely chopped	25g	1oz	2tbs
dark brown sugar	150g	5oz	²/₃ cup
milk	15ml	1tbs	1tbs
cold butter	150g	5oz	1¹/₄ sticks
a few whole almonds			
small egg, lightly beaten	1	1	1

Sift the flour, salt and baking powder into a large mixing bowl. Add the spices, ground almonds and citrus peel. Dissolve the brown sugar in the milk and add to the flour. Add the butter cut into little cubes. Knead quickly and lightly until well mixed and the dough forms a ball. Add a little extra milk if required. Allow this to stand in a cool place for at least a day or two.

If you have one, dust a carved wooden mould with cornflour and press the dough into it. Scrape away any excess dough and tap out the shapes on to a well greased baking tray.

Alternatively, roll out the dough 1cm (a little under ¹/₂ in.) thick and cut into rectangles 5 x 7cm (2 x 3in.). To make 'lovers', cut out figures of men and women 18cm (7in.) tall.

Decorate the shapes with whole almonds gently pressed into the dough. Brush with the lightly beaten egg to give a lovely glaze when cooked. Bake at 160°C (325°F/Gas 3) for 15–20 minutes.

Gevuld spekulaas

SPEKULAAS WITH ALMOND FILLING

quantity of spekulaas dough	1	1	1
quantity of almond paste	1	1	1

Divide the *spekulaas* dough into two portions and roll each out thinly on a floured board to fit a large baking tray. Place one portion on a well greased baking tray. Roll out the almond paste to the same size and lay on top of the layer of dough on the tray, shaping it to fit. Lay the second rolled out portion of *spekulaas* dough on top of the almond paste. Bake in a moderate oven at 160°C (325°F/Gas 3) for 30–40 minutes. When cool cut into triangles or squares and keep in an airtight container.
Makes 24.

Banketletter

PASTRY INITIALS

These are often used as place cards at the St Nicholas coffee table.

puff pastry	350g	12oz	12oz
almond paste	350g	12oz	1¹/₂ cups
egg, beaten PLUS a little water	1	1	1

On a floured board roll the almond paste into sausages 2.5cm (1in.) in diameter. Wrap in waxed paper and chill.
Roll out the chilled puff pastry into strips 9cm (3¹/₂ in.) wide and 3mm (¹/₈ in.) thick. Place an almond paste roll in the centre of each strip and fold the dough over, sealing the join and ends with water. Shape the strips into the required initial and place seam down on a well greased and floured baking sheet. Brush with beaten egg. Bake at 190°C (375°F/Gas 5) for 25–30 minutes until golden-brown.

Pepernoten

SPICY BISCUITS

These spicy biscuits (cookies) are a speciality of St Nicholas Eve, and are carried by St Nicholas' helper, Swarte Piet, in a large bag. On entering a room Swarte Piet throws a handful of *pepernoten* to each child.

self-raising flour	175g	6oz	1¹/₂ cups
mixed (pumpkin) spice	15ml	1tbs	1tbs
pinch of salt			
dark brown sugar	50g	2oz	¹/₄ cup
unsalted butter	25g	1oz	2tbs
golden syrup (dark corn syrup)	15ml	1tbs	1tbs
egg	1	1	1
milk	10ml	2tsp	2tsp

Sieve the dry ingredients into a large mixing bowl. Rub in the butter and bind with the egg and syrup. Mix well until the mixture forms a ball, adding a little milk if necessary. Break the dough into tiny, marble-sized balls and place them on a greased baking sheet. Bake in a cool oven at 150°C (300°F/Gas 2) for 20 minutes. Leave in the oven to cool. Makes 30.

Bisschopswijn
BISHOP'S WINE

This is a warming mulled wine drunk on St Nicholas' Eve.

orange	1	1	1
whole cloves	10	10	10
water	750ml	1¼ pints	2⅓ cups
blades of mace	2	2	2
cinnamon stick	1	1	1
lemon, sliced	1	1	1
sugar	50g	2oz	¼ cup
bottle red wine	1	1	1
lemon and orange slices			

Wash the orange and stick the cloves into it. Pour the water into a saucepan, add the orange, mace, cinnamon and lemon slices and bring to the boil. Cover and simmer for 30 minutes. Sieve the mixture before returning it to the pan with the sugar and the wine. Heat thoroughly but *do not boil*. Serve in glasses with a slice of lemon or orange in each.

FRANCE

France has throughout hisotry chosen Christmas Day to celebrate important events. In AD800, Charlemagne, king of the Franks, was crowned emperor of the Holy Roman Empire during Christmas mass at St Peter's.

Today Christmas in France is primarily a religious celebration, a family holiday that mostly confines gift giving to children. The frivolity and merrymaking is kept until *le Jour des Étrennes* or gift-giving day. This is New Year's Day, when adults exchange gifts and socializing takes over.

Gift giving of another sort, the custom of giving Christmas bonuses to the various trades-people who call at the house, is deeply entren-ched in France, where weeks before Christmas the requests for *étrennes* (tips) begin. The word *étrenne* is derived from the Latin *strenae*. These were gifts of sacred branches given during the Kalends.

Christmas trees are not usually put up in public places, but the shops make a special effort with their window displays. Every French child who has been on a shopping trip has stood entranced before the windows of the big department stores watching the amazing ani-mated displays.

For a French family the Christmas celebra-tions centre around midnight mass on Christ-mas Eve. The 24 December is a day of tremendous excitement for the children, start-ing with decorating the tree in the morning and culminating in being allowed to stay up late and place the Christ child in the crib of the *crèche* (nativity scene) which they will so carefully have set out a week or so before. The *crèche* has a prominent place in the living room. Little terracotta figures (*santons*) are grouped around the manger representing not only the familiar nativity figures but all the people of the village as well.

The older children are allowed to stay up and go to midnight mass but the younger ones go to bed. Their final act before sleep overwhelms them is to put their shoes by the fireside in the hope that *Père Noël* or *le petit Jésus* will come while they are asleep and leave some gifts for them and hang a few extra candies and fruits on the tree.

The Christmas Eve mass itself includes echoes of pagan ceremonies. At *Les Baux* in Provence the adoration of the Christ child is combined with the local shepherds bringing a real lamb to the crib and requesting fertility for their flocks. This candlelit procession takes place in the twelfth-century church of St Vincent to the singing of choirs accompanied by drummers.

Another shepherd's mass, held at Rouen, is a survival of a ninth-century service. It is inter-esting to note that these simple religious dramatizations gradually developed into full-scale religious dramas, *mystères*, and were the foundations of the modern French theatre.

Modern French Christians celebrate the warmth and regeneration symbolized by the arrival of the Christ child.

French families return from mass to enjoy the *réveillon*. This traditionally was the meal to break the pre-Christmas fast. In a museum in Arles, there is a recreation of *le réveillon* where the father signals the start of the meal by making the sign of a cross on the bread before breaking it. He keeps a quarter in case a beggar should call. The actual feast today varies from area to area. In some parts the family return to *pot au feu*, a stew made with a boiling hen and twelve other meats and vegetables. In Gascony they are likely to have *l'etouffat de boeuf*, a rich beef and brandy stew, and in Alsace roast goose is usually the

main course. The Bretons serve buckwheat pancakes with sour cream, and turkey roasted with chestnuts, long a favourite in Burgandy, is now becoming popular throughout France.

In Paris and the Île de France region, oysters and *foie gras* (goose liver pâté) are traditionally found on the *réveillon* menu.

In a typical Parisian family the father buys the oysters fresh from a café on his way home from work. He then opens them carefully with a special knife and arranges them on a bed of seaweed ready to be served with a dash of lemon and a loaf of fresh bread, and a glass of champagne. The seaweed comes from the barrel in which the oysters are sold.

As a Christmas extravagance the oysters are followed by a half dozen *escargots* (snails) for each person, served in bubbling garlic butter, or with a slice of pâté. Genuine *pâté de foie gras* is a very expensive delicacy. Jean-Joseph Close is said to have been the first to make it in 1762, and to have won all manner of favours from the military governors because of their fondness for his pâté! It is made from livers of geese specially fattened for this purpose.

Some families prefer to have velvety *boudins blancs*, which are pork, chicken and veal sausages not unlike the white puddings of Great Britain. As a festive touch both the *foie gras* and the *boudin* may be garnished with slivers of aromatic truffle.

A popular main course is roast goose served with apples stuffed with redcurrants or roast turkey either stuffed with, or just served with, chestnuts or a delicious smoked oyster stuffing. There is seldom any vegetable accompaniment to this course other than perhaps a simple salad. A fine Médoc wine would be considered sufficient to complete the course.

No French meal would be complete without

a *plateau de fromages* (cheese platter) and to end the meal on a traditionally sweet and festive note, a refreshing tangerine sorbet.

The Yule log, a legacy of pagan times, still features significantly in French Christmas celebrations. The symbolism of the Yule log goes back to an ancient belief that ancestral spirits were immanent in fire. Fires symbolized the sun's promise of warmth and regeneration and the triumph of light over darkness. Fire was also thought to have the power to keep evil spirits at bay.

Even today in many rural areas of Provence superstition dictates that the *Souche de Noël* (Yule log) must be cut from a tree that bears fruit containing a kernel such as a cherry or apricot. Where it is not possible physically to bring in a Yule log it nevertheless appears in edible form as rich chestnut dessert shaped and decorated like a log, the *bûche de Noël*.

In parts of Provence the symbolism of Jesus and the twelve apostles is carried through by having thirteen desserts to the *réveillon*, which are then eaten throughout the holiday.

Amongst the desserts served are the biscuits called *les quatre mendiants*. This, literally translated, means 'the four beggars' and recalls the time when the only way in which monks could get food was to go begging for alms. Each of the four orders of monks had a distinguishing colour of robe and similarly each biscuit is decorated with specific ingredients, each symbolizing one of the orders. Dried figs represent the Franciscans, sultanas the Dominicans, almonds the Carmelites and hazelnuts or walnuts the Augustinians.

Le nougat noir (black nougat) was a dessert even the poorest could afford because the basic ingredients of honey and almonds were readily available. Another dessert, *la pompe* or *gibassier*, was a round pastry made from flour and olive oil soaked in dessert wine. Pieces of this type of

galette were sometimes given by the baker to his customers. They would then go around to the wine merchant who would offer the dessert wine for them to dip it into.

The rest of the desserts are a selection of fruits, confections and cakes: dates, mandarins, oranges, fresh raisins, prunes, chocolates, glacé chestnuts, melon preserve, *beignets* (fritters), *calissons* (little cakes), or *biscottins* (small, crisp biscuits), *jujubes* (fruit jellies) and fondants wrapped in paper. *Bon-bons*, sugared almonds wrapped in twists of coloured paper, were very popular in Paris in the nineteenth century and inspired a visiting Englishman, Tom Smith, to invent the Christmas cracker.

Such a feast is a truly splendid affair—a luxury indeed, but also a wonderful way of celebrating the joyful message of Christmas.

A FRENCH 'REVEILLON'

ESCARGOTS À LA BOURGUIGNONNE
Snails stuffed with garlic butter

BOUDIN BLANC TRUFFÉ
Veal sausage

~

DINDE DE NOËL FARCIE
AUX HUÎTRES FUMÉES
Christmas turkey with smoked oyster stuffing

SALADE DE CHOUX ROUGE
ET LAITUE AUX NOIX
Salad of red cabbage, lettuce and walnuts

~

PLATEAU DE FROMAGES
Cheese platter

BÛCHE DE NOËL AUX MARRONS
Chestnut Yule log

Escargots à la Bourguignonne
SNAILS STUFFED WITH GARLIC BUTTER

S nails have been a French table delicacy since Roman times. They are usually presented on special plates (*escargotières*) but little rounds of brown bread serve equally well.

butter	175g	6oz	1½ sticks
chopped parsley	30ml	2tbs	2tbs
pressed garlic	10ml	2tsp	2tsp
shallots, pressed in the garlic press	20ml	1tbs heaped	1tbs heaped
Pernod	15ml	1tbs	1tbs
prepared snails either canned or frozen, plus shells	24	24	24

Cream the butter with the seasonings and Pernod until soft. Put a little butter into each snail shell, then push the snail back into the shell and cover the entrance with the seasoned butter.

Place the snails in *escargotières* or place on top of little circles of brown bread arranged in an oven-proof dish. Bake in a pre-heated oven at 190°C (375°F/Gas 5) for 20 minutes. Serve brown and bubbling.

Boudin blanc truffé
VEAL SAUSAGE

double cream (US: whipping)	150ml	¼ pint	½ cup
breadcrumbs	100g	4oz	1 cup
filleted chicken breast	225g	8oz	1 cup
lean veal	225g	8oz	1 cup
fatty pork	225g	8oz	1 cup
onion, finely chopped	1	1	1
eggs	3	3	3
ground allspice	5ml	1tsp	1tsp
salt and white pepper to taste			
pork intestine or sausage casing	1¼ m	1½ yards	1½ yards
water	1.5 litres	2½ pints	5 cups
milk	600ml	1 pint	2½ cups

Scald the cream and pour over the breadcrumbs. Leave to cool. If the sausage casing is dry and stiff, soak in cold water to soften. Either mince the meats and onion finely in a food processor, or put the meats through a mincer, adding the onion at the second mincing. Stir in the eggs, soaked breadcrumbs and allspice, and season well with salt and pepper—sausages need to be quite spicy. Beat this mixture well with a wooden spoon until it is smooth and comes away from the sides of the bowl.

By now the sausage skin should be pliable, so tie one end and, using a sausage stuffer or funnel, spoon in the filling. Do not pack too tightly or the sausages will burst during cooking. Tie into 15cm (6in.) sausages. (If you find the whole business of stuffing the skins too fiddly, find a kindly butcher to stuff them for you!)

Bring the milk and water to the boil and gently poach the sausages for 18–20 minutes. Leave them in the liquid to cool a little, then remove and cool completely. They can be kept in a refrigerator for up to 24 hours. Before serving, pan fry in a little butter for 5 minutes until golden brown. Excellent served with potato purée or hot apple slices or wine-soaked prunes.

Dinde de Noël farcie aux huîtres fumées

CHRISTMAS TURKEY WITH SMOKED OYSTER STUFFING

For instructions on roasting turkey, see Great Britain.

Stuffing

smoked oysters	275g–350g	10–12oz	10–12oz
onion	1	1	1
unsalted butter	100g	4oz	1 stick
fresh white breadcrumbs	150g	5oz	1 cup
sticks celery, finely chopped	3	3	3
grated rind of 1 lemon			
mixed herbs	5ml	1tsp	1tsp
chopped parsley	30ml	2tbs	2tbs
salt and pepper to taste			

Chop the onion finely and melt 25g (1oz/2tbs) of the butter in a saucepan. Add the onion and cook over a low heat until golden brown.

Add the rest of the butter, melt and take off the heat. Stir in the breadcrumbs and mix well until all the butter has been absorbed. Empty into a bowl, add the finely chopped celery, lemon rind, the parsley, herbs and seasonings.

Drain the smoked oysters and cut up roughly. Stir in the breadcrumbs and celery mixture and stuff the bird with it.

Bûche de Noël aux marrons

CHESTNUT YULE LOG

This classic French Yule log is far removed from the butter-icing-and-sponge confection made in Britain. It is served as a dessert to the Christmas meal and because it is extremely rich only a thin slice is served to each guest.

dark chocolate	100g	4oz	4oz
icing (confectioner's) sugar	100g	4oz	3/4 cup
unsalted butter, creamed	75g	3oz	3/4 stick
cognac	15ml	1tbs	1tbs
can of chestnut purée, unsweetened	450g	1lb	2 cups

Decoration

dark chocolate	100g	4oz	4oz
icing sugar			

Melt the chocolate in a double boiler. Remove from the heat and add the sifted icing sugar, creamed butter, cognac and chestnut purée. With a wooden spoon or electric beater, beat until thoroughly mixed.

Line a loaf tin with grease-proof (or waxed) paper and spoon in the mixture. Refrigerate for approximately 1 hour, until firm enough to mould. Turn the 'loaf' on to another sheet of greaseproof paper and shape into a log. Work quickly while the paste is cold, as it is impossible when it is tacky. Use a blade dipped in hot water to smooth the surface. Refrigerate again while you melt the 100g (4oz) chocolate. Allow this to cool a little before spreading over the log. Using a fork dipped in hot water, create a bark effect. Chill thoroughly.

Before serving decorate with a holly sprig, perhaps a little mushroom (very French) and a dusting of icing sugar.

~ EXTRA RECIPE ~

Galette des Rois aux amandes

ALMOND-FILLED TWELFTH-NIGHT CAKE

Twelfth Night is an important festival in France, signalling the end of the Christmas festivities. To mark this festival friends and relatives are invited to share in the ritual of cutting the *Galette des Rois* (Kings' cake). This is a pastry, often with an almond filling, in which a *fève*, or bean, is hidden. The cake is topped with a golden paper crown. The person finding the *fève* in his or her slice (without breaking a tooth) is crowned Bean King or Queen for the day and has the rest of the party at his or her command.

This recipe is for a light pastry with a delicious almond filling.

unsalted butter	100g	4oz	1 stick
caster sugar (US: granulated)	100g	4oz	1/2 cup
egg yolks	3	3	3
seeds of 1 vanilla pod			
ground almonds	100g	4oz	1/2 cup
kirsch	45ml	3tbs	3tbs
packet of frozen puff pastry	450g	1lb	1lb
icing (confectioner's) sugar			

Cream the butter and sugar until light and fluffy. Whisk in two of the egg yolks, the vanilla seeds and the ground almonds. Stir in the kirsch and allow to stand.

Divide the pastry in half and roll each half into a circle of approximately 20cm (8in.) diameter. Place one circle on a greased baking tray. Spoon the filling on to the circle keeping to within 3–4cm (2in.) of the edge. Don't forget to tuck in the *fève*. Beat the remaining yolk with a little water and paint the edges of the base. Place the second circle of pastry on top, gently pushing the edges together. Chill for 45 minutes. Decoratively pierce the top pastry layer with cuts in a star or lattice pattern. Snip through the edges every 5cm (2in.) or so and pinch to form a decorative edge. Brush with the egg yolk mixture and bake in a pre-heated oven at 190 C (375 F/Gas 5) for 30–40 minutes.

As a finishing touch, dust the top with sifted icing sugar and pop under the grill for a minute until brown. When cool, serve with a golden paper crown on top.

GREAT BRITAIN

Grisaille Window - detail. C13th Lincoln Cathedral.

Great Britain revels in *Christmas celebrations drawn from its vast heritage. The history of the Christian church in Britain has been littered with attempts to restrain the ancient pagan customs which have always been intertwined with Christian ones. St Augustine and his forty monks brought Christianity to the Anglo-Saxons when they landed in Kent in the south-east of England in AD596. The newly-converted Christians were, understandably, reluctant to give up their magnificent Festival of Yule—a festival in honour of the Norse god Odin—so, to ensure the success of their preaching, the missionaries encouraged them to continue celebrating in the way they always had, but in honour of Jesus' birth instead.*

Nevertheless, there were later attempts to restrict the festivities. Just over 300 years ago, in 1642, the celebration of Christmas was outlawed by the Puritans at the beginning of the Civil War. Anyone caught enjoying Christmas festivities was prosecuted; there were no church services on Christmas Day; and shops had to stay open.

In 1644, Parliament published an 'ordinance for the better observation of the Feast of the Nativity of Christ': it wanted Christmas Day to be a fast day and not a feast. The Puritan motive was to remind everyone that Christmas had an important spiritual side. However, their method was unpopular, and when Charles II came to the throne at the Restoration of the monarchy in 1660, Christmas feasting and gaiety were allowed to return. However, it wasn't until the reign of Queen Victoria that Christmas celebrations evolved into the two days of family-centred festivities that the British now think of as a traditional Christmas.

The Sunday nearest 30 November, St Andrew's Day, is affectionately known as 'Stir-up Sunday' because the Anglican prayer book reading for that day begins, 'Stir up we beseech Thee, O Lord, the will of thy faithful people.' Traditionally this is the day for making the Christmas pudding. Everyone in the house is supposed to stir the mixture from east to west in honour of the wise men who travelled in that direction.

Today's Christmas pudding, which has a long and interesting history, evolved from two sources: one was a porridge called frumenty (from the Latin *frumentum*, corn), associated with breaking the fast at the beginning of religious festivals for centuries. Frumenty is the equivalent of the Russian *kutya* and similar grain dishes eaten all over Europe at Christmas. Frumenty gradually developed into plum porridge, which at one time contained meat. The other source was a long round pudding—'hackin'—made from chopped meat, suet, oatmeal and spices and boiled in a length of sheep's or pig's gut. Hackin was served hot at the beginning of the meal and was probably a cousin of the Scottish haggis. By the sixteenth century the pudding tasted more like the one we know today and was boiled in a bag, hence its name 'bag pudding'.

Advent, with its spiritual preparation for Christmas, progresses and on 21 December, St Thomas' Day, charity money is distributed in some areas in accordance with the old custom of Thomassing, when poor women or children went from house to house offering sprigs of holly or mistletoe in return for enough flour to make not only their Christmas fare but, so they hoped, their bread for the rest of the winter too.

Christmas cards are an English invention. They were first sold in the early 1840s, a commercial variant of 'Christmas pieces'—

bordered cards written in laborious copperplate handwriting and given by schoolboys to their parents. Originally cards were not displayed until Christmas Eve, when their snow scenes, carol singers and nativity stables brightened mantelpieces and walls nationwide. Many cards glow with the flame of the robin's breast—a symbol of mid-winter fire and the bonfire which legend says the robin's wings fanned to warm Jesus.

In parts of Ireland after sunset on Christmas Eve there are caraway seed cakes for everyone and a tall thick candle is put in the largest window and lit by the youngest member of the family (in honour of Jesus). It burns all night to light the way of any passers-by who—like Mary and Joseph—are looking for shelter. As in much of Europe, candlelight is also used to symbolize the idea of Jesus' coming as being a bright light in a dark world.

Evergreens are as popular today for Christmas decorations as they have ever been. In pre-Christian times evergreens featured in the pagan mid-winter festival of Yule. However, when 25 December was designated the day to celebrate Christ's birth, the holly took on a new symbolism. Its prickles are said to represent the crown of thorns placed on Jesus' head at his crucifixion and the red berries the blood he shed on the cross.

Paper and foil garlands are popular but the favourite decoration is the Christmas tree. Known in England since the early nineteenth century, when it was introduced by German merchants living in Manchester, and then popularized by Victoria's consort, Albert, the tree has a place of honour in the living-room. Tinsel, shiny baubles, a fairy doll at the top of the tree and fairy lights make the tree a thing of wonder each year.

The most important part of Christmas Eve for children is when they put their Christmas stockings out ready for Father Christmas to fill that night. Some hang them at the mantelpiece by the fire, while others put them at the end of the bed. Carrots for the reindeer and a glass of something for the old man himself are thoughtful courtesies in some homes. Father Christmas has come to Great Britain by sleigh through the night sky every year since the 1870s, but may

not stop if children are looking out of the window for him. People give their children and each other presents as a symbol of their love. Christians remember that Jesus was a gift to us from God the Father as a sign of his love for us.

Shortly before 12 p.m., many people go to a midnight service in church. In Dewsbury, Yorkshire, the church bell ('Black Tom of Soothill') is rung the same number of times as the number of years since the birth of Jesus. This 'Devil's Knell' is a warning to the Devil that he has been overcome by the Prince of Peace. The atmosphere in church is expectant and joyful as the bell tolls midnight to signal the beginning of Christ's birthday.

And so the first day of Christmas dawns— too early for parents of young children who clamber into their bed in the early hours to empty their stockings. Different families have different customs—some eat their main Christmas meal at lunchtime while others save it for the late afternoon or evening. Presents too are exchanged at various times. Church in the morning is a time-hallowed custom—for some people the only time they go to church in the year. Many churches have a Christmas tree and a beautiful nativity scene too.

After church many return to homes fragrant with the smell of turkey roasting in the oven. Old and young wait while the cook makes his or her last-minute preparations and stirs the gravy, which is rich with the pan juices of the turkey. The table is laid with the best table linen and china or pottery. While Christmas is primarily a family occasion with relatives travelling long distances to be together, friends or acquaintances with no family of their own may be invited to join the gathering.

The meal may begin with something light

such as melon, smoked salmon with lemon or celery, or Stilton soup under a thin pastry 'hat'. Roast turkey is the most popular main dish today, though roast goose is a strong contender. Some cooks insist on cooking their bird in a very slow oven overnight but others wait until Christmas morning. Gilding the bird with a saffron glaze makes it look even more attractive. The turkey is accompanied by one or two stuffings, such as chestnut and bacon stuffing or sausage-meat stuffing, chipolata sausages and bacon rolls.

A sauce made from cranberries cooked with a port and orange flavoured syrup contrasts well with the rich turkey meat. Home-made bread sauce is traditional and is flavoured with cloves and nutmeg. Brussels sprouts are at their best at Christmas and are sometimes mixed with chestnuts or other nuts, or with breadcrumbs fried in butter. Delicious roast vegetables such as crunchy potatoes and caramelized parsnips add hugely to the delight—and calorie content— of the meal.

An interesting and delicious recipe that has been kept alive since the Middle Ages is cockatrice. This amazing Christmas festive dish consists of birds of decreasing size stuffed inside each other and separated by stuffings chosen to complement the flavour of each bird. In former times it was traditional to use seven birds, but three is a more realistic number. Choose from snipe, woodcock, quail, pigeon, poussin, guinea fowl, partridge, pheasant, chicken, capon, goose and turkey. As the birds are boned, the finished dish is easy to carve and it is also very pleasant served cold the next day.

The picture of the Christmas pudding being brought to the table flaming with brandy is a traditional image of the British Christmas lunch. It's prudent, though not as picturesque, to remove the sprig of holly from the top before setting light to the brandy-soaked pudding if one wishes to avoid the flames reaching too high. Brandy butter is all the lighter if some ground almonds are mixed into it, and some people like cream with their pudding as well. Those of weaker digestion may prefer a less traditional but lighter dessert such as a lemon soufflé, a fresh fruit salad—perhaps with a hint of liqueur—or a tipsy ratafia trifle.

Mince pies, port, Stilton cheese served from a jar and a choice of liqueurs make a fitting end to what is often the most elaborate meal eaten in most British homes in the year. Coffee and a chocolate or piece of Turkish delight add the finishing touches.

Christmas crackers are as popular in Britain today as they ever were. They date back to 1844 when a sweet shop proprietor named Tom Smith wrapped sugared almonds in tissue

paper twists, French bon-bon style. His customers loved them and so he took the idea a stage further and included love mottoes. These early bon-bons were bought by young men for their sweethearts. Tom Smith then developed them further, inspired—it is said—by a crackling log on the fire. He inserted a strip of cardboard impregnated with chemicals which exploded when the strip was pulled apart, and the log-shaped cracker was born.

Many families make sure their lunch is over by 3 p.m., when the Queen's speech is broadcast on television and radio. King George V started this custom back in 1932 and it has been popular ever since. Film of the Queen's family may be shown and the importance attached to this speech symbolizes the affection and esteem in which the monarchy is held by many of the British people.

Mince pies continue to be popular at Christmas time in Britain. They are descended from the large Christmas pie once always baked on Christmas Eve, which at one stage of its development contained plums.

Most children know the nursery rhyme about Little Jack Horner. 'Little Jack Horner sat in the corner, eating his Christmas pie. He put in his thumb and pulled out a plum and said "What a good boy am I."' Not so many know that Jack Horner was the steward to the Abbot of Glastonbury. One day he was told to take a Christmas pie as a present from the Abbot to King Henry VIII who was busy pulling down abbeys all over the country at the time of the Dissolution of the Monasteries in the sixteenth century. Under the pie-crust were the title deeds to twelve manor houses, intended as a bribe to the king so that he wouldn't order Glastonbury Abbey to be demolished. However, the king only received eleven deeds: Jack Horner had

obviously sat in his corner and pulled out a very nice plum—the deeds to the manor at Wells in Somerset.

December 26 in Britain is Boxing Day (also known as St Stephen's Day), the day when church alms boxes were given out to the needy, following a custom started by the Romans as part of their Saturnalia celebrations. Until recently it was traditional to give a 'Christmas box' on Boxing Day to service people and traders who regularly call at the house in recognition of their services. Today some householders give money or a present to these people just before Christmas in thanks for their year's work. In 1983, an article in *The Times* reported that the amount spent on Christmas tips was about £130 million! The Christmas season is also a time when many give to charitable organizations, sharing a little of their wealth with those who are less fortunate.

New Year, or Hogmanay, celebrations in Scotland rival Christmas for their gaiety. In some parts of Wales parties of people accompany a mock horse—the *mari lwyd* or 'grey mare'—from house to house, wassailing or singing a request for refreshment as they go. This is reminiscent of similar activities at the time of the ancient Roman new year festival of Kalends, when people used to run round the streets of ancient Rome dressed in animal skins. Some Christians have interpreted the event as commemorating the fable of the horse turned out of Jesus' stable to make room for the holy family.

The word 'wassail' stems from the Anglo-Saxon toast 'wes hal'—'Be whole!' or 'Your health!'—and wassailers drink and make merry around Christmas time to this day. Originally they went from house to house carrying a wooden bowl containing 'lambswool': ale which had been heated with eggs, sugar, nutmeg, cloves, ginger and roasted apples. On top floated pieces of toast (hence the expression 'to toast'), and sometimes the wassail bowl was decorated with ribbons and had a gilded apple floating in it. In Truro in Cornwall singers still go a'wassailing for alms over the twelve days of Christmas but elsewhere the more sedate carol singing before Christmas has replaced this pastime.

Twelfth Night marks the end of the twelve days of Christmas and is the eve of Epiphany, which celebrates the visit of the wise men to Bethlehem.

A special service at Epiphany in the Chapel Royal at St James' Palace in London has been conducted for the last 900 years to commemorate the wise men's gifts of gold, frankincense and myrrh. After the service a gift of money is donated to charity, frankincense is given to the church and myrrh is sent to a hospital.

Christian and pagan elements intertwine throughout the traditions of the British Christmas. Some people, jaded by all the excess, are highly critical of the festival. Yet, in the spirit of the early Christians in Britain who tried to reconcile these two sets of beliefs, Christmas can also be a time when people share Christian love and joy with those around them.

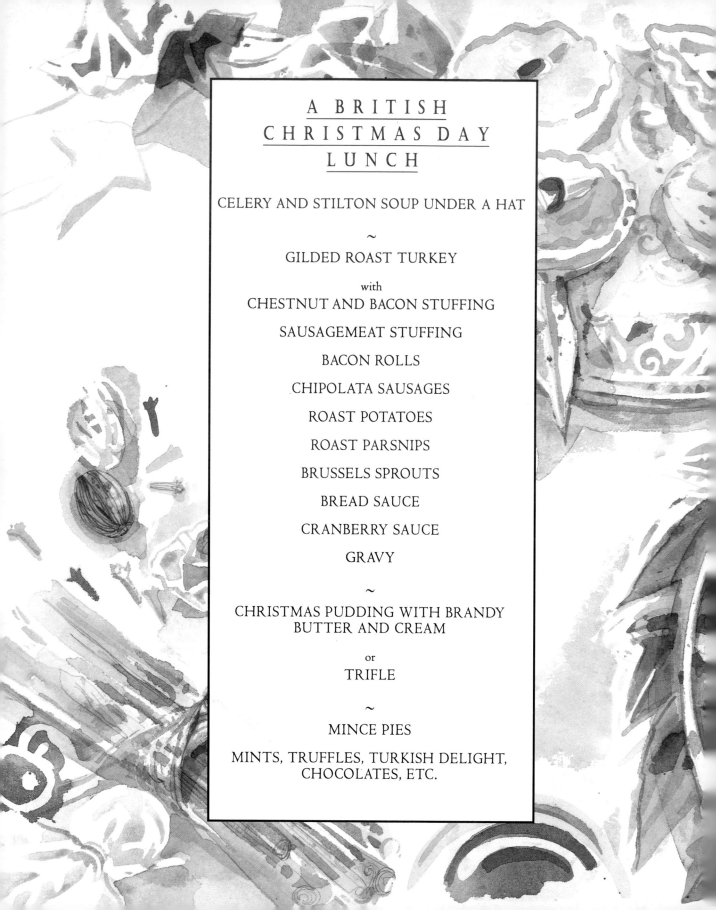

A BRITISH
CHRISTMAS DAY
LUNCH

CELERY AND STILTON SOUP UNDER A HAT

~

GILDED ROAST TURKEY

with
CHESTNUT AND BACON STUFFING

SAUSAGEMEAT STUFFING

BACON ROLLS

CHIPOLATA SAUSAGES

ROAST POTATOES

ROAST PARSNIPS

BRUSSELS SPROUTS

BREAD SAUCE

CRANBERRY SAUCE

GRAVY

~

CHRISTMAS PUDDING WITH BRANDY
BUTTER AND CREAM

or
TRIFLE

~

MINCE PIES

MINTS, TRUFFLES, TURKISH DELIGHT,
CHOCOLATES, ETC.

Celery and Stilton soup under a hat

T he unusual and delicious aroma from this soup is only released once the flaky pastry dome covering it is broken. Pieces of pastry fall into the bowl, adding to the flavour. This recipe serves 4 people.

sticks of celery, chopped	8	8	8
onions, chopped	2	2	2
butter	50g	2oz	1/2 stick
water	1.2 litre	2 pints	4 cups
salt and pepper to taste			
Stilton cheese, grated	75g	3oz	1/3 cup
flaky pastry (or dough for 2 pie crusts)	350g	12oz	12oz
egg yolks, beaten	2	2	2

Melt the butter in a large pan and sauté the onions and celery until the onions are softened. Add the water, salt and pepper to taste, and the Stilton cheese. Bring to the boil and simmer, covered, until the celery is tender—about 25 minutes. Strain or liquidize. Pour into individual straight-sided oven-proof soup bowls (the kind like small soufflé dishes). Divide the flaky pastry into four pieces and roll each out into a round large enough to cover the soup bowl and to overlap by 2cm (3/4 in.) all the way round. Brush the edges with beaten egg yolk and place, egg side inside, on top of the soup-filled bowl. Chill for 30 minutes. Brush the tops of the pastry covers with egg yolk and bake in the centre of a pre-heated oven at 200°C (400°F/Gas 6) for 10 minutes or until the pastry is well risen. Lower the temperature to 190°C (375°F/Gas 5) and bake for a further 12 minutes, until the pastry is golden-brown.

Gilded roast turkey

C hoose the weight of your turkey according to how many servings you need, both hot and cold. For each serving allow a minimum of 450g (1lb) oven-ready weight (including stuffings). A fresh free-range turkey tastes excellent but may be expensive. Dry-frozen birds are the best of the frozen ones. With any frozen bird it is essential to allow plenty of time for thawing. Boil up the giblets in water and use the resulting stock in the gravy.

Rinse out the inside of the turkey cavity with running water and pat the skin dry with kitchen paper.

Stuff the neck end of the bird with your chosen stuffing and secure the flap of skin over the stuffing with skewers. Some cooks also like to stuff the cavity of the turkey, though there has been some concern from health advisers that the centre of a stuffed turkey might not be adequately cooked.

Pre-heat the oven to 180°C (350°F/Gas 4). You can either cook your turkey covered in foil or in butter muslin (cheesecloth). Basting to keep the turkey moist is easier with muslin as you can baste through it, whereas you have to lift foil off. The turkey will cook quicker in muslin. Dot the bird with pieces of butter and cover with foil tucked around the sides of the roasting tin, or with a piece of double muslin large enough to tuck in at the sides of the bird. Baste once the butter has melted and again every hour during cooking.

Cooking times

	Muslin	Foil
5kg (10lb)	2 3/4 hrs	3 1/2–4 hrs
7.5kg (15lb)	3 1/4 hrs	4 1/2–5 hrs
10kg (20lb)	4 1/2 hrs	5 1/2–6 hrs
12.5kg (25lb)	4 3/4 hrs	6–6 1/2 hrs

Half an hour before the end of the cooking time remove the foil or muslin and cover the breast with slices of streaky bacon. Return to the oven. Remember to gild the bird if you wish. A cooked turkey will keep hot for 20 minutes as long as the skin is not broken.

In medieval times roast fowl was made to look an attractive golden colour by painting it with a gilding mix towards the end of the cooking time. Gilding was considered beneficial to the health. You can gild your Christmas bird, with a mixture of saffron and egg yolk. The yellow dye saffron comes from the stigma of the saffron crocus (*crocus sativa*), which can be grown only in those countries with warm enough summers to ripen the corms. Saffron Walden in England was a centre of saffron production for years, hence its name.

Gilding for roast turkey

butter	25g	1oz	2tbs
large pinch of saffron strands			
sugar	25g	1oz	2tbs
white wine vinegar	30ml	2tbs	2tbs
egg yolk	1	1	1

Melt the butter and add the sugar and the saffron strands. Heat, stirring, until the butter has taken on the bright yellow colour of the saffron. Cook until syrupy, then remove from the heat and stir in the vinegar and egg yolk. Heat gently without boiling until the mixture is thick. Ten minutes before the turkey is cooked, remove it from the oven and paint the gilding mixture all over its skin, using a pastry brush. Return to the oven for the final few minutes of cooking.

Chestnut and bacon stuffing

Stuffings are used in many countries for meat of various sorts and especially for poultry. Not only do they give meat a subtle flavour but they may also make it more succulent by preventing it from drying out during cooking.

butter	50g	2oz	1/2 stick
onion, peeled and chopped	1	1	1
green (unsmoked) bacon, chopped	100g	4oz	4–6 slices
turkey heart and liver, chopped			
mushrooms, sliced	175g	6oz	3/4 cup
chestnut purée	225g	8oz	1 cup
pâté de foie gras small can	1	1	1
stick of celery, chopped	1	1	1
fresh parsley, chopped	15ml	1tbs	1tbs
salt and black pepper to taste			
breadcrumbs	50g	2oz	1/4 cup

Melt the butter in a large pan and fry the onion, bacon, turkey heart and liver, and mushrooms until the butter is absorbed. Add the remaining ingredients and mix well.

Sausagemeat stuffing

Use the whole recipe as one of two stuffings for roast turkey, but use only half the quantities given if using it for cockatrice.

pork sausagemeat	675g	1 1/2 lb	1 1/2 lb
breadcrumbs	100g	4oz	1/2 cup
shallots, chopped	2	2	2
belly pork, minced	100g	4oz	1/2 cup
egg, beaten	1	1	1
salt and black pepper			

Mix all the ingredients together thoroughly.

Roast potatoes

Mastering the art of cooking crispy roast potatoes is a skill that no cook should be without.

old (US: baking) potatoes peeled and cut into 5cm (2in.) chunks	1kg	2¼ lb	2¼ lb
fat from around the roast meat			
corn oil or lard, if necessary			

Parboil the potato chunks by putting them into boiling water and simmering for 5 minutes. Drain, then cover the pan and shake to roughen the surface of the potatoes. If they won't roughen, score the surface of each potato with a fork. Pour some of the fat from the roasting tin into a separate tin (pan) for the potatoes. Aim to have a depth of about 5mm ($^1/_4$ in.) of fat. You can use dripping, lard or corn oil if you aren't roasting meat, or if you haven't enough fat around the roast meat. Move the roast meat to a lower shelf in the oven, if there is enough room in the oven, or remove it from the oven when it is cooked and keep it warm while the potatoes are cooked. (A large turkey holds its heat very well, especially if you insulate it with greaseproof [or waxed] paper covered with layers of newspaper.) Turn the oven temperature up to 220°C (425°F/Gas 7). Heat up the fat in the tin by putting it on the hob (stove) and, when it is sizzling, add the potatoes carefully to avoid splashing the fat. Spoon the fat over the potatoes, then put the tin in the oven. Roast for $^3/_4$–1 hour, turning and basting halfway through.

Roast parsnips

Parsnips take on an extraordinarily sweet flavour after the first frost of the year. This sweetness is brought out by roasting until the parsnips are almost caramelized.

Cook the parsnips exactly as for roast potatoes, though you needn't shake the pan after draining them. It's best to cook and serve the potatoes and parsnips separately so that the flavour of each can be appreciated.

Christmas pudding

Home-made puddings are usually far more delicious than shop ones. This recipe is the one my mother used to make. It makes enough for one pudding in a 1 litre (2 pint) basin, or two in 600ml (1 pint) ones. Guests always say it is the most delicious they have ever had. Queen Victoria rewarded her cook one Christmas by dropping a few sovereigns into the pudding as she stirred it. You may like to add silver coins to your pudding, or—to be even more traditional—charms. Old traditions say that to the finder a thimble means spinsterhood for a year; a button, bachelorhood; a ring, a wedding; and a coin, good fortune. Remember to wrap the charms or coins in foil first and tell everyone what they may find in their pudding.

shredded suet	100g	4oz	¾ cup
mixed (pumpkin) spice	2ml	½ tsp	½ tsp
pinch of grated nutmeg			
pinch of ground cinnamon			
self-raising flour	50g	2oz	½ cup
soft brown sugar	225g	8oz	1 cup
white breadcrumbs	100g	4oz	¾ cup
sultanas (golden raisins)	100g	4oz	½ cup
raisins	100g	4oz	½ cup
currants	225g	8oz	1 cup
almonds, chopped	50g	2oz	¼ cup
mixed citrus peel, chopped	25g	1oz	2tbs
grated rind of 1 orange and 1 lemon			
small cooking apple, peeled, cored and chopped	1	1	1
eggs, beaten	2	2	2
barley wine or stout	150ml	¼ pint	½ cup

rum	30ml	2tbs	2tbs
brandy	50ml	2fl oz	3tbs
sprig of holly, to decorate			

Mix the suet, spices, flour, sugar and breadcrumbs. Add the fruit, nuts, peel and orange and lemon rind and mix well. In another bowl mix the eggs, barley wine or stout and rum and pour this over the dry ingredients. Stir well and add any charms or coins. Cover the bowl and leave overnight. Grease the basin(s) the next day and fill to the top. Cover with grease-proof paper followed by a piece of cloth and tie round the rim(s) with string. Cook the pudding(s) by steaming in the top of a double boiler or by boiling in a pan with water coming halfway up the sides of the basin. Cook for six hours, remembering to replenish the water as necessary. When cool, replace the paper and cloth coverings with dry ones. Store the pudding(s) in a cool, dry place. When needed, steam for a further two hours. The long cooking times make these puddings particularly light.

To serve, turn the pudding out on to a dish and stick the holly on top. Warm the brandy in a little pan and pour it over the pudding, then light it and carry the pudding to the table flaming.

Brandy butter

B randy butter, or brandy hard sauce, is just the right accompaniment to Christmas pudding, especially if made with some ground almonds to give a fluffier, lighter texture.

unsalted butter	75g	3oz	3/4 stick
caster sugar (US: granulated)	75g	3oz	1/3 cup
ground almonds	75g	3oz	1/3 cup
grated rind of half an orange			
brandy	45ml	3tbs	3tbs

Cream the butter with a wooden spoon, then beat in the sugar, ground almonds and grated orange rind. When well mixed, add the brandy and stir till thoroughly incorporated. Pile into a serving dish and chill till needed. This brandy butter freezes very well.

Trifle

R ecipes for trifle abound and can be very different from each other. This trifle is far removed from the sort made from sponge cake, tinned fruit, packet custard and red packet jelly, but it is sure to please. Basically it is a syllabub mixture poured over a macaroon base. It has quite a lot of alcohol and a slightly lemony tang.

broken macaroons, ratafia biscuits or amaretti	225g	8oz	1 cup
apricot jam, warmed	60ml	4tbs	1/4 cup
sweet sherry	50ml	2fl oz	3tbs
brandy	50ml	2fl oz	3tbs
double cream (US: whipping)	225ml	8fl oz	1 cup
juice of 2 lemons			
caster sugar (US: granulated)	25g	1oz	2tbs
flaked almonds, toasted	25g	1oz	2tbs
angelica	25g	1oz	2tbs

Pour the jam over the macaroons or biscuits in a glass serving bowl. Mix the sherry and brandy and pour half the quantity over the macaroons. Whisk the cream, lemon juice, sugar and the rest of the sherry and brandy until thick. Pile on top of the trifle and chill. Decorate with the almonds and angelica.

Mince pies

Three hundred and fifty years ago, mince pies were baked in an oblong shape and had a little pastry figure nestling on top to represent Jesus in the manger. One was eaten for each of the twelve days of Christmas. The Puritans put a stop to such fancies and thereafter mince pies were round and with no figure on top. Today's pies are stuffed full with dried fruit, spices and sugar but originally mince pies were known as 'shrid pyes' and contained 'shredded' (minced) chicken or beef tongue, hence our name 'mincemeat'. Some say that the spices in mince pies are reminders of the spices given to Jesus by the wise men.

This recipe is made with a mouthwatering pastry flavoured slightly with lemon and almond. It makes 24 pies.

plain flour	275g	10oz	2½ cups
ground almonds	25g	1oz	2tbs
butter	175g	6oz	1½ sticks
icing sugar (confectioner's)	75g	3oz	⅓ cup
grated rind of 1 lemon			
egg yolk	1	1	1
milk	45ml	3tbs	3tbs
mincemeat	225g	8oz	1 cup
brandy	15ml	1tbs	1tbs
beaten egg white			
caster sugar (US: granulated)			

Mix the flour and ground almonds in a large bowl. Quickly rub the butter into the flour with the fingertips. Sift in the icing (confectioner's) sugar and add the grated lemon rind. Mix the egg yolk and milk and stir into the dry ingredients. Mix and knead lightly. Cover and leave in a cool place for 30 minutes. Roll out the pastry thinly on a floured surface and stamp

out 24 circles of pastry with a 6cm (2½ in.) round fluted cutter. Line 24 greased patty (or muffin) tins with these rounds, then stamp out 24 smaller rounds for the tops with a 5cm (2in.) cutter. Mix the mincemeat with the brandy and put a teaspoonful into each pie. Dampen the edges of the pastry rounds and press the tops on neatly. Prick the tops with a fork. Brush with a little beaten egg white and sprinkle with caster sugar. Bake at 200°C (400°F/Gas 6) for 15–20 minutes, then remove from the tins and cool on a wire rack. Mince pies will keep in an airtight tin for 2–3 weeks and also freeze well.

~ EXTRA RECIPES ~

Cockatrice

This unusual Christmas bird is in fact not one but three! Ask your butcher well in advance of Christmas to choose fresh birds of suitable size for the finished weight you require, then ask him to bone them for you. Tell your butcher that only the largest bird, the turkey, needs to be boned from one end. The smaller ones can be split open down the back. This recipe uses a pheasant inside a capon inside a turkey. Using even a small turkey you will have enough for a hot meal, a cold meal and plenty over for the freezer even if you have as many as ten guests.

The stuffings chosen complement the flavours of each bird and provide colour. Stuff and prepare your birds as soon as you bring them home from the butcher, then parcel the finished 'bird' in foil and store it in the freezer.

Remember to allow plenty of time for thawing before you want to cook it. Cook it from fresh if you like, but check with your butcher that he has time to bone the birds if it is a day or two before Christmas. He could, of course, bone fresh birds some time before Christmas and store them for you in his freezer if you don't have one.

turkey, boned	1	1	1

capon, boned	1	1	1
pheasant, boned	1	1	1
chestnut and bacon stuffing (see page 209)			
apricot and brown rice stuffing (see page 213)			
sage and onion stuffing (see page 214)			
sausagemeat stuffing (see page 209; use half quantities)			
streaky bacon to cover turkey	225g	8oz	8oz

Keep the giblets of the turkey to make the chestnut and bacon stuffing. Use the heart and liver from the capon and pheasant, together with the bones from all the birds, to make home-made soup for Boxing Day.

Stuff the pheasant with sage and onion stuffing or with apricot and brown rice stuffing as described opposite. Re-form it roughly and put it inside the capon. Put apricot and brown rice stuffing around the pheasant inside the capon as evenly as you can, then re-form the capon. There is no need to sew up the pheasant or the capon.

Put the stuffed capon inside the turkey, trying not to tear the opening too much. Squeeze chestnut and bacon stuffing between the capon and the turkey, trying to do it as evenly as possible. Any remaining stuffing can be cooked separately. Use the sausagemeat stuffing to fill the neck end of the turkey and secure the skin flap with two skewers. Sew up the open end of the 'bird' with a large needle (a trussing needle if you have one) and thick thread, using large stitches which will be easy to see and remove. You could use skewers for speed if you wish. Shape the 'bird' so as to look as much like a plain turkey as possible, and cover with streaky bacon rashers (slices).

When ready to cook, cover with foil and wrap the foil around the rim of the roasting pan. Put the tin plus 'bird' on the bathroom scales, or else work out the combined weight of the birds plus stuffings you've used, then put into a pre-heated oven for the required cooking time. Allow about 15 minutes per 450g (1lb) at 160°C (325°F/Gas 3). Work out your cooking time to allow 1 hour before you want the turkey ready for the table. When the cooking time is up, remove the

foil, turn the oven up to 200°C (400°F/Gas 6), and cook for a further half an hour. Remove from the oven and allow to rest with a covering of foil, so as to make carving easier. The bird will stay hot for much longer. It is essential not to undercook cockatrice.

You may like to cook your 'bird' overnight, in which case put it into a very slow over at 11 or 12 o'clock and leave it there until half an hour before serving. This works very well.

When carving, a good tip is to cut the 'bird' into four quarters, then give each person a slice from the middle and a slice from the outside. Don't expect to see neat layers of bird and stuffing—this doesn't happen.

All the usual trimmings go very well with cockatrice, and it's a dish that everyone will remember.

Apricot and brown rice stuffing

This amount is sufficient to stuff a pheasant for cockatrice. If you wish to use it for a larger bird, increase the amounts given. The sweet, nutty flavour contrasts well with dark, gamey pheasant meat.

brown rice	50g	2oz	1/4 cup
dried apricots	100g	4oz	1/2 cup
medium onion	1	1	1
butter	25g	1oz	2tbs

Cook the rice. Cover the apricots with water in a pan, bring to the boil and simmer for 10 minutes, then drain. Melt the butter in a pan and sauté the onion gently for 5 minutes. Mix together the cooked rice, apricots, onion and any remaining butter.

Sage and onion stuffing

butter	50g	2oz	1/2 stick
onions, chopped	225g	8oz	1 cup
wholemeal breadcrumbs	225g	8oz	1³/₄ cups
fresh sage, chopped OR	10ml	2tsp	2tsp
dried sage	5ml	1tsp	1tsp

Melt the butter in a pan and gently cook the onions for 5 minutes. In a bowl mix the onions and butter, wholemeal breadcrumbs and sage, and stir well.

Pigeon pie

An old favourite, this pigeon pie is made with tender breast meat and given even more flavour with bacon and onion. The pie freezes well and can be eaten hot or cold.

pigeons (or squabs)	4	4	4
red wine	600ml	1 pint	2¹/₂ cups
good chicken stock	600ml	1 pint	2¹/₂ cups
large carrot, sliced	1	1	1
shortcrust or flaky pastry (pie crust dough) made with 225g (8oz/2 cups) of plain flour			
butter or dripping	50g	2oz	1/2 stick
medium onions, chopped	2	2	2
cloves of garlic, crushed	2	2	2
rashers (slices) streaky bacon, diced	3	3	3
plain flour	50g	2oz	1/2 cup
tomato purée	10ml	2tsp	2tsp

OR tomato ketchup	15ml	1tbs	1tbs
fresh parsley, chopped OR	10ml	2tsp	2tsp
dried parsley	5ml	1tsp	1tsp
salt and pepper to taste			
egg yolk PLUS	1	1	1
cold water	15ml	1tbs	1tbs

Don't pluck the pigeons but part the feathers on the breast and slit with a sharp knife down over the breastbone. Peel the skin back each side. Make a small cut in the skin at the base of the breastbone. Lay the pigeon on its back, hold its tail with one hand and put the index finger of the other hand under the lower part of the breastbone. Pull the breastbone with the breast meat off in one easy movement. Put the breasts, still on the bone, into a large saucepan and cover with the red wine and stock. Add the chopped carrot. Bring to the boil and simmer for 2 hours, covered, or until the meat falls away from the bone easily. Strain the liquor from the meat and carrots and reserve.

While the pigeons are cooking, make the pastry and chill. Melt the butter or dripping in a large saucepan and sauté the onions, garlic and bacon until the onions are well browned and soft. Stir in the flour. Add enough of the liquid in which the pigeon breasts were cooked to make a thick sauce, then add the tomato purée or ketchup, parsley and salt and pepper to taste.

Pre-heat the oven to 180°C (350°F/Gas 4). Remove the meat from the bone and break into large chunks.

Lay the meat and carrots in a greased pie dish and pour over the sauce.

Roll out the pastry and cut a 2¹/₂ cm (1 in.) strip long enough to place round the rim of the pie dish. Press this strip round the rim and moisten with water. Lay the rest of the pastry over the pie and press down round the rim on to the moistened pastry strip. Cut off the excess pastry round the sides and fork or crimp the edge of the piecrust. Use the trimmings to cut out pastry decorations to put on top of the pie. Stick these on with some of the egg glaze made by mixing the egg yolk and water together well. Glaze the pie by brushing with the rest of this egg glaze.

Bake the pie for 40–45 minutes or until the pastry is crisp and golden-brown on top.

Christmas cake

A rich dark fruit cake, covered with marzipan and white icing and then decorated, is an essential part of Christmas for many families. The Christmas cake probably springs from the older tradition of the Twelfth Night cake baked for Epiphany on 6 January. This recipe includes thick marzipan but you can halve the amount if you wish. Ideally, bake the cake six weeks before Christmas and cover it with marzipan a week before icing it. Before making the cake, soak the dried fruit overnight in brandy. The quantities given are for a cake 20cm (8in.) in diameter.

currants	225g	8oz	1 cup
raisins	275g	10oz	1¼ cups
sultanas (golden raisins)	275g	10oz	1¼ cups
glacé cherries	100g	4oz	½ cup
mixed citrus peel, chopped	50g	2oz	¼ cup
angelica, chopped	15g	½ oz	1tbs
brandy	50ml	2fl oz	¼ cup
grated rind and juice of 1 small lemon			
butter, to grease the tin	25g	1oz	2tbs
self-raising flour	225g	8oz	2 cups
salt	2ml	½ tsp	½ tsp
mixed spice	2ml	½ tsp	½ tsp
pinch of grated nutmeg			
ground cinnamon	2ml	½ tsp	½ tsp

ground cloves	2ml	½ tsp	½ tsp
ground almonds	75g	3oz	⅓ cup
almonds, chopped	100g	4oz	½ cup
butter	225g	8oz	2 sticks
soft dark brown sugar	175g	6oz	¾ cup
large eggs, beaten, plus 1 extra egg, if needed	5	5	5
a few teaspoonfuls of brandy			
home-made marzipan (see recipe) OR bought marzipan	1kg	2lb	2lb
apricot jam			
recipe royal icing (see recipe) OR fondant icing			
decorations			

The night before you make the cake, put the dried fruit, peel and angelica into a bowl and pour over the brandy and lemon juice. Stir, cover and leave to soak. The next day, butter the cake tin, line with a double layer of grease-proof paper, then brush the paper with melted butter. Tie a double layer of brown paper round the outside of the tin, allowing a large overlap above the tin.

Sift the flour, salt and spices into a large bowl and add the ground almonds, soaked fruit, peel and angelica, and chopped almonds. Mix well.

In another bowl, cream the butter, sugar and lemon rind until fluffy. Beat in the beaten eggs, a little at a time. Stir this mixture into the flour and fruit. The resulting mixture should be soft and moist but, if not, add an extra beaten egg and stir well. Spoon into the tin and cover with a double layer of brown paper with a 1cm (½ in.) diameter hole cut in the centre to allow moisture to escape.

Bake in a pre-heated oven at 140°C (275°F/Gas 1) for 4–4½ hours. The cake is done when it begins to shrink from the sides. During the last two hours add an extra layer of brown paper to prevent burning.

Remove from the oven and cool slightly before turning the cake out on to a wire rack. When cold, wrap in foil to store.

A few weeks before Christmas, make some holes with a thick needle (a skewer is too thick) and pour in a few teaspoonfuls of brandy. Rewrap and leave until ready to cover with marzipan.

Marzipan

ground almonds	450g	1lb	2 cups
icing sugar (confectioner's sugar), sifted	225g	8oz	1³/₄ cup
caster sugar (US: granulated)	225g	8oz	1 cup
almond essence (extract)	2ml	¹/₂ tsp	¹/₂ tsp
lemon juice	5ml	1tsp	1tsp
sherry	15ml	1tbs	1tbs
egg yolks, plus 1 extra if necessary	4	4	4

Mix the ground almonds, icing (confectioner's) sugar and caster sugar. Add the remaining ingredients and mix well. Knead until moist and smooth. If the mixture is still too dry, add another egg yolk. Use at once or wrap in plastic food-wrap till needed.

Warm some apricot jam and brush it over the top and sides of the cake, discarding any pieces of apricot.

Take about half the marzipan and roll it out on a floured board to roughly fit the top of the cake. Put the cake carefully on to the rolled-out paste and trim the paste to fit the top. Roll out the other half of the marzipan into an oblong the length of the circumference of the cake and the width of the height of the cake. Cut this in half for easier handling, then roll up one half and unroll on to the side of the cake, pressing firmly. Repeat with the other half of the oblong to finish covering the side of the cake. Turn the cake the right way up and smooth the surface and the joins of the marzipan with a rolling pin.

Ideally leave the cake to dry for a week before icing to avoid staining the icing as the marzipan dries.

Royal icing

icing sugar, (confectioner's sugar) sifted	500g	1lb 2oz	4 cups
egg whites, beaten till stiff	4	4	4
glycerine	5ml	1tsp	1tsp

Stir the sugar into the egg whites a little at a time, beating thoroughly after each addition. When the icing forms soft peaks when pulled up with a wooden spoon, stir in the glycerine, which keeps the icing from setting hard. Ideally, leave the icing to rest for 24 hours before using, then beat it again before icing the cake. You can get a smooth finish with royal icing but if you prefer a 'snow' effect, apply the icing then whip it up into peaks with a fork. Add the decorations before the icing sets.

S P A I N

Detail of tiles from 'Caso de Pilato'- Andalucia-Spain.

Spain celebrates the birth of the King of Kings with tangible reminders of the first Christmas. As the festival time approaches market stalls are set up in every town—from the Plaza Mayor in Madrid to the cathedral steps of Barcelona. They carry on the centuries-old tradition of selling little nacimiento (nativity) figurines. Every family has a Belen (Bethlehem) scene, a symbolic reminder to Spanish Christians that Christ has come to dwell among people.

In wealthier homes an entire room may be set aside for a scene made with priceless antique figurines. In other homes children have hours of fun arranging the models made of clay, wood or plastic in a special corner of the living-room, the Christ child and the wise men being absent until the appropriate day. Spanish children address their Christmas letters to one of the wise men—usually the favourite, Balthazar. They know that on the eve of Epiphany, 6 January, he will leave gifts in their shoes put out on the windowsill.

As the majority of Spaniards are Catholic the focus of the festival is on the Christmas Eve mass, the Misa del Gallo, so called because, like the cockerel, it ushers in Christmas morning. There is also a Christian tradition which says that the cock was the first living creature to proclaim Christ's birth. The village churches and city cathedrals are packed to capacity and the happy sounds of organs, guitars, tambourines and choirs combine to welcome the Christ child. As in other places there are echoes of pagan fertility rituals interwoven with the Christian celebrations, although today they are done with religious intent. Fire, noise and dancing to ward off evil spirits remind us of the ancient origins of winter festivals.

Before going to mass, families gather for a special supper, the Cena de Nochebuena, lit-erally the 'supper of the good night'. In Spain a meal is more than just a means of getting nourishment. It is a family rite of love and respect, feeding the soul as well as the body. The deeper meanings of sharing food are never more important than on this night.

Being a land of such contrasts, Spanish cuisine is very regional. Whether the Christmas meal takes place in the snowbound Pyrenees or in the fragrant warmth of Valencia, it will reflect these contrasts. The availability of local ingredients will also to a certain extent determine the meal. *Fiesta* means feast, and the generosity, joy and abundance with which this feast of feasts is celebrated reflects the vitality and exuberance of the Spanish people.

Although there is no one Christmas meal as such, clear favourites do emerge. It is common in coastal areas particularly to begin the meal with a fish dish using bream, eel or *mariscos* (shellfish). The pink-fleshed sea bream is baked in olive oil, herbs, wine and garlic to make *Besugo al arriero*. Large, plump *langostinos a la plancha* (langoustines) will be flash-fried in a little garlic and olive oil and served with *esparragos* (asparagus) and lemon mayonnaise or marinated *alcachofas* (artichokes) and perhaps a little pile of fried almonds served on a colourfully painted plate. In inland areas such as La Maragateria, dried fillets of cod are an expensive delicacy. They are well soaked and then cooked until tender. The fish is often served with a dish of fine white cabbage, red pepper and garlic. In the warmer regions such as Granada, there are echoes of the Moorish heritage with a cold, creamy almond soup, *sopa de almendras* to start the meal.

The main course again varies from region to region. Turkey is very popular and it is not to be forgotten that it was the Spanish *conquistadores*

who brought this bird back from their New World journeys. In the inland area of Ampurdán the festive turkey is stuffed with *butifarras* (sausages), raisins and pine nuts. In the Balearic islands a tender, succulent roast sucking pig, *cochinillo asado* is likely to grace the table. The piglet used is usually a small milk-fed one and is often stuffed with a tasty mixture of sausage-meat, mushrooms and herbs. This glossy piglet, served with an apple in its mouth, is an impressive sight on the Christmas table. For many centuries sheep farming was vital to the Spanish economy and in parts of Spain lamb is still the favoured celebratory dish.

A Castilian speciality is *lechazo asado*, a tender milk-fed lamb traditionally roasted in a brick oven fuelled by fragrant oak or jara wood. These roasts are usually served with fried potatoes or fried cauliflower dusted with paprika. A crunchy endive, red pepper and orange salad, dressed with the classic *alioli* (garlic, lemon and olive oil dressing) makes a colourful accompaniment. A Spanish wine such as a robust *rioja* is drunk by all, including the children.

Rice is not generally thought of as being a product of Spain but in areas like Levante there are huge rice paddies and in these areas rice is served instead of potatoes as an accompaniment to the roast. Alternatively it is found on the menu as a rich, creamy rice pudding sprinkled with cinnamon *arroz con leche* for dessert. A rich but delicious end to the meal is *crema Catalana* (crème caramel) with a sugar topping that is caramelized by melting it with a hot iron specially made for this purpose.

Another dessert that will always be served is the famous *turrón*. This delicious nougat was at one time made specially for Christmas but as most holiday-makers know it is now a year-round favourite. It is sometimes sold from door to door and it is thought churlish to refuse to buy it. There are many variations but two of the nicest are a brittle kind from Alicante made from chopped toasted almonds, honey, sugar and egg whites or the softer *turrón de Jijona* made from pine kernels, egg whites and coriander. A rich chocolate version is also very good. The small town of Jijona north of Alicante is largely given over to the making of *turrón* and the streets are heady with the fragrance of honey and almonds. Carthaginians who ruled Spain in 200 BC are known to have offered sweet cakes to one of their goddesses and it is thought that the giving of *turrón* may be a survival of that ritual. It is also possible that it stems from a later Roman custom of giving something sweet at the Kalends to ensure that the coming year would be full of sweetness.

Another almond confection given and eaten at Christmas is marzipan. The word comes from the Arabic *mawthapan*. Legend has it that Alfonso VI was the first to make it during the siege of Toledo. In Spain marzipan is made into shapes, usually of animals and flowers, and painted with a little colouring. The enjoyment of marzipan spread to the rest of Europe and it has become a traditional part of Christmas food in most European countries. The nuns in many of the convents across Spain are busy at Christmas baking sweets and little cakes to recipes handed down over hundreds of years. People will travel long distances to buy these *dulces caseros* (home bakes) because, although the ingredients are simple they say the love and devotion with which they are made gives them a special flavour.

A large platter with an assortment of sweets and cakes and of fresh fruits such as dates, figs, grapes and oranges as well as dried and candied fruits and nuts is kept constantly filled during the Christmas week, when there is open house. Visitors are welcome to help themselves from it, and also to eat marzipan and *membrillo*, a delicious Sevillian quince paste.

At the end of the Christmas meal this platter is passed around together with *polvorones*, small rounds of rich almond shortbread, liberally dusted with icing (confectioner's) sugar and wrapped in twists of paper. They are served with a glass of sherry or *aguardiente* (Anís brandy) or one of the many Spanish liqueurs. Sherry (fortified wine) is native to Spain, originating in the wine-producing region around the town of Jeréz. True sherry is unique to this region and has been exported to England since the twelfth century.

It is interesting to note what a large contribution Spanish conquistadores and Spanish cuisine have made to European culinary style. Not only the pre-lunch sherry, the turkey, potatoes and tomatoes and peppers in the salad, the mayonnaise on the shrimp cocktail, the nutmeg in the Christmas pud, and the Christmas chocolates, but also table settings and the custom of serving meals in courses— all were introduced to Europe by the Spaniards.

Later there will be more celebrations, when the guitar, tambourines and castanets are brought out. An impromptu circle is formed to dance some of the lively traditional dances. Each region has its own dances such as the Catalonian *sardana*. Many of the movements of these dances have long-forgotten symbolic and religious meanings of which today's dancers are largely unaware. Singing is very much part of the evening—carols being sung before and after the meal.

Spanish Christmas carols, *villancicos*, are cheerful and homely and reflect the Spanish identification with the essential humanity of the divine family. With delightful simplicity they sing of Mary drying the nappies on a rosemary bush and of birds nesting in the stable to watch over the Christ child. Indeed, in the northern rural parts of Spain, the Yule log and the hearth play an important role in a similar legend. The log is left to burn all night. People say it is so that the Virgin Mary will have somewhere warm to rest and to dry the holy infant's nappies. Sometimes a chair is put out for her to sit on and on Christmas morning the children look for her footprints in the ashes. Until very recently it was common to leave the front door unlocked on Christmas Eve so that the holy family could enter. Sadly this lovely custom has fallen victim to the high crime rate and today few leave their doors open.

But Christmas is far from over. The arrival of

the wise men is not celebrated till Epiphany. Each day it is the task of the children to move the little *nacimiento* figures of the magi a little closer to the crib. Frequently the nightly singing around the nativity scene will continue until the magi finally reach the stable at Epiphany and the celebrations and the Christmas story are complete.

A SPANISH CHRISTMAS EVE MEAL

BESUGO AL ARRIERO
Baked sea bream

or

LANGOSTINOS A LA PLANCHA CON ALCACHOFAS
Langoustines with marinaded artichokes

~

LECHAZO ASADO
Roast baby lamb

ENSALADA SEVILLANA
Endive salad

~

CREMA CATALAN
Caramel topped custard

TURRÓN DE JIJONA
Jijona Christmas nougat

POLVORONES SEVILLANOS
Christmas almond shortbread

FRESH FRUIT: GRAPES, DATES, FIGS, ORANGES, DRIED FRUIT AND NUTS

Besugo al arriero
BAKED SEA BREAM

In many parts of Spain the Christmas Eve meal begins with sea bream and every family has its own way of cooking it. This recipe produces a delicious sauce with undertones of garlic and paprika that allows the flavour of the fish to come through.

bream	1–1.5kg	2–3lb	2–3lb
(red mullet or bass are good substitutes)			
salt and black pepper			
large lemon	1	1	1
bay leaf	1	1	1
onion, quartered	1	1	1
chopped parsley	15ml	1tbs	1tbs

Sauce

olive oil	30ml	2tbs	2tbs
clove of garlic, roughly chopped	1	1	1
plain flour	10ml	2tsp	2tsp
sweet paprika powder	10ml	2tsp	2tsp
dry white wine	150ml	1/4 pint	1/2 cup
fresh breadcrumbs, optional	30ml	2tbs	2tbs

Wash and dry the cleaned bream and place on a sheet of baking foil. Squeeze the juice of half the lemon over the fish. Season well with salt and black pepper. Sprinkle the chopped parsley over the fish and tuck in the bay leaf and onion quarters. Wrap into a loose parcel and bake at 160°C (325°F/Gas 3) for 20 minutes. Reserve the liquid and keep the fish warm while you make the sauce.

Heat the olive oil in a pan and fry the garlic until golden. Discard the garlic and add the flour to the oil with the paprika and wine, adding a little of the reserved fish stock if necessary. Check the seasoning before pouring over the bream. If you like, you can sprinkle the breadcrumbs over the fish and pop it under the grill until the crumbs are lightly toasted. Serve garnished with lemon wedges.

Langostinos a la plancha con alcachofas
FLASH-FRIED LANGOUSTINES WITH MARINADED ARTICHOKES

fresh langoustines	12	12	12
(king prawns or jumbo shrimp)			
clove garlic	1	1	1
olive oil	10ml	2tbs	2tbs
ground black pepper			

Shell and clean the langoustines. Press the garlic and mix with the olive oil and black pepper. Coat the langoustines in oil and flash fry—preferably on a very hot frying pan or, failing that, grill—until cooked, turning once.

Serve with *alcachofas*.

Alcachofas

can artichoke hearts	1	1	1
tomato juice	150ml	1/4 pint	1/2 cup
fresh coriander	15ml	1tbs	1tbs
OR			
generous pinch of dried coriander			
sugar	5ml	1tsp	1tsp
salt and pepper			
zest of 1 orange			
chilli powder or to taste	2ml	1/2 tsp	1/2 tsp
olive oil	45ml	3tbs	3tbs

Drain the artichokes and pat dry. Blend all the other ingredients thoroughly, adding chilli powder to taste. Pour over the artichokes and leave to stand, preferably overnight. Drain excess marinade before serving.

Lechazo asado

ROAST BABY LAMB

There can be few more succulent roasts than milk-fed baby lamb roasted in the traditional Spanish way—in a baker's oven. Although lacking the charm of the baker's oven, a very delicious roast can be achieved at home in a conventional oven and it makes a welcome alternative to turkey.

Rub the prepared lamb with the lard, salt, pepper and a little sweet paprika. Preheat the oven to 230°C (450°F/Gas 8). Place the lamb in a large roasting tin (pan) and roast for half an hour. Mix the garlic, onion, rosemary, parsley and bay leaves with half the wine and pour over the roast. Reduce the heat to 160°C (325°F/Gas 3) and cook, basting frequently. After an hour add the rest of the wine and the lemon juice and continue to baste as before until done (when pierced with a skewer the juices should run clear). Leave to rest on a heated platter and prepare the gravy. Drain off the fat from the roasting pan. Stir in the flour and over a low heat cook until reduced and thickened. Blend in the stock. Simmer a few minutes longer, adjust the seasoning, then strain and serve with the lamb accompanied by cauliflower and potatoes 'Castilian' style, which means sautéed with garlic and dusted with paprika.

whole baby lamb, if available OR	1	1	1
1/2 lamb	2.5–3.5kg	5–7lb	
lard	75g	3oz	1/3 cup
salt and freshly ground black pepper			
sweet paprika			
cloves of garlic, finely chopped	2	2	2
large onion, grated	1	1	1
a few sprigs of rosemary or marjoram			
parsley	15ml	1tbs	1tbs
bay leaves, crushed	3	3	3
dry white wine	300ml	1/2 pint	1 cup
juice of 1 lemon			
plain flour	20ml	1tbs heaped	1tbs heaped
lamb or vegetable stock	100ml	4fl oz	1/3 cup

Ensalada sevillana
ENDIVE SALAD

Conventional salad greens are expensive in northern countries at Christmas but this salad combines winter endive with tart Seville oranges to make a colourful and refreshing salad.

head of curly endive, washed	1	1	1
red pepper, sliced	1	1	1
small onions, sliced in rings	2	2	2
Seville oranges	2	2	2
black olives, stoned (pitted)	12	12	12

Dressing

olive oil	60ml	4tbs	4tbs
white wine vinegar or tarragon vinegar	30ml	2tbs	2tbs
salt and freshly ground black pepper			
clove of garlic	1	1	1
a pinch of fresh or dried tarragon			

Slice the oranges into thin rounds. Try to use thin-skinned oranges and leave the skin on, otherwise peel them first if you must. Mix all the ingredients together in a large salad bowl.

Press the garlic and mix with the olive oil, vinegar and tarragon and season to taste. Allow to stand for at least an hour before pouring over the salad. Toss well and serve.

Crema Catalan
CARAMEL TOPPED CUSTARD

The Catalan cook will have a special iron with which to caramelize the sugar but the same effect can be achieved by putting the ramekins under a hot grill for a few minutes.

egg yolks	5	5	5
cream	600ml	1 pint	2½ cups
caster sugar (US: granulated)	30ml	2tbs	2tbs
vanilla essence (extract)	2ml	½ tsp	½ tsp
cornflour (corn starch)	15g	1tbs	1tbs
granulated sugar	225g	8oz	1 cup

In a bowl mix the caster sugar (2tbs sugar), egg yolks, vanilla essence and cornflour (corn starch) until smooth.

Meanwhile heat the cream until it is just about to boil. Add to the egg yolk mixture and return to a low heat, stirring constantly until the mixture thickens. Pour into flame-proof ramekins and leave to set. When cool refrigerate for 2–3 hours.

To make the caramel topping spread a generous layer of the granulated sugar on top of each ramekin and place under a hot grill until the sugar melts.

Serve once the caramelized sugar has cooled and hardened.

Turrón de Jijona
JIJONA CHRISTMAS NOUGAT

Giraboix, or *turrón* as it is popularly known, was originally a Moorish delicacy. Although difficult to reproduce at home it would be inconceivable not to give a recipe for *turrón*, which is synonymous with Christmas in Spain. This makes a soft nutty nougat—kinder on the teeth than the hard Alicante nougat.

blanched almonds or pine nuts	125g	4 1/2 oz	1/2 cup
hazelnuts	125g	4 1/2 oz	1/2 cup
egg whites	3	3	3
honey	100g	4oz	1/2 cup
caster sugar (US: granulated)	100g	4oz	1/2 cup
pinch of coriander or cinnamon, optional			
bittersweet covering chocolate, optional			
sheets rice paper	8	8	8

Over a high heat scorch the hazelnuts quickly in a frying pan, then remove the skins by rubbing in a cloth. Toast the almonds or pine nuts lightly in the oven. Grind the nuts very finely—a liquidizer is easiest. Beat the egg whites until stiff peaks form and fold in the ground nuts and cinnamon or coriander if desired. Bring the honey and sugar to boil in a saucepan and as soon as it boils add the egg and nut mixture. Lower the heat and cook for 10 minutes, stirring all the time with a wooden spoon and watching it carefully as sugar burns very easily. Line the sides and bottom of a rectangular mould such as a small swiss-roll tin with grease-proof (or waxed) paper and then with rice paper. Pour the mixture into the mould and cover with another layer of rice paper. Place a flat heavy weight (the bread-board is ideal) on top and allow to cool. When completely cool you can cover it with melted chocolate and decorate with pine nuts and almonds or just dust with a little cinnamon and icing (confectioner's) sugar and cut into bite-sized bars.

Polvorones Sevillanos
CHRISTMAS ALMOND SHORTBREAD

Looking like British Christmas crackers wrapped in twists of paper, these delicious shortbreads are passed around with the sherry after the Christmas meal.

plain flour, sifted	225g	8oz	2 cups
ground almonds	50g	2oz	1/4 cup
icing sugar, sifted	175g	6oz	3/4 cup
cinnamon	10ml	2tsp	2tsp
butter	175g	6oz	1 1/2 sticks
few drops of brandy or anis liqueur			
icing (confectioner's) sugar to dust			
tissue paper			

Lightly toast the flour on a baking sheet in an oven pre-heated to 230°C (450°F/Gas 8) for a few minutes. When completely cool mix all the dry ingredients in a large mixing bowl. Rub in the butter and add a few drops of brandy or liqueur to make a smooth pastry. Refrigerate for 20 minutes. On a floured board roll out to 12mm (1/2 in.) thickness and cut into small rounds. An upturned sherry glass makes just the right size! Place the rounds on a well greased baking sheet and bake for 10–15 minutes in an oven pre-heated to 200°C (400°F/Gas 6) until lightly golden. When cool, dust liberally with icing sugar and, as a final touch, wrap each one in a twist of tissue paper. A box of these would make an attractive Christmas gift.

~ EXTRA RECIPE ~

Hot chocolate drink

At Christmas hot chocolate is served with the Epiphany cake and often at the end of the Christmas Eve revelry it is served with *churros* for an early morning breakfast. This recipe makes 4 small cups of very rich hot chocolate.

dark cooking chocolate	100g	4oz	4oz
custard powder (US: vanilla instant pudding)	15ml	1tbs	1tbs

milk	450ml	¾ pint	1½ cups
pinch of freshly grated nutmeg			
whipped cream			

Over a low heat warm half the milk. Break the chocolate into pieces and add to the milk, stirring until melted. Mix the remaining milk with the custard powder and add to the chocolate. Stir constantly until you have a thick hot chocolate but *do not boil*. Whisk the chocolate until frothy. Serve topped with a blob of cream and a grating of fresh nutmeg, cinnamon or grated chocolate. (You could omit the custard powder for a less rich version.)

GHANA

A warp-faced 'Keto' cloth - woven by the Ewe people of Ghana.

Ghana in December is hot and dry, cooled only by the evening drop in temperature and by the breezes along the Gold Coast of the south.

Ghanaian Christians show their joy at the festival of Jesus' birth with lively exuberance. Their celebrations are based on local traditions, but express a faith shared by millions around the world.

Whether celebrated in a city or its suburbs, in a rural town or in a tribal village, Christmas is important to African Christians. There is almost none of the commercial hype that surrounds the festival in many more developed countries, but some of the stores in Accra have a Father Christmas. The level of Europeanization of Christmas customs and food depends on a family's experience, wealth and background, and on the availability of food in a land used to food shortages because of drought, fire, distribution problems and shortages of seed and fertilizers.

An ordinary family living in the outskirts of Accra starts thinking about Christmas only a week or so before the big day, when the parents go to the local daily market to choose a turkey or—even more special—a goat. Bargaining over the price is a skilful business demanding patience and a sense of humour. Usually the buyer starts by offering half the price he is prepared to pay. The animal is taken home alive and fattened up to be in peak condition for 25 December.

In Ghana both 25 and 26 December are public holidays, but the festivities begin on Christmas Eve. After supper, at around six in the evening, parcels wrapped in special paper bought from the market are handed out. A woman may receive a new dress—a 'cloth'—and children sweets or a new cloth. Balloons make the home look bright and festive.

Supper is based on *foo-foo*, which is made from yam, plantain, cocoyam (taro), or cassava, alone or in any combination. The roots are boiled in a clay pot and then pounded with a wooden pestle until smooth. Cassava (manioc or yucca) is a starchy, dense, potato-like tuber from whose flour tapioca is made and it is a staple food in Ghana, as are yams. *Foo-foo* is light and slightly elastic and sticky in texture, and *foo-foo* balls are eaten with either palmnut soup or stew or groundnut (peanut) soup or stew. *Foo-foo* and a spicy soup are the basic food of many African Ghanaians.

Palmnut soup or stew is a special treat. Palmnuts grow in clusters at the top of the palm oil tree. When these little red fruits are ripe, they are cooked in boiling water for fifteen minutes then pounded with water to make a pulp. The pulp is squeezed through a net, the resulting juice being rich in orange-gold, nutty-flavoured palmnut oil, which is a characteristic ingredient of African cooking. To this oily juice is added crushed raw tomato, African pepper, salt and crushed onions. To make a stew from this soup, dried fish from the market is added. The soup or stew is then boiled for half an hour before being served with the *foo-foo*.

The African pepper used is *pilli-pilli*, also known as *piri-piri* in Mozambique and *ber-beri* in Ethiopia. It's similar to, but stronger than, cayenne pepper and in parts of Africa it's said that a husband can judge how much his wife loves him by the amount of this pepper she uses. If his food is bland, her ardour must be dying!

Some families choose a dark groundnut soup or stew to have with their *foo-foo* instead of using palmnuts, but both are traditional accompaniments to the starchy staple food. Peanuts were probably first brought to Africa by Portuguese traders from Brazil. The plants belong to the legume family and the nuts are dug out of the soil (hence 'groundnuts'), where they have ended up after the flower stalks have bent right over. High in protein and oil, peanuts are used in sauces, sweet dishes and in soup or stew—especially in the 'cold' season. Because meat will be eaten on Christmas Day, fish is likely to be used in the stew. One of the most popular dishes served in African restaurants in Europe is groundnut stew containing fish or meat and served with rice.

At sunrise on Christmas Day the mother of the family goes to buy the day's food from one of the many stalls or 'kiosks' dotted along each street in the suburbs. The street sellers are almost all women and are given the respectful name of 'mammy'. According to tradition, these women are very powerful because in Ghana goods are more valuable than money. Breakfast foods bought early in the morning include *kenkey*—ground maize (corn) mixed with salt and water, boiled for an hour, and parcelled up in balls in corn husks rather like the *tamales* of Mexico. Some *kenkey*—*fanti kenkey*—is brown and comes wrapped in plantain leaves. Being fermented, it has a taste all of its own. Each adult usually eats one or two balls.

Along with the still-warm *kenkey* are bought loaves of white leavened bread—usually shaped like short French sticks; little fish ready-fried in coconut oil; and ready-made sauce to eat with the *kenkey*. The sauce is a typically hot African sauce made from ground African pepper (*pilli-pilli*), rock salt, crushed raw onion and crushed raw tomato.

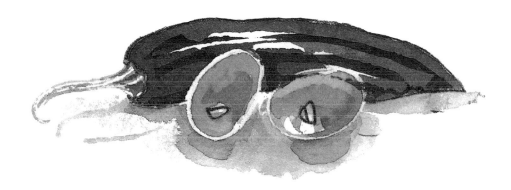

Back at home, the breakfast *kenkey*, pepper sauce, fried fish and bread are washed down with water, Coca-cola, or cocoa. The cocoa industry in Ghana is in decline because of a shortage of fertilizers, because of poor transport to the ports and because trees are not being replaced fast enough, but cocoa is still a popular drink. All beverages are known in Ghana as 'tea'. Cocoa is therefore called 'cocoa-tea', tea is 'tea-tea'; and coffee is 'coffee-tea'.

The next task of the day is to start preparing the festive meal. The male head of the family—nowadays often a younger man than in the days when several generations of a family were likely to live together in tribal conditions—first has to kill the chosen fattened animal. He slits the goat's throat with a knife with all the family watching. If the family were to eat a turkey, he would kill that but a large chicken would be killed by a woman.

If a goat is to be eaten, it is prepared very early in the morning—around 7 a.m.—and a wood fire is made in the yard so that the animal can be barbecued. As the fire is heating up, the goat is skinned, then threaded from head to tail on to a spike or spit. The word 'barbecue' comes from the French *barbe à queue*: 'beard to tail'. The goat is rotated from time to time during the morning by turning a wheel at one end of the spit, and a drip pan catches the fat. The mixed fragrances of wood smoke and barbecuing goat flesh waft through the air as the African morning heats up and everyone starts getting ready for church.

First the children are washed and dressed in their best clothes. The girls are dressed in a single piece of brightly coloured cloth crossed over in front and tied behind their necks. The boys have trousers and a T-shirt. The adults dress in their best too. In the cities some Ghanaians wear Western clothing but on Christmas Day most wear their national dress, which is based on pieces of brightly patterned and coloured material called cloths. The finest cloths are the Kente cloths, with silk and cotton threads woven in six-inch strips joined together to make a large rectangle. The patterns all have meanings: some are particular to certain tribes while others tell stories in pictures. The women wear a cloth round their waist, a T-shirt on top, a smaller cloth round their waist or shoulder to carry a baby, and a head-cloth. The men's cloth is worn like a toga, with trousers underneath. A sign of wealth is a full Kente dress. Second best is a cloth with Kente trimmings.

Hair must be plaited afresh for the day. If no one in the family can plait, people can go to a plaiter in the market. Gold earrings and jewellery complete the attractive outfits.

At around 8.30 it's time for church, which is an important social as well as a spiritual event. There is a great deal of singing during the long service and in the suburbs there may be organ music. In the villages there is clapping and dancing to Christian Christmas music played to insistent African rhythms. When the children have had enough, they can slip out and play back at home.

Later on, after the worship, a palm leaf and some flowers such as forget-me-nots and roses are gathered. The flowers are threaded between the fronds of the leaf and then the flowered leaf is put over the front door. A large table is laid for the gathering of friends and family with a patterned cloth kept for best and with plates and glasses. There is no cutlery because eating with a hand is the norm. Indeed, all social rituals such as shaking hands, passing food, giving gifts and eating are done with the right hand.

Soon family and guests begin to congregate for the Christmas lunch amidst a warm welcome and much shaking of hands. The food prepared is similar to the festive food chosen for any special occasion.

White-fleshed yams are peeled and sliced, then boiled for twenty minutes before being pounded into *foo-foo*, and rice is cooked in water with some salt added. Rice tends to be eaten only in towns and, because it's expensive, it's saved for special occasions. The barbecued goat is cut up by the head of the family and at about 12:30 the meal is ready. The goat, hot *pilli-pilli* sauce, yam balls and rice are washed down with Coca-cola, locally brewed beer, or water.

The feast continues at a leisurely pace. Fresh pineapple or a fruit salad is served for dessert; and the adults may sing traditional European carols such as 'O Come all ye faithful' and 'We wish you a Merry Christmas' as they sit around the table, the children playing at their feet.

The afternoon is spent visiting neighbours and relatives or being visited. Sooner or later someone will start tapping a drum and then others will dance, even in the heat of the afternoon. Gatherings are friendly and open, and all are welcome to join in with the festivities. Such generous hospitality is widespread in Ghana, but at this time of year is a special reminder of Jesus' message of love and concern.

A GHANAIAN CHRISTMAS EVE MEAL

FOO-FOO

GROUNDNUT (PEANUT) SOUP OR STEW

or

PALMNUT SOUP OR STEW

A GHANAIAN CHRISTMAS DAY LUNCH

BARBECUED GOAT

YAM BALLS

GHANAIAN RICE

PILLI-PILLI SAUCE

AFRICAN FRUIT SALAD

Groundnut (peanut) soup

Soups in Ghana are classified as either light or dark. Peanut soup is a dark soup and is served either hot or cold, according to the weather. Peanut soup served with *foo-foo* (mashed, boiled cassava, yam or other starchy tuber) is a staple food for many families in Ghana. It is customary to take some *foo-foo* with the right hand and dip it into the soup-bowl to soak up some of the rich, flavoursome liquid. Freshly ground roast peanuts give a better flavour than commercially processed peanut butter.

fish fillets (herring, mackerel, flounder, sole, or red snapper)	900g	2lb	2lb
large onion, peeled	1	1	1
carrots, peeled	2	2	2
salt	5ml	1tsp	1tsp
pinch of ground black pepper			
water	1.2 litres	2 pints	4 cups
tomato purée OR	75g	3oz	1/3 cup
fresh tomatoes, finely chopped	450g	1lb	2 cups
freshly ground roast peanuts OR	100g	4oz	1/2 cup
peanut butter	100g	4oz	1/2 cup
pinch of cayenne pepper			
pinch of chilli powder			

Put the fish, onion, carrots, salt, pepper and water into a large saucepan and bring to the boil. Simmer for 30 minutes, then remove the fish, onion and carrot with a perforated spoon and keep in a cool place for use in a peanut stew. Add the tomato purée or chopped tomatoes, ground peanuts or peanut butter, cayenne pepper and chilli powder, and simmer for a further 20 minutes. Skim off the oil that has risen to the top of the liquid and discard. Reserve 300ml ($^1/_2$ pint/1 cup) of the soup to make stew. Serve the peanut soup in small bowls with plenty of mashed cassava, plantain of yam (*foo-foo*), or mashed potatoes.

Groundnut (peanut) stew

Follow the recipe for groundnut (peanut) soup, removing and reserving the fish, onion and carrots. Normally the soup is made and eaten the day before the stew is needed but about 300ml ($^1/_2$ pint/1 cup) of the soup is reserved and kept in a cool place. To assemble the stew, cut the fish, onion and carrots into small chunks and add the remaining soup.

Palmnut soup or stew

Ghanaians consider palmnut soup or stew more special than groundnut soup or stew for festive occasions. If you have access to palmnuts, you can make these delicious recipes yourself. Follow the recipe for groundnut (peanut) soup or stew but make two changes. First, omit the freshly ground roast peanuts (or peanut butter). Second, include the pulp and oil from 450g (1lb/2 cups) of palmnuts when you cook the fish.

To prepare the palmnuts, put them into plenty of boiling water in a large saucepan and cook for 15 minutes. Mash them well. Add 300ml ($^1/_2$ pint/$1^1/_4$ cups) of cold water and mix thoroughly with your hands. Push the mixture through a sieve or through butter muslin to collect the pulp and oil. Discard the skins caught in the sieve or muslin.

Yam balls

Cooked yam is often mixed with egg for special occasions such as Christmas in Ghana. Although yam is a much-loved staple food, eggs are precious in most families and indeed are sometimes used instead of currency to buy goods. This recipe makes 8 yam balls, enough for 4 people.

fresh yams, cooked	675g	1 1/2 lb	3 cups,
small eggs, beaten	2	2	2
evaporated milk	50ml	2fl oz	3tbs
small onion, finely chopped	1/2	1/2	1/2
garlic cloves, peeled and crushed	2	2	2
salt	2ml	1/2 tsp	1/2 tsp
flour	30ml	2tbs	2tbs
oil (such as peanut oil) for deep-frying			

Peel the yams, cut into chunks, and cook in plenty of boiling salted water in a large saucepan until tender. Drain and mash well until smooth. Add the beaten eggs, evaporated milk, onion, garlic, salt and flour and mix well. Chill until cold. Divide the mixture into 8 pieces and form each piece into a ball. Heat the oil until a crumb of bread dropped in immediately rises to the surface of the oil, sizzling. Deep-fry the yam balls for about 3 minutes or until golden-brown.

Ghanaian rice

R ice is a luxury throughout most of Ghana and is only eaten for festive occasions. It is a perfect accompaniment to barbecued meat and mops up every last bit of the hot tomato *pilli-pilli* sauce.

rice	8oz	225g	1 cup
chicken stock	600ml	1 pint	2 1/2 cups
bay leaves	2	2	2
salt	5ml	1tsp	1tsp
pinch of pepper			
pimento-stuffed olives, chopped	50g	2oz	1/4 cup
roasted peanuts	100g	4oz	1/2 cup

Wash the rice well. Bring the chicken stock to the boil in a large pan and add the rice, bay leaves, salt and pepper. Cover the pan and simmer until the rice is cooked but not too soft. Remove the bay leaves. Stir in the olives and peanuts and serve.

Pilli-pilli sauce
HOT TOMATO SAUCE

T he small, fiery red pepper known as the *pilli-pilli* in Ghana is called the *piri-piri* in areas of Africa with a Portuguese influence and the chilli pepper in many other parts of the world. The *pilli-pilli* is an integral part of African cooking.

tomato sauce	450ml	3/4 pint	13oz can
lemons	2	2	2
large onion, finely chopped	1	1	1
garlic cloves, peeled and crushed	2	2	2
small, fresh red chilli pepper, finely chopped	1	1	1
tomatoes, finely chopped	3	3	3

Mix all the ingredients well and keep in a cool place until needed.

African fruit salad

This exotic salad has an unusual flavour from the sweet-and-sour lime dressing.

enough raw salad leaves (such as lettuce, chicory or spinach) to line four salad bowls generously

small pineapple	1/2	1/2	1/2
mango	1	1	1
orange	1	1	1
lemon	1	1	1
avocado	1	1	1
strawberries	100g	4oz	4oz
banana	1	1	1
roasted peanuts, chopped	50g	2oz	1/4 cup

Lime dressing

limes	2	2	2
mayonnaise	75ml	6fl oz	2/3 cup
double cream (US: whipping), lightly whipped	150ml	1/4 pint	1/2 cup
caster sugar (US: granulated)	15ml	1tbs	1tbs

Wash the salad leaves, remove the stems and tear into pieces, use to line four individual salad bowls.

Put the pieces of fruit into a large mixing bowl as you prepare them. Peel the pineapple, cut into slices and then into finger-shaped pieces. You may prefer to discard the central core as it is sometimes a little stringy. Peel the mango and cut the flesh from the stone in large strips. Cut the orange into very thin slices with a sharp knife, leaving the skin on. Squeeze and reserve the juice from the lemon. Cut the avocado in half, remove the stone and peel each half, then cut the flesh into strips and dip them into the lemon juice. Hull the strawberries. Peel the banana and cut it into chunks, dip them into a little of the mayonnaise reserved for the dressing, then roll them in a bowl of chopped roasted peanuts.

Grate the rind of the limes and squeeze out their juice, then mix the grated rind and the juice with the remaining mayonnaise, whipped cream and sugar. Put the fruit salad into the leaf-lined bowls and pour some of the dressing into each bowl.

BRAZIL

Brazil is famous for the huge statue of Christ towering above Rio at Corcovado. *With arms outstretched, the statue seems to welcome the people of Rio. It is with a similar warmth and affection that the Brazilians embrace the birth of the Christ child and Christmas celebrations.*

Crib scenes (*presépios*) are set up in many churches, schools and homes and in an unusual concession to the twentieth century the *presépios* often feature miniature planes, motorbikes, trains and even factories among the traditional pastoral figurines. Although Brazil enjoys hot summer days in December, Christmas traditions from northern countries have been adopted. Most homes have a Christmas tree, and *Papai Noel* arrives at the Rio stadium, sweltering in his red suit with fur trimmings, and distributes gifts to excited children.

Although the stores vie for the custom of Christmas shoppers with their enticing window displays there is little evident commercialization of Christmas, even in the big cities. The spirit of Christmas moves people to give generously to aid organizations who bring a little Christmas cheer to the impoverished families living in the *favelas* (shanty towns), which crowd the hillsides surrounding the cities. In wealthier homes it has become a modern custom for the maids to be taken to the supermarket just before Christmas to fill a trolley for their own families as a gift from their employers.

In the rural areas, particularly in the north, there are many other colourful, exciting celebrations. Here the cultural influences of the Africans, Indians and indigenous Tupi have so modified the original Portuguese-Catholic observance of Christmas that they have created a celebration uniquely Brazilian. In the smaller towns such as Bahia and Ceara in the weeks preceding Christmas there are carnival-like festivities in the open air. People take to the streets, singing and dancing the samba, batucada and other rhythmic dances to the sounds of the *pandeiro* (tambourine), drum, rattle, guitar and accordion.

Traditional dramas are enacted; curiously half-Christian, half-pagan pageants, full of primitive superstition. The satirical sketches *Bumba Meu Boi* (Whoa, My Ox) begin at Christmas and last until Epiphany. A colourful ox, made from wood, calico and papier mâché, is held aloft and capers about to the delight of the crowd who often join in the singing of the verses which make up the play.

Another drama enacted at this time is the *Fandango*, involving huge bonfires, fireworks and a play about a ship endangered by bad weather until the devil is thrown overboard.

More in keeping with the Christian origin of the Christmas celebration are the beautiful *Pastorinhas* (folk plays) and the *Folia dos Reis* (the frolic of the wise men) enacted at Epiphany. All these celebrations bear witness to the variety of cultures in Brazil.

In both rural and urban areas on Christmas Eve people attend midnight mass. This mass is called *Missa do Galo* (Mass of the Cockerel). The cock is widely connected with the corn spirit and the harvest and this bit of mythology may have been imported to Brazil from Europe—showing how pagan myths and rituals have been intermingled with the religious practice. There is also a Christian tradition which says that the cock was the first living creature to proclaim the birth of Jesus Christ at Bethlehem by crowing *Christus natus est*, and since then it is said that cocks have crowed throughout the night of 24 December.

The traditional Christmas *Ceia,* or supper, is usually eaten before midnight mass. Although this is usually an intimate family occasion, it is not uncommon to invite strangers who find themselves away from their own families to share in the celebrations. They will sit down at a table richly decorated with colourful fruits and flowers. The food is equally exotic with bold flavouring: chilli, garlic and coconut are used in abundance.

The cuisine of Brazil, like its Christian customs and folklore, shows the influence of the Africans, Portuguese, Indians, Spaniards, Germans and Italians. Brazil is a vast country and the tropical African-style food of the north is very different from that of the cosmopolitan cities. In the north for their Christmas meal, as for their daily meals, the Brazilians will utilize the resources of the giant Amazon river and the lush forests. A popular Christmas meal consists of fish or roast pig, either cooked in the oven or roasted over an open fire, or perhaps *Pato no tucupi*—roast duck with a sauce made with the juice of grated manioc (cassava), garlic and chicory.

As a treat, lobsters (*lagosta*) may be served as a first course. Flash fried in a fiery chilli and tomato paste, they are doused with coconut milk to make a creamy sauce. Served with rice this dish sets a special tone for the *Ceia.*

Over much of the rest of the country, particularly in the cities, turkey is still a favourite. *Peru a Brasileira* (turkey Brazilian-style) is marinaded in *Vinha d'alho* made from garlic, celery, white wine and oil, before roasting. The turkey is always served with *farofa*, either as a stuffing or served separately. The principal ingredient of *farofa* is *farinha* (manioc meal) which is a staple in Brazil and appears at nearly every meal in one form or another—sometimes

sprinkled over food from a shaker. At Christmas it is combined with butter, olives, chopped nuts, ham and seasonings to make a savoury stuffing to fill the crop of the bird, and mixed with carrots, raisins or prunes and melted butter to serve as a nutty accompaniment.

Glazed, baked ham served with pineapple may be served in addition to the turkey if the family is a large one. This may be accompanied by a beet-and-potato salad with a French dressing or a colourful avocado salad with lettuce, chopped celery, ham, tomato, black olives and prunes, served with mayonnaise. Rice is almost always served, either plain or cooked with tomato and onion. *Môlho de limâo*, a hot lime relish, is served on the side.

A selection of drinks may be served with the meal, including the refreshing *Guarána*. This drink, made from the fruit of a Brazilian shrub, is as popular as Coca-Cola and many claim that it has wonderful health-giving properties. Mixed with fruit juices and mineral water it forms the basis of a delicious punch.

For dessert *rabanadas* (French toast) is traditional. Slices of bread are soaked in sugar and port, dipped in egg and fried in butter until golden brown. These slices are served hot with a sprinkling of sugar and cinnamon.

In a sophisticated version of *rabanados*, *jabuticaba*—a plum-like fruit found in Brazil—is layered with bread and baked in a rich custard sauce. *Pudims* are a variation of baked custard. Usually they are made with nuts, fruits, or coconut and set in a mould. When turned out they are decorated with cream, fruits or nuts and are an attractive and delicious way to end the meal.

Bôlo de Nozes, a walnut cake with a rich coffee- and chocolate-cream filling might be an alternative choice for dessert. A simpler choice would be a fruit salad of papaya, melon, pineapple, banana, orange and lime, with a dash of port. To satisfy the very sweet-toothed Brazilians *goiabada*—a paste made from boiled guava and sugar—is served with curd cheese to end the meal.

Being a nation of coffee growers, the Brazilians are expert at brewing a good strong cup of coffee. The family sit and drink cup after cup of *cafezinho*, aromatic little demitasses of freshly ground coffee, black and well sweetened. They idly crack a few nuts from the bowl of walnuts, Brazil nuts and hazelnuts sitting on the table, and chat and laugh and tell stories until the small hours of the morning.

Family laughter, good food, open-handed generosity and a cheerful willingness to embrace a wide variety of traditions, irrespective of their origin: these are characteristic of Christmas in Brazil.

A BRAZILIAN CHRISTMAS CEIA

LAGOSTA COM LEITE DE COCO
Lobster in coconut milk

PERU À BRASILEIRA
Marinaded turkey Brazilian style

RECHEIA BRASILEIRA
Savoury manioc meal stuffing with nuts and olives

FAROFA DE CENOURAS
Carrot, raisin and manioc meal stuffing or accompaniment

MÔLHO DE LIMÂO
Hot lime relish

SALADA DE BETERRABAS E BATATAS
Beetroot and potato salad

or

SALADA DE ABACETES
Avocado salad

ARROZ
Rice

~

RABANADAS
Port-wine French toast

PUDIM JABUTICABA
Bread pudding with jabuticaba

BÔLO DE NOZES
Nut cake with coffee filling

SALADA DE FRUTAS
Fruit Salad

~

GLACÉ FRUIT AND NUTS

Lagosta com leite de coco
LOBSTER IN COCONUT MILK

B y altering the amount of cayenne pepper you can make this as fiery as you wish.

medium lobster tails, shelled and cleaned	4	4	4
olive oil	30ml	2tbs	2tbs
juice of lemon OR juice of lime	$1/2$ 1	$1/2$ 1	$1/2$ 1
grated onion	15ml	1tbs	1tbs
tomato paste	30ml	2tbs	2tbs
cloves garlic, crushed	1	1	1
thick coconut milk	150ml	$1/4$ pint	$2/3$ cup
avocado	1	1	1
salt and black pepper to taste			
cayenne pepper to taste			

Squeeze the lemon or lime juice over the lobster tails. In a heavy frying pan heat the olive oil and add the onion, garlic, tomato paste and cayenne pepper. Add the lobster tails and cook for 5 minutes. Lower the heat and add the coconut milk. Taste and adjust the seasoning. Cook for a further 5–7 minutes stirring gently. Serve with rice and garnish with a few slices of avocado with lime juice.

Peru à Brasileira
MARINADED TURKEY BRAZILIAN STYLE

F or something a little different—marinaded in *Vinha d'alho* before roasting makes it very succulent and delicious.

whole turkey, plus giblets	7kg	15lb	15lb

Marinade *Vinha d'alho*

cloves garlic, crushed	3	3	3
stalk celery, chopped	1	1	1
onion, grated	1	1	1
chopped parsley	45ml	3tbs	3tbs
salt	2ml	$1/2$ tsp	$1/2$ tsp
dry white wine	500ml	16fl oz	2 cups
juice of lemons	6	6	6

In a very large bowl mix all the marinade ingredients together. Clean and prepare the turkey. Pour a little of the marinade inside the bird to coat the whole cavity. Place the bird breast-down in the marinade and leave overnight.

The following morning remove the bird from the marinade, pat dry and stuff with the nut, olive and bacon stuffing. Truss and rub all over with salt and butter.

Follow the general instructions for roasting in this book and baste the bird frequently.

Recheia Brasileira

SAVOURY MANIOC MEAL STUFFING
WITH NUTS AND OLIVES

This is used as a stuffing for the Christmas turkey or as an accompaniment or both. The principal ingredient is manioc meal (or farina), which is available at good health stores. It is combined with any number of ingredients. The recipe given here is for a rather unusual stuffing. The nuts give it a crumbly texture, best for the crop of the turkey.

olive oil	90ml	6tbs	6tbs
chopped parsley	45ml	3tbs	3tbs
clove garlic	1	1	1
onion, chopped	1	1	1
dried sage	10ml	2tsp	2tsp
manioc meal (or farina)	100g	4oz	1/2 cup
mixed nuts, finely chopped	150g	5oz	3/4 cup
finely chopped ham or bacon steak	100g	4oz	1/2 cup
olives, stoned (pitted)	15–20	15–20	15–20
stock	45ml	3tbs	3tbs
salt and black pepper to taste			

Spread the manioc meal on a baking sheet and toast lightly in the oven. In a large frying pan heat the oil and sauté the garlic, onions and ham. Remove the garlic and add the toasted manioc meal and the chopped nuts, turning well to coat. Add the olives and sage and check the seasoning. Add the stock if the mixture is too crumbly. Stuff the neck of the turkey with the mixture and skewer the neck closed. Stuff the body cavity with a conventional pork and apple or chestnut stuffing and roast in the usual way.

Farofa de Cenouras

CARROT, RAISIN AND MANIOC MEAL
STUFFING OR ACCOMPANIMENT

This is a light *farofa*, the carrots giving it a sweet and nutty texture that is excellent with poultry.

large carrots, grated	3	3	3
butter	60ml	4tbs	4tbs
salt and pepper to taste			
raisins and sultanas (or golden raisins)	100g	4oz	1/2 cup
manioc meal (or farina)	150g	6oz	3/4 cup

Using half the butter sauté the carrots for about 7 minutes. Add the rest of the butter and gradually add enough manioc meal for the mixture to resemble breadcrumbs. Season, and add the raisins or sultanas. Heat thoroughly, turning constantly. Serve as an accompaniment to the roast turkey.

Môlho de limâo

HOT LIME RELISH

Served as a side dish, this is a sharp and fiery sauce made with malagueta peppers. If you prefer, you can use the milder capsicum.

juice of limes	3	3	3
cloves of garlic, crushed	1	1	1
onion	1	1	1
malagueta peppers, without stem and seeds OR	3	3	3
mild, green capsicum, without pith and seeds	2	2	2
salt to taste			

Blend the garlic, onion and peppers well in a blender. Stir in the lime juice. Add salt to taste.

Rabanadas

PORT-WINE FRENCH TOAST

Not the usual French toast—this is a much richer version, dipped in port wine and sugar, and is as traditional to the Brazilian Christmas meal as Christmas pudding is to England.

port wine	175ml	6fl oz	2/3 cup
caster sugar (US: granulated)	20ml	1 tbs heaped	1 tbs heaped
slices French bread	8	8	8
eggs	2	2	2
butter or margarine	75g	3oz	3/4 stick
ground cinnamon	15ml	1tbs	1tbs
caster sugar (US: granulated)	30ml	2tbs	2tbs

Mix the 20ml (1 heaped tbs) sugar with the port and soak the slices of bread in it.

Beat the eggs and pour into a shallow dish. Carefully dip the bread in the beaten eggs, coating both sides well. Melt the butter in a large frying pan and fry the bread on both sides until golden brown. Serve the *rabanadas* warm with a generous sprinkling of sugar and cinnamon, mixed together.

Pudim jabuticaba
JABUTICABA BREAD PUDDING

The plum-like jabuticaba is a Brazilian fruit and can be layered with bread and baked in a creamy custard to make a delicious variation of *rabanadas*. Blackberries, although not as delicate in flavour, make a suitable substitute.

jabuticaba	600ml	1 pint	2¹/₂ cups
OR			
blackberries	600ml	1 pint	2¹/₂ cups
white bread, slices, without crusts	8–10	8–10	8–10
double cream (US: whipping)	300ml	¹/₂ pint	1¹/₄ cups
milk	150ml	¹/₄ pint	¹/₂ cup
sugar	100g	4oz	¹/₂ cup
eggs	3	3	3
egg yolk	1	1	1
vanilla essence (extract)	10ml	2tsp	2tsp
zest of orange	1	1	1
icing sugar (US: confectioner's)	30ml	2tbs	2tbs

Generously butter a 2 pint/1 litre oven dish, or for a festive effect, butter a ring mould. Cut each slice of bread into quarters. In a bowl whisk together the eggs and the extra egg yolk, milk, cream, sugar, orange zest and vanilla essence. Line the dish or mould with a layer of bread, followed by a layer of fruit and half the egg mixture.

Repeat until all the ingredients are used and the bread is well soaked in custard.

Bake at 190°C/375°F for about 50 minutes until well set.

If cooked in a mould, turn out and serve dusted with icing sugar and decorated with fresh fruit.

Bôlo de nozes
NUT CAKE WITH CHOCOLATE COFFEE FILLING

This has a rich chocolate and coffee filling and is best made and eaten on the same day.

Cake

walnuts, ground to a powder	175g	6oz	³/₄ cup
OR			
hazelnuts, ground to a powder	175g	6oz	³/₄ cup
eggs, separated	6	6	6
caster sugar (US: granulated)	175g	6oz	³/₄ cup
self-raising flour	50g	2oz	¹/₂ cup

Beat the egg yolks and caster sugar until very light. Mix the flour and finely-ground nuts together before folding into the egg mixture. Whisk the egg whites with a balloon whisk until very stiff. Gently fold into the egg mixture.

Pour into two well-greased and preferably lined cake tins and bake for 30–35 minutes in the centre of the oven at 190°C (375°F). When cooked allow to cool before removing from the tins.

Filling

plain bitter chocolate	225g	8oz	8oz
double or whipping cream	225ml	8fl oz	1 cup
instant coffee, dissolved in water	30ml 15ml	2tbs 1tbs	2tbs 1tbs
eggs, separated	2	2	2

Melt the chocolate in a double boiler. Add the instant coffee and beat in the egg yolks one at a time. Remove from the heat and allow to cool while you whisk the egg whites and beat the cream. When cool, fold in the cream and the egg whites. Use as a filling and topping for the cake.

BARBADOS

Barbados *is a tropical island set in the emerald of the Caribbean. There can be few people who, in the middle of a cold, seemingly endless, grey winter haven't longed to escape to such a place. Yet for some, Christmas wouldn't seem right without snow, holly, frosty nights and candles. So what would it really be like to celebrate it basking in sunshine, with the Caribbean gently lapping at your toes?*

For the Bajans Christmas is a time of great festivity. In the days of the British Empire their island was deservedly called the 'brightest jewel in the English crown'. Being a British colony for more than three centuries means that the English traditions are quite strong but not dominant. Dutch, African, American and Portuguese influences have all contributed to making a unique Bajan culture.

Christmas in Barbados means new curtains, and probably new covers on the lounge suite too. Fortunately the curtains are light nets and readily renewed. It is not uncommon to repaint the house both inside and out in preparation for Christmas. Thus there is a grand early spring clean all over the island in readiness for the big day. It is also a family occasion and those living abroad try to get home to share the festivities.

The Bajans are very community-minded and, if it is known that a family is suffering hardship at Christmas, a chicken and a few gifts will mysteriously be left on the doorstep.

Church plays an important role in the life of the Bajans, and on Christmas morning the churches are packed for the 5 a.m. services. People celebrate this happy festival by wearing new outfits. Everyone gets at least one, and on Christmas morning Bajans can be seen walking to and from church looking immaculate. After church most young people congregate in Queen's Park to hear the Royal Police Band perform.

Back home willing hands help prepare lunch. An egg-nog helps to keep hunger at bay. The overwhelming impression of a Bajan Christmas meal is the abundance of food. Dishes of yam pie, potato, avocado, green and beet salads, roast chicken, 'doved peas' (rice, bacon and green peas) and baked ham are crammed buffet-style on the table. The central meat dishes are usually chicken or turkey and glazed ham, baked with ginger and pineapple. This is nearly always served with the traditional Christmas *jug-jug*, a dish aptly described as a Caribbean haggis. There is a theory that *jug-jug* was an attempt by seventeenth-century Scottish exiles on Barbados to recreate the haggis of their homeland. It is equally possible that it is an 'unevolved' Christmas pudding because it bears great similarities to 'plum porridge', the forerunner of the British Christmas pudding.

Another delicacy, fried flying fish, if obtainable, is served separately at a side table.

There is a loaf or two of coconut bread on the table, jugs of rosy sorrel drink and perhaps a potent rum punch.

For dessert there is a selection of ice-creams such as mango, coconut or vanilla, fresh fruit salad, mince pies and Christmas cake. This is a very dark, moist cake, heavy with rum-soaked fruit, almost like a pudding.

The table cloth is a festive one—not that you can see very much of it under the laden table. The Bajan hostess only has to step outside to gather an armful of frangipani, poinsettia and hibiscus to make a flamboyant centre-piece for her table.

Although the meal is served buffet-style, after helping themselves everyone sits down around the table to eat and chat.

Lunch is an extended affair when everyone

somehow finds room for just another little portion. Finally there comes a point when, suitably satiated, there is a drift to the sparkling, newly decorated sitting room.

In the corner of the room there is a Christmas tree, usually an artificial one as real trees have to be imported and are consequently very expensive. The tree is decorated a few days before Christmas with tinsel, glitter and baubles. The family exchanges gifts and sits and catches up on family news. This is a lovely relaxed time.

The younger set sit and gossip and then get ready to go to one of the many house parties or 'fêtes'. This is an opportunity to wear another new outfit and to dance away the night to the rhythm of a steel band.

Most homes have 'open house' on Christmas evening for friends to pop in and sample a bit of Christmas fare, exchange greetings, gossip and 'lick-back' the rum, chased with a soft drink and soaked up by coconut bread.

A century or so ago this relaxed scene would have been interrupted by an itinerant band of 'scrubbers'. For instruments these bands of three or four minstrels would use an ordinary comb covered with tissue paper, a tin whistle or a guitar, all of which were played with more enthusiasm than skill. In return for their vivacity (or to get rid of them) they received a drink and a bit of Christmas fare. Today scrubbing is hardly known but you still find itinerant 'tuk' bands around at Christmas time.

Boxing Day (26 December) is a day for families and friends to pack a huge picnic basket with food left over from the previous day and to head for one of the beautiful beaches encircling the island. There they will meet to discuss the previous evening's fêtes, play beach cricket or just laze in the sun.

The Bajans have an endearing way of repeating adjectives to place emphasis on something and it would be fair to say that Christmas in Barbados is fun, fun fun! With characteristic generosity and in the true spirit of Christmas, the Bajans ensure that the fun is shared by all.

A BAJAN
CHRISTMAS DAY
LUNCH

ASSORTED SALADS

FRIED FLYING FISH

~

GLAZED HAM WITH GINGER
AND PINEAPPLE

ROAST CHILLI CHICKEN

CARIBBEAN HAGGIS
Jug-jug

DOVED PEAS

COCONUT BREAD

~

MANGO SHERBET

or
COCONUT ICE-CREAM

and
EXOTIC FRUIT SALAD WITH RUM CREAM

Fried flying fish

A side dish of flying fish is a highlight of the Bajan Christmas table.

filleted fish (substitute whiting or haddock)	4	4	4
juice of 3 limes or lemons			
pinch of thyme			
egg, beaten	1	1	1
generous pinch of chilli powder			
generous pinch of ground ginger			
flour	50g	2oz	1/2 cup
salt and pepper to taste			
oil for frying			

Marinade the fish fillets in the lime juice and thyme for 20 minutes while you mix the flour and seasonings. Pat dry, dip the fillets in the beaten egg, toss in seasoned flour and fry in hot oil for 3–4 minutes each side until golden brown and crisp.

Glazed ham with ginger and pineapple

This dish makes a glossy, succulent centre-piece to the Christmas table.

ham, soaked overnight	4.5–5kg	10lb	10lb
carrots	2	2	2
whole onions	2	2	2
peppercorns	10	10	10
bay leaves	3	3	3

Wash the ham well, then place in a pot with enough water (or half-beer, half-water) to cover the above ingredients. Simmer for $4^1/_2$ hours until tender. Preheat the oven to 180° C (350° F/Gas 4).

Remove the skin and score the fat underneath it. Stud decoratively with cloves and glaze with the following:

Glaze			
pineapple syrup	125ml	$4^1/_2$ fl oz	1/3 cup
brown sugar	100g	4oz	1/2 cup
ground ginger	10ml	2tsp	2tsp
tinned pineapple slices	10	10	10
sweet red pepper	1	1	1
slivers of ginger, optional			

Melt the pineapple syrup reserved from the tin, the brown sugar and the ground ginger in a pan over a low heat. Pour over the ham and bake for 40 minutes, basting whenever you think of it. About 5 minutes before it is ready, add the pineapple slices, and the red pepper cut into strips. Serve the ham, crisp and glossy, garnished with the pineapple, red pepper slices and, if you like, slivers of ginger.

Roast chilli chicken

When there is going to be a big family gathering a Bajan hostess will often serve a plump spicy chicken such as this in addition to the ham.

roasting chicken	2–2.5kg	4–5lb	4–5lb
lemon	1	1	1
butter	50g	2oz	1/2 stick

ground chilli (or sweet paprika, which is milder)	2ml	1/2 tsp	1/2 tsp
clove garlic, pressed	1	1	1
ground coriander	2ml	1/2 tsp	1/2 tsp
salt and pepper to taste			

Clean the chicken and rub with the quartered lemon and season with salt and pepper. (Don't throw away the quartered lemon, instead pop it inside the chicken cavity.)

Mix the chilli, garlic and coriander with the butter. Smear over the bird. Roast in a roasting tin (pan) (on its back is best).

Use a cooking time of 20 minutes per 500g (1lb). At the end, turn the bird over and add an extra 15 minutes to give the skin a chance to crisp. To check if it is done pierce the thigh and the juices should run clear.

Jug-jug
CARIBBEAN HAGGIS

Whether you think this dish is an 'unevolved' Christmas pudding or an 'evolved' haggis, serve it as an accompaniment to ham or roast chicken.

Pigeon peas, also known as gungo peas, are sold either canned or dried. If you are using dried peas, soak them overnight before using.

lean pork or chicken, cut into large chunks	50g	2oz	1/4 cup
salt beef, cut into large chunks	50g	2oz	1/4 cup
pigeon peas	225g	8oz	1 cup
large onion, finely chopped	1	1	1
sprig of parsley, finely chopped	1	1	1

spring onions (green onions), bulbs and blades	2	2	2
bunch of mixed herbs OR mixed dried herbs	5ml	1tsp	1tsp
salt and ground black pepper to taste			
pinch of chilli (optional)			
millet	25g	1oz	2tbs
butter	25g	1oz	2tbs

Bring the pork or chicken to the boil in enough salted water to cover. Add the salt beef. Reduce the heat and simmer covered for 30 minutes. If you are using fresh pigeon peas, add these to the meats and cook until they are soft. (If you are using canned peas, add only when the meats are cooked and then cook only for a further 5 minutes to heat through.) Strain, reserving the stock.

Return the pan of stock to the heat and add the chopped onion, spring onions, parsley, herbs and the millet. Season to taste. Cook this over a low heat for about 10–15 minutes, stirring constantly.

Mince the meat and pea mixture, add to the pan and cook for a further 15–20 minutes until the jug-jug is fairly stiff. Check the seasoning. Stir in half the butter and spoon the jug-jug into a serving dish. Spread the rest of the butter over the top and serve piping hot.

Doved peas

A Bajan cook would use pigeon (Gungo) peas for this dish. They are available dried but they must be soaked overnight before using. Regular green peas, while not traditional, make an agreeable substitute.

fresh pigeon peas or green peas	275g	10oz	1 1/4 cups
bacon rashers (slices) or ham slices, chopped	4	4	4

small onion, finely chopped	1	1	1
red pepper, finely chopped	1/2	1/2	1/2
clove garlic, pressed	1	1	1
cooked rice	225g	8oz	1 cup
butter	50g	2oz	1/2 stick
generous pinch of marjoram			
salt and pepper to taste			

Cook the peas in lightly salted water until tender, reserve the water.

In a frying pan heat half the butter, add the chopped ham or bacon, onion, red pepper, garlic, marjoram and salt and pepper. When nicely browned stir in the peas, water and rice. Leave to simmer until the water has evaporated.

Stir in the remaining butter and serve with the Christmas turkey or ham.

Coconut bread

This is a sweet bread with a lovely nutty texture. This recipe makes 2 loaves.

plain flour	350g	12oz	3 cups
baking powder	15ml	1tsp	1tsp
salt	5ml	1tsp	1tsp
sugar	150g	5oz	3/4 cup
fresh coconut, finely grated	225g	8oz	1 cup
melted unsalted butter	100g	4oz	1 stick
vanilla essence (extract)	5ml	1tsp	1tsp

milk and coconut water	150ml	5fl oz	1/2 cup
egg, well beaten	1	1	1

Sift the flour, baking powder and salt. Stir in the sugar and coconut. Add the rest of the ingredients and mix thoroughly. The mixture will be very wet. Fill two well-greased loaf tins two-thirds full. Before baking, sprinkle the tops of the loaves with sugar. Bake for 50–60 minutes at 180°C (350°F/Gas 4). Allow the loaves to cool a little before turning out on a rack.

Mango sherbet

A refreshing and exotic note on which to end a meal.

mango pulp	600ml	1 pint	2 1/2 cups
gelatine	15ml	1tbs	1tbs
lime juice	45ml	3tbs	3tbs
caster sugar (US: granulated)	100g	4oz	1/2 cup
egg white	1	1	1

Sieve the mango pulp. Sprinkle the gelatine on a little cold water then dissolve over a low heat. Allow to cool before adding the mango purée, lime juice and sugar. Freeze until syrupy then beat until light and fluffy. Gently fold in the very stiffly beaten egg white and freeze again.

The sherbet is best removed from the freezer 5 minutes before serving.

Coconut ice-cream

Coconuts are plentiful in Barbados and often feature in cooking. Here coconut is used to make a wonderful, creamy ice-cream that is a perfect contrast to the more tangy mango sherbet. If you can get hold of a fresh coconut, use the freshly grated flesh in preference to the desiccated kind.

desiccated coconut (shredded or flaked)	175g	6oz	3/4 cup
double cream (US: whipping)	450ml	3/4 pint	2 cups
milk	450ml	3/4 pint	2 cups
gelatine	15g	1/2 oz	1tbs
caster sugar (US: granulated)	100g	4oz	1/2 cup
pinch of cream of tartar			
coconut, for toasting	30ml	2tbs	2tbs
icing sugar (confectioner's sugar)	15ml	1tbs	1tbs

Put the milk and 150ml (1/4 pint/1/2 cup) of the cream into a saucepan. Add the coconut and heat but do not boil. Remove from the heat and leave to stand for 15 minutes. Dissolve the gelatine in 45ml (3tbs) of water over a low heat. Add the gelatine, sugar and a pinch of cream of tartar to the coconut milk. Liquidize or blend in a food processor for a minute or so. Then sieve the milk into a bowl, pressing out as much flavour as you can from the coconut. Leave to stand until cold and thick. Whisk the remaining 300ml (1/2 pint) of cream until stiff. Lightly whisk the coconut mixture to get rid of any lumps and then gently fold in the whipped cream. Pour into a lightly oiled 1 litre (2 pint) pudding basin or mould and freeze for several hours.

Transfer the ice-cream from the freezer to the refrigerator an hour before required. Mix the icing sugar and coconut and spread on a baking sheet. Toast in the oven at 160°C (325°F/Gas 3) until golden brown. Sprinkle over the ice-cream before serving.

Exotic fruit salad with rum cream

The black granadilla pips make a delightful contrast to the coral pinks and yellows of the other fruits. Deliciously wicked served with a dollop of rum cream or a scoop of coconut ice-cream.

Fruit salad

papaya	1	1	1
OR			
paw-paw	1/2	1/2	1/2
granadillas (passion fruit)	2	2	2
oranges	2	2	2
bananas	2	2	2
juice of half a lime			

Slice the papaya (or paw-paw) in half and discard the pulpy centre and pips. Peel. Cut into chunks and put into a serving bowl. Slice the granadillas in half and using a teaspoon scoop the pulp into a bowl. Quarter the oranges and slice the fruit into chunks, add together with the sliced bananas.

Finally squeeze the juice of 1/2 a lime over the salad. Gently mix with a large spoon so as not to damage the soft papaya flesh and serve with rum cream.

Rum Cream

double or whipping cream	150ml	1/4 pint	1/2 cup
caster sugar (US: granulated)	30ml	2tbs	2tbs
rum (depending on how wicked you feel)	15–30ml	1–2tbs	1–2tbs

Whip the cream until fairly stiff then whip in first the caster sugar, one tablespoon at a time, then the rum.

~ EXTRA RECIPES ~

Egg-nog

This is a popular drink to serve while waiting for the Christmas lunch.

eggs, separated	6	6	6
sugar	225g	8oz	1 cup
milk	300ml	1/2 pint	1 1/4 cups
cognac	100ml	4fl oz	1/2 cup
rum	150ml	1/4 pint	1/2 cup
double cream (US: whipping)	300ml	1/2 pint	1 1/4 cups
grated rind of 1 orange			
grated rind of 1 lime			
pinch of freshly grated nutmeg			

Whisk the egg yolks and sugar until light and creamy. Stir in the milk, cognac and rum. Fold in the stiffly beaten egg whites and chill for a couple of hours. Before serving fold in the cream and the lime and orange rinds and serve with a grating of nutmeg.

Sorrel drink

This is always served at Christmas parties. The sepals of the sorrel plant from which it is made mature at this time of year in Barbados.

sorrel sepals	350g	12oz	1 1/2 cups
OR			
sorrel syrup made up according to the label (obtainable from West Indian grocers)			

fresh ginger root, crushed	25g	1oz	2tbs
cloves	2–3	2–3	2–3
sugar	450g	1lb	2 cups
boiling water	2.25 litres	4 pints	10 cups
dried orange peel	10ml	2tsp	2tsp
dark rum	175ml	6fl oz	3/4 cup

Wash the sorrel and put it into a jug with the ginger, cloves, peel and sugar. Pour the boiling water over and allow to stand overnight or longer. Strain through a fine sieve. Add the rum and chill well before serving.

Rum punch

In 1731, because of discipline problems, Admiral Vernon of the British navy ordered all rum rations to be diluted. The admiral in question was nicknamed 'Old Grog' because he always wore a grogram cloak. The new drink was called 'grog'. Today in the West Indies you still 'fire a grog'. Here is a recipe to help you do the same.

One of sour (one part fresh lime juice)
Two of sweet (two parts sugar)
Three of strong (three parts rum)
Four of weak (four parts ice and water)

Serve with a dash of angostura bitters over crushed ice and with a suitably festive cherry.

MEXICO

Based on an Aztec relic.

Mexico *is the land of fiestas and none is more important than the one at Christmas. The word* fiesta *literally means 'feast', and feast the Mexicans certainly do!*

The preparation for Christmas begins with Advent, when each household lights the first red candle in the Advent ring made of ivy that sits on their dining table. Each Sunday another is lit until all four are alight by Christmas Eve.

The real excitement begins when the markets fill up with Christmas fare at the end of the first week in December. Little clay figures from the nativity story can be bought, for each family has its own large and beautiful nativity scene (*nacimiento*) at home. There are toys in abundance as well as flowers, sweets, baskets, cakes, nuts and crystallized fruit.

Most important and most colourful of all are the *piñatas*. These are large containers made of clay and covered with papier mâché shaped and decorated to resemble animals (such as pandas and lions), stars, rockets, cradles, planes and other objects. Inside each *piñata* are sweets, peanuts, *jícamas* (sweet fruit) and mandarin oranges. Each family buys a *piñata* to be opened when it is their turn to hold a *posada*.

For nine days—from December 16th to Christmas Eve—the *posadas* are held. *Posada* means 'lodging' and *posadas* are parties which commemorate the journey of Mary and Joseph from Nazareth to Bethlehem and their search for a place to stay. Each family has a turn to hold a *posada* to which their friends and relatives are invited. Many people go to a different house each night and both adults and children take part. Before holding a *posada*, the house is decorated with Spanish moss and Canadian pine, and with Christmas embroideries in flamboyant Mexican colours. Poinsettias enliven every room with their bright red colouring and beautiful candles are put on the window-sills.

As soon as it is dark, at about 6 or 7 o'clock, a procession of guests, each holding a candle, is led by two children carrying a nativity scene with clay figures of Mary, Jesus and Joseph on a litter. Singing all the way they arrive at the house where the party is to be held.

'Joseph' then sings a request for lodging. Traditionally, the man of the house (the 'inn-keeper') tells them to go away, that everyone is asleep and that he will beat them if they don't go. Eventually, when he realizes the importance of the travellers, he opens his door and there is great rejoicing. Once inside, there are prayers and more songs in front of the nativity scene.

The children ask their hostess for sweets by reciting comical poems to her, then the refreshments are served. The food is kept relatively simple. There may be savoury and sweet *tamales* (corn dumplings served in the husk) with *atole*— a sweet drink similar to a thick milk shake. Other dishes popular with old and young alike are *tacos* (filled *tortillas*) or *enchiladas* (*tortillas* dipped in a sauce and then lightly fried before being filled). *Tortillas* are rather like pancakes but made with white maize flour (*masa harina* or Mexican cornflour). This flour has been specially treated with lime and ordinary cornflour doesn't give the same results. *Tortillas* are either soft or crunchy, depending on how they are cooked. Unfilled, they replace bread at the table, and filled they are the basis for many Mexican meals. *Ponche* (fruit punch) is often drunk with *tortillas* and the children may have drinks coloured a bright pink with pomegranate juice.

After the food comes dancing and then the part the children have been looking forward to all evening—the breaking of the *piñata*. The

piñata is suspended on a thick cord held by two people and the children form a queue. Blindfolded, the first child is spun around to make him or her dizzy and is then allowed several attempts to break open the *piñata* with a stick. Usually all the children have had at least one go before it finally bursts open to release a flood of goodies for them.

Throughout the nine days of joyful celebration before Christmas, the streets of the towns are alive with gaiety. Roast chestnuts are on sale, as are huge brightly-coloured balloons decorated with spots and stripes. The street decorations include coloured lights and large ornaments hung above the roads. December 23rd, 24th and 25th are public holidays in Mexico.

Christmas Eve is the most important day of the Christmas period. On that morning the children wake as excited as anywhere in the world. Breakfast is as usual: egg with beans and ham or bacon accompanied by sweet bread or *tortillas* with coffee. The morning is spent preparing for the special meal in the evening and lunch is a minor event, perhaps with some soup, a little meat and some fruit. The Christmas Eve *posada* is particularly special and some people even dress up in national costume. As this night is the night of the nativity, a special song is sung and half an hour before midnight nine 'Ave Marias' are said. Someone is chosen to be the 'godfather' of Jesus and places a figure of the Christ child in the manger of the nativity scene. Sometimes the smallest children are dressed as shepherds and they stand by the manger as the figure of Jesus is placed there and then sung to sleep.

After midnight mass the streets explode with excitement. Fireworks light the night sky, church bells ring loudly and people blow little tin whistles, dance and sing.

Now is the time for the Christmas dinner and even the smallest children stay up. Families who haven't been to church may have their meal earlier, at around 10.30. The table looks festive, with the Advent ring alight with its four candles and with flowers—especially poinsettias—everywhere.

A favourite starter is *sopa de frijol* (bean soup). This can be followed by either *bacalao* or *romeritos*, or both. *Bacalao* is dried salted cod and is cooked for Christmas in a tomato sauce with chillies, olives and potatoes. A popular dish—sometimes known as *revoltijo*—is *romeritos* (the leaves of a rosemary-like plant) cooked in chilli sauce with shrimps and prickly pear.

Next on the menu is turkey. This can be roasted with a stuffing made from beef mincemeat or almonds and raisins, and served with courgettes (*zucchini*), peppers and corn (*calabacitas con rajas y elote*). Alternatively, the turkey can be cooked with a chocolate and chilli sauce—a dish called *mole poblano*—perhaps Mexico's most famous dish, best accompanied by *tortillas* and rice. Turkey was first brought to Europe by the Spaniards, who discovered it in 1519 in Mexico. *Ensalada navideña* (Mexican Christmas salad) is a traditional accompaniment and makes a festive-looking dish with the pink from the beetroot mixed with the colours of the fruit, nuts and

lettuce, and avocado dip (*guacamole*) is a must. To finish the meal there may be meringues, chocolate cake, fresh fruit, *buñuelos* or *mueganos* (fried *tortillas* or sweet puffs with muscovado sugar syrup) or *capirotada* (Mexican bread pudding). Throughout the meal, the wine, tequila (a spirit distilled from a succulent plant) or fruit juice flow.

Santa Claus has been coming to Mexico for more than twenty years but he doesn't yet call at all the homes. He leaves presents at midnight on Christmas Eve and puts them around the Christmas tree. Mexico has large areas of forest, so there is no shortage of real trees to decorate the homes, though some people prefer an artificial tree. On the tree are little dolls made from wood, straw and felt, together with coloured lights and lots of angel hair.

When Christmas Day dawns, the children are up bright and early to open their presents. Today is a day for visiting friends and no special meals are prepared, though there will probably be many good things left over from the *posadas*. December 26th is not a holiday in Mexico.

On 6 January, Epiphany, the churches are alight with candles and bursting with the sound of music. Epiphany is the time when some children find gifts of sweets left by the wise men under the Christmas tree. Later in the day the tree is taken down.

The person elected 'godfather' to Jesus at Christmas gives a party at his house today. A special cake is bought (or, occasionally, made at home) called a *Rosca de Reyes* (three kings' ring). During the afternoon friends and family gather to eat a slice of this sweet, spiced fruit bread and to drink coffee, hot chocolate or limeade. To commemorate the gifts taken by the wise men to the infant Jesus, some special surprises are hidden inside the cake. There is a ring, a coin, and crystallized fruits to represent jewels. The baby is represented by a small china or plastic doll (*el niño*). If your slice contains the ring, tradition says there will be a wedding in the family. The coin is supposed to foretell good luck and prosperity during the coming year. If you get the doll, however, you must give another party for everyone present on Friendship Day, 2 February.

Throughout the festive season Mexicans remember the grudging way in which Jesus was found a place to stay, and now welcome him and each other with joy and celebration.

A MEXICAN
CHRISTMAS SUPPER

SOPA DE FRIJOL
Bean soup

~

BACALAO A LA VIZCAINA
Salted cod with potatoes, olives and peppers in tomato sauce

and/or

REVOLTIJO
Romeritos in chilli sauce with shrimps and prickly pear

~

MOLE POBLANO
Turkey in chilli and chocolate sauce

ENSALADA NAVIDEÑA
Mexican Christmas salad

GUACAMOLE
Avocado dip

RICE

TORTILLAS

~

FRESH FRUIT/MERINGUES/
CHOCOLATE CAKE

BUÑUELOS, SOPAIPILLAS OR MUEGANOS
Deep-fried tortillas or sweet puffs with muscovado syrup

CAPIROTADA
Mexican bread pudding

Sopa de frijol
BEAN SOUP

Beans are an essential part of Mexican cooking. This recipe uses red kidney beans, but you could use whichever beans are your particular favourite, and tinned beans are fine. If you can't get fresh coriander, use parsley instead.

oil	15ml	1tbs	1tbs
small onion, chopped	1	1	1
garlic clove, crushed	1	1	1
cooked beans	425g	15oz	1³/₄ cups
chicken stock	600ml	1 pint	2¹/₂ cups
tomato purée	15ml	1tbs	1tbs
fresh green chilli, chopped	1	1	1
fresh coriander leaves, chopped	60ml	4tbs	4tbs
pinch of salt			
pinch of black pepper			
pinch of sugar			

Heat the oil in a large saucepan and gently fry the onion and garlic until softened. Add the remaining ingredients, reserving 30ml (2tbs) of the coriander leaves, and bring to the boil. Simmer for 20 minutes. Pass through a sieve or blend till smooth, and serve sprinkled with coriander.

Bacalao a la vizaina
SALTED COD WITH POTATOES, OLIVES AND PEPPERS IN TOMATO SAUCE

This dish is Spanish in origin and is often served on Christmas Eve. Its base is a home-made tomato sauce, which is the base of most Mexican sauces. Hot chillies aren't usually used with fish in Mexico. Use instead the long, pale, mild chillies. You can make the sauce in advance and freeze it to save time on Christmas Eve.

Bacalao

salted cod from a good fishmonger or a West Indian food shop	275g	10oz	10oz
butter	50g	2oz	¹/₂ stick
oil	15ml	1tbs	1tbs
onion, finely sliced	¹/₂	¹/₂	¹/₂
red pepper, finely sliced	1	1	1
stuffed green olives, sliced	15	15	15
tomato sauce (see below)	250ml	9fl oz	1 cup
tomato purée	15ml	1tbs	1tbs
new potatoes, cooked and diced	225g	8oz	1¹/₂ cups
pinch of dried oregano			
pinch of sugar			

Soak the fish for 8 hours or overnight in cold water, drain and cover with fresh cold water, then bring to the boil. Simmer for 15 minutes then discard the water and cover with more water. Simmer again for 15 minutes then drain and cool. Flake the fish as finely as possible, removing the bones. Heat the butter and oil in a frying pan and cook the onion and red pepper for 3 minutes, then add the fish and remaining ingredients, mixing well. Cover and simmer for 5 minutes. Serve hot.

Salsa para enchiladas *Tomato sauce*

cooking oil	30ml	2tbs	2tbs
onion, finely chopped	1	1	1
cloves garlic, crushed	2	2	2
mild chillies, long, pale green	4	4	4
tomatoes, peeled (drop them in boiling water to split the skins)	900g	2lb	4 cups
tomato purée	45ml	3tbs	3tbs
capers	45ml	3tbs	3tbs
sprigs fresh coriander	4	4	4
chicken stock cubes	2	2	2
pinch of freshly ground black pepper			
pinch of sugar			

Heat the oil in a frying pan (a heavy-based one will help prevent the tomato sauce from burning) and sauté the onion, garlic and chillies until the onion is soft. Squash the tomatoes with a potato masher and add to the pan with the remaining ingredients. Simmer for 20 minutes. When the chillies are a dull green colour and the mixture has thickened, the sauce is ready. Discard the chillies and the sprigs of coriander.

Revoltijo
ROMERITOS IN CHILLI SAUCE WITH SHRIMPS AND PRICKLY PEAR

This is a traditional dish for Christmas Eve in Mexico. *Romeritos* is similar to the rosemary bush in appearance but its leaves are softer and shrink to almost nothing when cooked. You can copy this recipe using spinach instead of *romeritos*. Mexican shops are full of *romeritos* around Christmas time. Dried shrimps are available from Chinese or Indian shops. *Nopales* are the little 'paddles' from the prickly pear and must, of course, have their sharp thorns removed. They are boiled before being used in the recipe. You can sometimes find canned *nopales*, or your greengrocer may be able to order them for you (but take care that they have not been bruised during their long journey). French beans make an acceptable substitute.

romeritos or finely chopped spinach	450g	1lb	2 cups
water	300ml	1/2 pint	1 1/4 cups
nopales or cooked French beans	300g	11oz	1 1/2 cups
salt	30ml	2tbs	2tbs
pinch of bicarbonate of soda (baking soda)			
dried shrimps	100g	4oz	1/2 cup
egg white	1	1	1
oil	15ml	1tbs	1tbs
recipe dried chilli sauce (salsa adobada), see below	1	1	1
new potatoes, peeled, boiled and quartered	225g	8oz	1 1/2 cups

Clean the *romeritos*, removing any roots. Wash and boil with the water in a pan for 10 minutes. Drain and squeeze. If using spinach, cook for 5 minutes in only the water clinging to its leaves after washing.

Cut the *nopales* into 12mm ($^{1}/_{2}$ in.) squares. Soak in plenty of water with the salt for 3 hours. Drain and wash under running water. Cover with plenty of water in a large pan and bring to the boil. Add a pinch of bicarbonate of soda and simmer for 20 minutes until tender, skimming frequently. Drain.

Clean the dried shrimps, discarding the shells, heads and whiskers, then blend or pound until smooth. Whisk the egg white until stiff, then fold in the shrimps. Heat the oil in a frying pan and fry the shrimp mixture, 15ml (1tbs) at a time, turning each patty once. Drain and keep warm. Heat the chilli sauce and add the *romeritos* or spinach, *nopales*, shrimp patties and potatoes. Bring slowly to the boil and serve hot.

Salsa adobada *Dried chilli sauce*

This makes a good barbecue sauce and is the sauce needed for *revoltijo*. It can also be used as an easy version of the sauce for *mole poblano*, the well known Mexican celebration dish of turkey in chilli and chocolate sauce. Added to potato and chorizo sausage in a *tortilla* it makes a tasty snack. Its dark red colour comes from the dried chillies and the chocolate serves only to sweeten and darken it slightly.

cloves garlic	3	3	3
cinnamon stick	1	1	1
large onion, chopped	1	1	1
cooking oil	30ml	2tbs	2tbs
tomato purée	75ml	3fl oz	1/4 cup
chicken stock	750ml	1 1/4 pints	2 1/2 cups
plain chocolate, grated	15ml	1tbs	1tbs
mole powder (a special sort of chilli powder) OR	75ml	3fl oz	1/4 cup
chilli powder	45ml	3tbs	3tbs
sugar	2ml	1/2 tsp	1/2 tsp

Put the garlic, cinnamon and onion in a blender and blend to a paste, or use a pestle and mortar if you have no blender. Heat the oil in a large pan and add the onion paste. Cook, stirring constantly, for about 5 minutes. Add the remaining ingredients and simmer until the sauce thickens—about 20 minutes.

Ensalada navideña
MEXICAN CHRISTMAS SALAD

This attractive red, white and green salad combines fruit and nuts with lettuce and beetroot and looks festive for the Christmas Eve supper. The *jícama* (a turnip-shaped tuber with juicy, sweet, white flesh and brown skin) is sometimes available from good greengrocers. Acceptable alternatives are water chestnuts or even tart green cooking apples.

Webb's (crisp) lettuce, very finely chopped	1/2	1/2	1/2
small cooked beetroot, sliced thinly	4	4	4
large orange peeled and thinly sliced, with the pith removed	1	1	1
red apple, thinly sliced	1	1	1
ripe bananas, sliced	2	2	2
jícama, peeled, sliced and cut into small pieces	1	1	1
peanuts, shelled	50g	2oz	1/4 cup
pine nuts or flaked almonds	15g	1/2 oz	1tbs
juice of 1 lemon			
sweet sherry	150ml	1/4 pint	1/2 cup
pinch of salt			
pinch of cayenne pepper			

On a bed of lettuce on a large flat dish arrange all the vegetables and fruit in circles of colour. Garnish with the peanuts and pine nuts. Mix the lemon juice and sherry with the salt and spoon it over the salad. Sprinkle with cayenne pepper.

Guacamole

AVOCADO DIP

Guacamole is hugely popular in Mexico, where avocado pears have been cultivated since 7000BC. The mashed avocado flesh is flavoured with tomatoes, onions and chilli or green pepper, and accompanies the Christmas turkey. Ripe avocados which yield to the touch are the best. Encourage an over-firm fruit to ripen by putting it in a brown paper bag for a day or two.

juice of 1/2 lime or lemon			
tomatoes, finely chopped	2	2	2
onion, finely chopped	15ml	1tbs	1tbs
fresh green chillies, deseeded and finely chopped	2	2	2
salt	2ml	1/2 tsp	1/2 tsp
black pepper			
avocados	2	2	2

Squeeze the juice from the lime or lemon and put into a bowl. Add the tomatoes, onion, chillies, salt and some black pepper. Peel the avocados and remove the stones, then mash the flesh and add to the other ingredients. This is best done last as the flesh tends to blacken on exposure to the air, but lemon or lime juice helps preserve the colour. Mix well and either serve at once or cover tightly with plastic food wrap until needed.

Buñuelos, Sopaipillas or Mueganos

DEEP-FRIED TORTILLAS OR SWEET PUFFS WITH MUSCOVADO SYRUP

On Christmas Day these sweetmeats are sold in Mexico City's main square. The first person to buy is wished 'Good luck' and in return replies 'May you sell plenty'. You can make *buñuelos* by deep-frying *tortillas* (see recipe on page 273), and pouring muscovado syrup (see below) over them. Large sweet puffs are popular in the United States, where they are known in 'Tex-Mex' language as *sopaipillas*. Smaller puffs, popular in Mexico, are called *mueganos*. This recipe is for *sopaipillas*. Remember to make the dough shapes at least 2 hours before you wish to fry them.

Batter			
plain flour	75g	3oz	3/4 cup
baking powder	5ml	1tsp	1tsp
pinch of salt			
lard	15g	1/2 oz	1tbs
warm water	50ml	2fl oz	3tbs
oil for deep frying			

Syrup			
muscovado sugar (unrefined)	225g	8oz	1 cup
water	150ml	1/4 pint	1/2 cup
cinnamon stick	1	1	1
rind and juice of 1 orange			

Sift the flour, baking powder and salt into a bowl and rub in the lard. Add the warm water to make a dough. Knead till smooth. Roll the dough out on a floured board to about 2mm (1/8 in.) thick and cut into rectangles about 5 x 7.5cm (2in. x 3in.). Put the shapes on to waxed paper and cool in the fridge for 2 hours.

Make the syrup by heating the ingredients together in a pan and simmering for 5 minutes. Remove the cinnamon stick and keep the syrup warm. Heat the oil in a deep-sided pan to 190°C (375°F) and deep-fry one shape at a time until puffed and golden. Drain on kitchen paper and keep warm in the oven while you cook the other shapes.

Pour the syrup over the puffs and serve.

Capirotada
BREAD PUDDING

Many Mexicans enjoy this sweet and simple pudding at Christmas time.

firm white bread	350g	12oz	2 cups
butter	100g	4oz	1 stick
apples	3	3	3
raisins	175g	6oz	3/4 cup
almonds, chopped	100g	4oz	1/2 cup
Cheddar cheese coarsely grated	225g	8oz	1 cup

Syrup

brown sugar	450g	1lb	2 cups
cinnamon stick	1/2	1/2	1/2
cloves	2	2	2
water	1 litre	1 3/4 pints	4 cups

Cut the bread into 1.5cm (3/4 in.) cubes. Melt the butter in a large frying pan and toss the cubes in the melted butter until golden brown. Peel, core and slice the apples thinly. Grease an ovenproof dish with butter and build up alternate layers of bread cubes and of apple slices, raisins, almonds and cheese. Make the syrup by melting the brown sugar in a large pan, adding the cinnamon, cloves and water, and simmering

for 30 minutes. Remove the cinnamon and cloves. Pour the syrup over the layers of bread in the dish. Bake in a pre-heated oven at 180°C (350°F/Gas 4) for 45 minutes.

~ EXTRA RECIPES ~

Chorizo toluqueno
SPICY SAUSAGE

Chorizo sausage meat can be put into casings as sausages or can be used on its own in various dishes, often crumbled before being cooked. You can buy *chorizo* sausage at most delicatessens, but the homemade version is not only delicious but also avoids the use of preservatives. You can keep this mixture in the fridge for up to two weeks. The recipe below is authentic but you may find it very spicy. The first time you cook it, it would be safer to halve the quantities of spices.

pork, finely minced	450g	1lb	1lb
pork fat, finely minced	175g	6oz	6oz
malt vinegar	60ml	4tbs	4tbs
salt	5ml	1tsp	1tsp
black pepper, freshly ground	5ml	1tsp	1tsp
cloves garlic, crushed	4	4	4
cayenne pepper	15ml	1tbs	1tbs
paprika	30ml	2tbs	2tbs
coriander seeds	5ml	1tsp	1tsp
cinnamon stick, crushed	13cm	5in.	5in.

dried oregano	5ml	1tsp	1tsp
dried marjoram	5ml	1tsp	1tsp
nutmeg	2ml	½tsp	½tsp
ground cloves	2ml	½tsp	½tsp

Mix the meat and fat with the vinegar, salt and pepper then add all the remaining ingredients and mix well. Refrigerate for 4 days in a plastic or glass bowl, stirring daily and draining off any juices at the same time. Stuff into sausage casings and tie every 13cm (5in.) or leave as it is. You can cook the loose *chorizo* by crumbling it into hot oil and frying for 6–7 minutes.

Tortillas

*T*ortillas are the Mexican cornflour pancakes found on the table at most meals, often taking the place of bread. They may be soft or crispy, filled or plain, sweet or savoury, according to the recipe used. Shaped into a shell and filled, they become tacos; filled and sealed into a parcel, they are *quesadillas*. *Enchiladas* are filled *tortillas* covered in sauce, while *enfrijoladas* are fried *tortillas* covered with beans plus a topping. *Tostadas* are deep-fried *tortillas* which can be topped with a choice of beans, lettuce, chicken, tomatoes, onions, soured cream, cheese, pickle or *guacamole*. The very versatility of *tortillas* is partly why they are so popular today.

You can buy *tortillas* or *taco* shells ready made, canned, or frozen, but if you make your own you'll find them not only tastier but also cheaper. A *tortilla* press gives neater and easier results. White maize flour is the only suitable flour to use: cornflour or cornmeal (polenta) are not good substitutes.

masa harina (white maize flour)	120g	4½oz	1 cup
plain flour	40g	1½oz	⅓ cup
warm water	100ml	4floz	½ cup

Mix the flours in a large bowl and gradually add the warm water, mixing constantly with your hands. Work the dough for 10–20 minutes, adding a little more flour if the sides of the bowl are sticky and a little more water if the dough cracks when formed into a ball. Divide the dough into 10 pieces and put each one between two sheets of waxed paper. Roll out on a floured board with a rolling pin or press with a *tortilla* press to give rounds of about 15cm (6in.) diameter. Heat an ungreased, heavy frying pan over a moderate heat, then gently lower the *tortilla* into the pan. Cook for 2 minutes on each side, remove from the pan, and wrap in a tea towel to keep warm while cooking the others. *Tortillas* can also be cooked by frying in shallow or deep oil. Cooked *tortillas* can be eaten as they are or filled. They may be refrigerated or frozen to store.

Quesadillas de chorizo y papàs
TORTILLAS FILLED WITH CHORIZO AND POTATOES

*T*hese little *tortilla* parcels are often served at a *posada* and can be eaten in the fingers, buffet-style.

oil	5ml	1tsp	1tsp
onion, finely chopped	½	½	½
green chilli, chopped (optional)	1	1	1
chorizo, crumbled or thinly sliced if in sausage form	100g	4oz	½ cup
potatoes boiled and either mashed or cut into small (5mm/¼ in.) chunks	225g	8oz	1 cup
salt and pepper, to taste			
cooked tortillas	8	8	8

Heat the oil and fry the onion and the chilli until the onion is yellow and soft. Add the *chorizo* and fry until dark red. Add the potatoes and seasoning. Warm the *tortillas* (if cold) by heating them in a dry, hot frying pan for about 30 seconds, then put some of the *chorizo* and potato mixture on top of each. Wrap each *tortilla* around its filling to make a parcel and seal the edges by pressing them together. Cook in a dry, hot frying pan for about 45 seconds on each side and serve at once.

Mole poblano

TURKEY IN CHILLI AND CHOCOLATE SAUCE

Turkey in chilli and chocolate sauce is a very popular Mexican fiesta dish and was favoured by the Aztecs who were living in Mexico before Christopher Columbus arrived there in 1492. The Aztecs gave chocolate its name and allowed only men of high rank to eat or drink it. The chocolate in *mole poblano* lends only a little colour and sweetness rather than flavour. This is one of the easier of the many recipes for the dish.

turkey portions	4	4	4
malt vinegar	45ml	3tbs	3tbs
salt	5ml	1tsp	1tsp
black pepper			
sugar	2ml	$\frac{1}{2}$ tsp	$\frac{1}{2}$ tsp
salsa adobada (see earlier recipe for quantities)			
sesame seeds	25g	1oz	2tbs
almonds	25g	1oz	2tbs
peanuts	25g	1oz	2tbs
oil	60ml	4tbs	$\frac{1}{4}$ cup
raisins	50g	2oz	$\frac{1}{4}$ cup

Put the turkey portions into a bowl and sprinkle with the vinegar, salt, pepper and sugar. Leave to marinade for 1 hour. Make one recipe quantity of *salsa adobada* but omit the 20 minutes of simmering at the end. Put the sesame seeds, almonds and peanuts into a frying

pan. Dry fry them, turning frequently, for about 4 minutes, until golden.

Heat the oil in a large, heavy-based casserole and fry the marinaded turkey pieces until golden on all sides. Add the *salsa adobada*, fried sesame seeds, almonds and peanuts, and the raisins. Cover the casserole and bake in a pre-heated oven at 180°C (350°F/Gas 4) for about $1^3/_4$ hours. Stir occasionally to prevent burning.

Rosca de Reyes

THREE KINGS' RING

This spicy, sweet fruit bread ring is traditionally served at Epiphany along with soft drinks, hot chocolate and coffee in the afternoon. Take care when eating a piece, as you may come across one of the three kings' gifts! Most Mexicans buy their rings from bakers' shops, whose windows are full of them at Epiphany.

strong (regular) flour	350g	12oz	3 cups
dried yeast **OR**	5ml	1tsp	1tsp
fresh yeast	15g	$\frac{1}{2}$ oz	1tbs
granulated sugar	100g	4oz	$\frac{1}{2}$ cup
warm milk	125ml	$4\frac{1}{2}$ fl oz	$\frac{1}{3}$ cup
butter	100g	4oz	1 stick
pinch of salt			
pinch of cinnamon			
eggs, beaten	2	2	2
egg yolks, beaten	2	2	2
grated rind of 1 lemon			
candied peel, roughly chopped	50g	2oz	$\frac{1}{4}$ cup
candied pineapple, roughly chopped	50g	2oz	$\frac{1}{4}$ cup

glacé cherries, roughly chopped	50g	2oz	1/4 cup
flaked almonds, roughly chopped	25g	1oz	2tbs

Topping and glazing

granulated sugar	25g	1oz	2tbs
butter	25g	1oz	2tbs
plain flour	25g	1oz	2tbs
egg white, lightly beaten	1	1	1
icing sugar (confectioner's sugar)	75g	3oz	1/3 cup
milk or water	30ml	2tbs	2tbs

Gifts: 1 small doll (a jelly baby wrapped in foil or a small china or plastic doll), a ring and a coin

Place 225g (8oz/2 cups) of the flour in a mixing bowl, reserving the rest. Cream together the yeast and 2ml (1/2 tsp) of the sugar. Add the warm milk and about one third of the flour from the bowl. Beat well and leave in a warm place for 15 minutes. Rub the butter into the rest of the flour in the bowl and stir in the salt and cinnamon. Make a well in the centre and add the beaten eggs and yolks, lemon rind and yeast batter. Mix well. Turn the dough on to a board floured with some of the reserved flour and knead well for 10 minutes. Place in a greased bowl and cover with a damp cloth. Leave to rise for about 5 hours in a warm place or overnight in a cool place, until doubled in size. Knead again on a floured board (using some of the reserved flour) until smooth. Add the fruit and almonds, reserving some for decoration, and mix well. Roll the dough into a sausage about 56cm (22in.) long. Join the ends to form a ring and place on a greased baking sheet. Cover and leave to rise in a warm place for about 30 minutes.

Make cuts around the ring with a pair of scissors, about 5cm (2in.) deep and 7.5cm (3in.) apart

Make the topping by creaming the butter and sugar together until light and fluffy, then adding the flour to make a paste. Divide the paste into as many pieces as the number of cuts you made in the top of the ring and shape the pieces into small fingers. Place a finger between each cut. Glaze the ring with the egg white. Bake at 200°C (400°F/Gas 6) for 25–30 minutes until golden-brown.

When the cake is cool, insert the gifts into the cooked cake via small cuts. Mix the icing sugar and milk or water and glaze the ring, making sure the cuts for the gifts are covered. Decorate with the remaining candied fruit and almonds.

Tamales dulce

FRUIT-FILLED CORN DUMPLINGS IN PINK CORN HUSKS

*T*amales have been eaten in Mexico since the time of the Aztecs and some shops today sell nothing but *tamales*. They are a traditional fiesta dish of the Mexican Indians. They can be sweet or savoury and are traditionally served at the *posada*. Sweet *tamales* are coloured pink. Corn husks are the outer leaves of corn cobs. If you can't buy them ready dried, 20cm (8in.) squares of kitchen foil with waxed paper squares on top will do instead.

There is *no* substitute for *masa harina* (white maize (corn) flour) but it can be bought in specialist grocers' shops.

A good helping of happiness while cooking is said to make *tamales* light and fluffy!

dried corn husks	24	24	

Tamale dough

masa harina (white maize flour)	225g	8oz	2 cups
warm water	450ml	3/4 pint	1 1/2 cups
lard, softened	75g	3oz	1/3 cup

baking powder	5ml	1tsp	1tsp
granulated sugar	15ml	1tbs	1tbs

Sweet fillings

glacé cherries, chopped AND	4	4	4
slices crystallized pineapple, chopped AND	2	2	2
raisins OR	15ml	1tbs	1tbs
raisins	30ml	2tbs	2tbs
per tamale			

cochineal (red food colouring) to colour husks

Soften the husks by soaking overnight in water or by covering with water, bringing to the boil and draining. Tear twenty 5mm ($^1/_4$ in.) strips from four of the husks and set aside for tying the *tamales*. Mix the *masa harina*, water and lard in a large bowl. Add the baking powder and beat until bubbles start to appear. If ready, a little dough dropped in cold water will float and stick together. If it sinks, and breaks up, beat some more. Stir in the sugar. Next combine the dried fruit. Put two husks together with wide ends overlapping by 5cm (2in.) and put 15ml (1tbs) of the dough on top. Add 15ml (1tbs) of fruit, the same again of dough, followed by the same again of fruit. Wrap the husks over the filling to make a parcel and tie each end with the reserved strips. Dab the *tamales* with cochineal to colour them pink. If using foil and waxed paper instead of husks, there is no need to tie up the foil parcels—just fold the edges together. Arrange the *tamales* in the top of a steamer and cover with grease-proof (waxed) paper. Cover and steam for $1^1/_2$ hours or until light and fluffy. This recipe makes 10 *tamales*.

Atole

MAIZE (CORN) DRINK

*A*tole is a thick, sweet drink flavoured with fruit or chocolate and is served with *tamales* at the *posada*. If chocolate is used as the flavouring, the drink is known as *champurrado*. Strawberry and chocolate *atole* mixes can be bought in Mexican shops and simply need the addition of milk.

masa harina or cornflour	50g	2oz	$^1/_4$ cup
water	600ml	1 pint	2 cups
milk	1 litre	1$^3/_4$ pints	4$^1/_2$ cups
caster sugar (US: granulated)	175g	6oz	$^3/_4$ cup
fresh fruit, puréed	225g	8oz	1 cup
pinch of cinnamon			

Dissolve the *masa harina* or cornflour in a little of the water. Bring the milk to the boil and pour over the dissolved *masa harina*, stirring constantly. Pour the mixture back into the pan and add the remaining water. Simmer for 3 minutes, stirring constantly, then add the sugar and fruit purée. Sprinkle a little cinnamon on each mug of *atole* before serving.

For *champurrado*, replace the fruit purée with 100g (4oz/$^1/_2$ cup) of grated plain chocolate and heat the milk with a cinnamon stick. Remove the cinnamon before stirring in the chocolate.

CANADA

Canada is a true cultural mosaic. Before Christianity arrived in Canada native religions flourished among the Indian population. It was the early missionaries and pioneers who brought the message of Christianity with them. There can be few more incongruous scenes than those of early Canadian Christmases spent amongst the native Indians. Picture an isolated bronze-skinned Huron community of 1620 on the shores of one of Quebec's many lakes. They are singing a Christmas carol in their own language, *'Jesus Ahatonhia'*—Jesus is born. Leading the singing is the composer, a bearded Jesuit priest, Jean Brébeuf.

'Twas in the moon of winter time
    when all the birds had fled,
That Mighty Gitchi Manitou
    sent angel choirs instead.
Before their light the stars grew dim,
    and wand'ring hunters heard the hymn,
Jesus, your King, is born;
Jesus is born;
    in excelsis gloria!'

Within a lodge of broken bark
    the tender Babe was found,
A ragged robe of rabbit skin
    enwrapped His beauty round.
And as the hunter braves drew nigh,
    the angels' song rang loud and high;
Jesus, your King, is born;
Jesus is born;
    in excelsis gloria!'

The earliest moon of winter time
    is not so round and fair
As was the ring of glory
    on the helpless Infant there.
And chiefs from far before Him knelt
with gifts of fox and beaver pelt.
Jesus, your King, is born;
Jesus is born;
    in excelsis gloria!'

A later account by Samuel de Champlain, one of the leading figures in the development of Canada during the French regime in the 1600's, tells of a Christmas feast held in his log cabin. The crude table was set with squares of birchbark and Indian bowls of polished basswood. Everyone brought their own knife but bark spoons were provided. They feasted on a great stew of eels, salmon and beans, cakes of corn bread, peas, baked squash, roast venison, deep squirrel pies, baked pigeons, owls and blackbirds. For dessert they dined on maple sugar cakes and a sweetmeat made of crushed nuts and sunflower seeds served with a berry sauce.

More than anything these remarkable stories illustrate the great feature of Canadian Christmas celebrations which is their *adaptability*.

After the American War of Independence, many English-speaking Loyalists migrated north. Since then Canada has continued to absorb vast numbers of immigrants. German, Dutch, French, Scottish, English and Irish hopefuls as well as many East Europeans, particularly Ukrainians, crossed the Atlantic to the New World. In this century, immigrants from all over the world have made Canada their home. They all brought with them their own cherished customs and traditions which have been adapted over the years. With a heritage of so many diverse cultures, Christmas in Canada is celebrated in many different ways: for some Christmas begins with St Nicholas on 6 December, whereas others of Ukrainian and Greek Orthodox descent celebrate a week after everyone else.

Many of the traditions of the French colonies have become a part of the Canadian way of life. Some of the original traditions continue to be honoured by Canada's many French-Canadian families, the majority of whom live in Quebec. Montreal is in fact the largest French-speaking city after Paris. Just as in France, many French-Canadian families set out a crèche (a nativity scene) under a decorated tree in the living-room. On Christmas Eve the younger children have to go to bed early so that they won't be too tired to enjoy the thrill of being allowed to go out in the middle of the dark snowy night to attend midnight mass. In earlier days they would have been bundled into the sleigh, covered with furs and skins with their feet keeping warm on heated stones or clay 'piggins' filled with hot water. Everywhere one could hear the jingling of the sleighbells and the swish of the sharpened runners as the people converged on the village church. The candles, the curé, the crèche, the choirs marching down the aisle singing the beautiful carol, 'Minuit, chrétiens', are all images of which memories are made.

As their French cousins across the Atlantic are finally going to bed, families in Quebec return home to the comfort of the hot réveillon. This meal varies from house to house but usually the dishes are served buffet-style. By tradition one of the dishes is tourtière, a pork pie with a delicious golden crust with which some families like to eat strawberry jam! Salads are usually served, perhaps a crunchy apple and pecan one with a lightly spiced mayonnaise or a refreshing jellied cranberry salad. Other traditional favourites include boulettes, little meatballs in a sauce, and créton, a pâté-like meat treat made from lean pork and spices, slices of which are served cold between pieces of French or rye bread. Galantine, a layered meat and vegetable brawn, is another dish often served at a réveillon. Some families go on to eat a dessert of fruit salad, fruit cake or a rich chestnut bûche de Noël (Yule log). There is no hurry for French-Canadians to rise on Christmas morning as it is not until New Year's Day that Père Noël arrives and gifts are exchanged.

After the conquest many British settlers chose the provinces of the Atlantic region to be their home. In Nova Scotia, New Brunswick and Prince Edward Island they were joined by Irish, German, French and Scottish settlers. The families living in these provinces today are still predominantly of Scottish, Irish and British descent, and in isolated fishing villages and farms in Nova Scotia Gaelic can still be heard.

Those early colonists brought with them many of the Christmas traditions that form the backbone of present day Canadian celebrations—shortbread, black pudding, plum pudding and brandy butter, and Christmas mince pies to mention but a few.

Possibly because of its isolation and the homogeneous Irish/English population, Newfoundland retained many old-world customs. One such custom was that of having a Yule log or 'black junk' burning from Christmas Eve until Twelfth Night—when a piece of it was thrown over the house. Tradition said that this would protect the inhabitants from fire during the coming year.

But their adoptive homeland offered new resources: the famous Grand Banks means that fish, especially cod, is plentiful throughout these provinces. Cod—which is also known as 'Christmas fish' is often eaten, sometimes salted, on Boxing Day in Newfoundland.

Cranberry sauce has its home here. Newfoundland has little arable land but the rocky barrens and marshes produce an abundance of wild berries including cranberries, known here as partridgeberries. Their lively colour and slight tartness enhance many delicious recipes such as cranberry syllabub, jellied cranberry salad, ruby punch, Christmas cranberry salad, cranberry relish and cranberry stuffing.

Unique to New Brunswick are 'fiddleheads'. They are an edible form of the ostrich fern and have a delicate flavour similar to asparagus. An early spring vegetable for pioneers, today they are often served as a treat at Christmas, with a light hollandaise sauce. New Brunswick children won't be surprised to find 'chicken bones' in their stockings—not the real things, of course, but a candy made at the famous Ganong's factory in St Stephens.

Contrasting with the Atlantic provinces is British Columbia on the Pacific shore. It is noted for its wonderful salmon and shellfish. Thanks to modern vacuum-packaging, Canadian smoked salmon is exported world-wide and has become, with Stilton cheese, inextricably linked to Christmas. Many Canadian cooks serve salmon either fresh or smoked as the first course of their Christmas meal. Little packages of light salmon mousse wrapped in smoked salmon and glossed with aspic make an impressive first course.

In strong contrast to such gourmet refinements is the picture of Vancouver in early Victorian days when it was still largely raw wilderness, inhabited mainly by rough, lonely loggers. Even they took time off to celebrate Christmas. They would gather in Vancouver's old Gastown and feast on venison and 'good ol' bunch grass beef', with plenty of ale, beer and whisky to wash it all down.

Next to British Columbia lie the prairie provinces: Alberta, Saskatchewan and Manito-ba. There are some delightful records of rather unusual Christmas meals that the men of the Hudson Bay Company consumed at the forts dotted across the prairies.

At one Christmas meal which was shared with the native Indians they ate boiled Buffalo hump, beaver tails, and other delicacies such as fish browned in buffalo marrow and mouffle—dried moose nose! Along with all this were served piles of potatoes, turnips and fresh loaves of bread.

At Christmas time the succulent broad-breasted grain-fed turkeys of Alberta are in great demand. An excellent stuffing can be made from another prairie speciality—Manitoba wild rice. Mixed with peppers, celery, onion and mushroom and cooked in chicken stock its nutty texture makes a delicious turkey stuffing and it is just as good served as an accompaniment. Apple jelly tarts and Manitoba poppyseed roll are two other Christmas specialities of this region. Northern Saskatchewan abounds in lakes and woods and many native berries which grow here are used in holiday cooking. A Saskatoon pie and blueberry muffins may well be eaten during the holiday season.

Ontario is a vast province, and over 1,000 miles from east to west. It is here in cities such as Ottawa, the federal capital, and Toronto, the commercial heart, that one comes across the less romantic aspect of Christmas—the commercialization and the pressure to buy! buy! buy! As early as 1882 *The Mail and Empire* newspaper gleefully reported that trade in Toronto shops was so brisk that over one million gifts were sold that year. Earlier in the century Christmas presents were sold by public auction.

As early as November the Santa Claus parades signal the start of city Christmas celebrations. These colourful parades started in 1905 in Toronto and were so popular that they are something of an institution in major cities across Canada.

Canadian hospitality is legendary and during the holiday season many homes will have open-house. Friends and neighbours and colleagues are welcomed in to exchange Christmas greetings and sample some of the tasty canapés such as roasted savoury pecan nuts, little rounds of pumpernickel topped with an olive-nut spread or roasted cheese slices made with mature Canadian cheddar. A festive bowl of ruby punch made with cranberries and ginger ale is refreshing and economical to serve at such a party. As the guests drink one another's health they are carrying on the ancient tradition of a wassail bowl—wes-hal being Anglo-Saxon for 'good health' or 'be whole'. Originally pieces of toast floated in this bowl, hence the phrase 'toast your health'.

Despite all the commercial trappings the true spirit of Christmas is also very much apparent in the generosity shown to Christmas charities and drives which help the poor. At this time many Canadians visit shut-ins and those in hospitals, and neighbours are on the receiving end of the holiday baking. Canadian women don't do the amount of baking they used to do. Changing food habits, the fact that more women are working outside the home and the availability of good quality pre-packed food are having their effect. There is also an increasing awareness that most countries are not as blessed with the abundance that Canadians enjoy.

Christmas Eve finds Canadian families gathered together snug in their homes despite the blanket of snow outside. Families and friends go to great lengths to be together for the celebrations and there is much fun and laughter as last-minute gifts are wrapped, the candy canes are hung on the tree, and preparations are made in the kitchen for the Christmas dinner to come. Homes are festooned with evergreens and ribbons, Christmas cards have been sent and received and there is an inviting wreath on the door. Children hang their stockings on the mantelpiece and scan the sky for Santa and his reindeer. There is an air of expectation that extends across Canada.

Not even those manning research and weather stations in the snowy Arctic wastelands are forgotten, with the national radio broadcasting messages and greetings to them from far-away friends and the airforce planes making 'drops' of Christmas mail, gifts and food. As these people stand and search the Arctic skies for the lights of the little plane one is reminded of another light all those years ago—that of the Bethlehem Star.

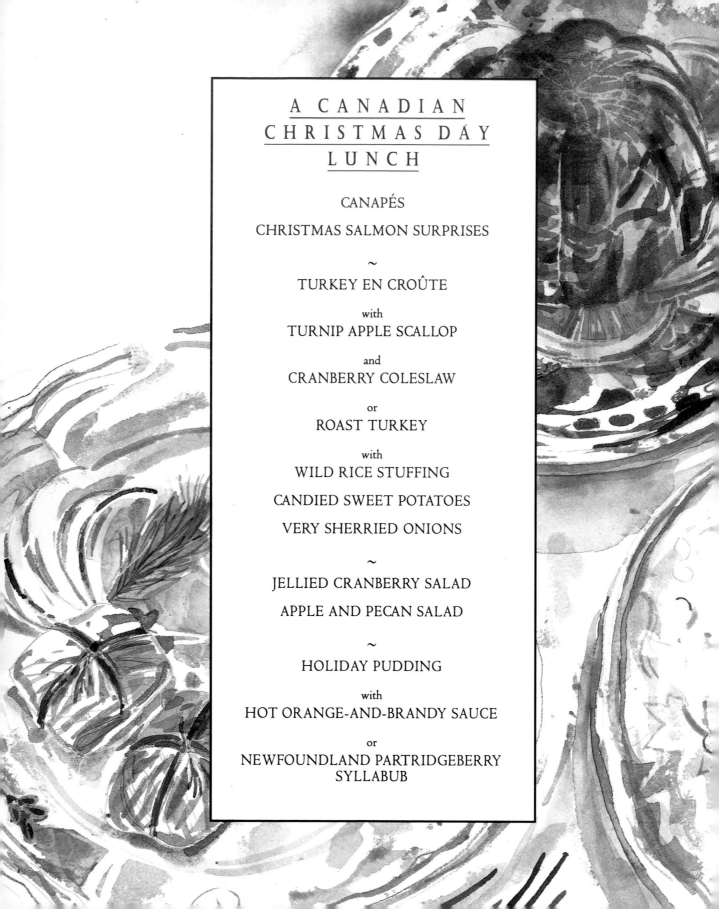

A CANADIAN
CHRISTMAS DAY
LUNCH

CANAPÉS

CHRISTMAS SALMON SURPRISES

~

TURKEY EN CROÛTE

with
TURNIP APPLE SCALLOP

and
CRANBERRY COLESLAW

or
ROAST TURKEY

with
WILD RICE STUFFING

CANDIED SWEET POTATOES

VERY SHERRIED ONIONS

~

JELLIED CRANBERRY SALAD

APPLE AND PECAN SALAD

~

HOLIDAY PUDDING

with
HOT ORANGE-AND-BRANDY SAUCE

or
NEWFOUNDLAND PARTRIDGEBERRY
SYLLABUB

Canapés

At some time or another during the holiday season most Canadian homes will have 'open house' for friends and neighbours to pop in, exchange greetings, taste the punch and sample a few canapés. Here are just a few of the favourites given to us from what seems to be an inexhaustible supply of recipes.

Spicy roasted almonds/pecans

unblanched whole almonds or pecan halves	225g	8oz	1 cup
butter	30ml	2tbs	2tbs
chilli powder	5ml	1tsp	1tsp
ground cumin	2ml	1/2 tsp	1/2 tsp
garlic salt	2ml	1/2 tsp	1/2 tsp
salt to taste			

Melt the butter in a frying pan and add all the spices. Toss the nuts in the mixture until coated, taking care not to scorch them. Spread the coated nuts on a baking sheet and bake in the oven at 160°C (325°F/Gas 3) for 20–30 minutes, turning every so often to avoid burning. Salt to taste. Prettily wrapped in foil, boxes of these make welcome gifts.

Olive nut spread

cream cheese	175g	6oz	6oz
mayonnaise	100ml	4fl oz	1/3 cup
chopped pecans	75g	3oz	1/3 cup
large green olives, chopped	175g	6oz	3/4 cup
brine from the olives	30ml	2tbs	2tbs
black pepper to taste			

Mix all the ingredients thoroughly and chill for 24 hours to let the flavours mingle. Serve on crackers or pumpernickel rounds.

Roasted cheese canapés

Ontario is Canada's cheese and wine province, being famous for its cheddar cheese which is exported world-wide. Ninety per cent of the wine produced in Canada also comes from the sunny south of the province. This recipe dates from 1847 and makes a quick and tasty snack to serve with pre-lunch drinks. Try adding asparagus tips or pimento for a different flavour.

mature Cheddar cheese, grated	100g	4oz	1/2 cup
egg yolks, lightly beaten	2	2	2
dry mustard	2ml	1/2 tsp	1/2 tsp
paprika	2ml	1/2 tsp	1/2 tsp
fresh breadcrumbs (granary tastes good)	150g	5oz	3/4 cup
butter	100g	4oz	1 stick
pinch of salt			
Worcestershire sauce	5ml	1tsp	1tsp
slices of toast, crusts removed	6–8	6–8	6–8

Combine all the ingredients (except the toast) and beat until smooth. Spread thickly on the toast and grill (broil). Cut into fingers or fancy shapes using cookie cutters.

Christmas salmon surprises

C anada produces some of the finest salmon in the world and for the Canadian cook it is a natural favourite for a Christmas treat. Because it is expensive it warrants the effort of making something as special as these elegant little parcels filled with light salmon mousse.

smoked salmon slices just over 25g (1oz) each	4	4	4
red pepper, cut into thin 'ribbons'	1	1	1
fresh dill or French parsley to garnish			

Mousse

salmon freshly cooked, with skin and bones removed **OR**	225g	8oz	8oz
can of salmon	225g	8oz	8oz
smoked salmon trimmings	25g	1oz	2tbs
tomato sauce	15ml	1tbs	1tbs
lemon juice	30ml	2tbs	2tbs
paprika	2ml	1/2 tsp	1/2 tsp
gelatine	15ml	1tbs	1tbs
fish stock	75ml	3fl oz	1/4 cup
double cream (US: whipping)	150ml	1/4 pint	1/2 cup
black pepper and salt to taste			

Aspic

gelatine	40g	1 1/2 oz	3tbs
juice of one large lemon			

Blend or sieve the salmon flesh, trimmings, tomato sauce, lemon juice and paprika. Add the gelatine,

dissolved in the fish stock, mixing well all the time to avoid lumps. Carefully whisk in the whipped cream. Taste and season.

Lay the slices of smoked salmon on a board and spoon a quantity of mousse in the centre of each piece. Wrap the salmon around the mousse to form neat parcels, tucking in the ends. Cover and chill. In the meantime cut strips from the flesh of a red pepper to form 'ribbons'.

Prepare the aspic by dissolving the gelatine in the lemon juice over a low heat. Stand the aspic over ice until it is thick and syrupy. Lay the 'ribbons' of pepper across the salmon parcels and carefully brush with the aspic. Finish off with a frond of fresh dill or parsley on top. Serve each parcel very simply with a few slices of cucumber and triangles of buttered brown bread.

Turkey en croûte

C hristmas is all about parcels and this time it is the turkey's turn to be spread with seasoning, covered in ham and then wrapped up in a golden puff of pastry. To keep things manageable, it is best to stick to a maximum 3kg turkey—ideal for the average family or for a small dinner party. This avoids having to eat turkey leftovers until New Year's Day!

turkey breast, boned and rolled	1–1.2kg	2–2 1/2 lb	
mild whole grain mustard	30ml	2tbs	2tbs
turmeric	2ml	1/2 tsp	1/2 tsp
pinch of curry powder			
freshly milled black pepper to taste			
thin slices ham	4–5	4–5	4–5
egg, lightly beaten	1	1	1
frozen puff pastry	375g	13oz	13oz

Let the pastry thaw at room temperature for about I hour. Roast the turkey joint according to its weight and the wrapper instructions (about I–I^1/$_2$ hours in a moderate oven). Cool and score all round. Mix all the seasonings together and use a knife to spread the mixture evenly over the entire joint. Press the ham slices around the joint and chill while you prepare the pastry.

On a lightly floured board roll out the pastry to about 40cm (16in.) square. Brush with beaten egg and place the chilled turkey roll in the centre. Make a diagonal cut from the ham to each corner of the pastry. Brush the rest of the joint with beaten egg and fold the end flaps of pastry over, encasing each end of the turkey. Now make a series of parallel diagonal cuts about 2 ^{1}/$_2$ cm (I in.) wide in the side pieces of pastry. By laying alternating strips of pastry across the top of the joint, plait the pastry until the turkey is completely enclosed. Roll out the pastry trimmings and cut out some diamond-shaped leaves or perhaps some festive stars for decoration. Keep these in place with a little of the beaten egg. Chill thoroughly before baking. Brush with the rest of the beaten egg. Bake on a heated baking sheet in an oven pre-heated to 220°C (425°F/Gas 7) for 40 minutes or until golden brown.

Turnip apple scallop

E ven the humble turnip when cooked this way becomes worthy of the festive table.

turnips, sliced and cooked	275g	10oz	1^1/$_4$ cups
cooking apples peeled, cored and sliced	225g	8oz	1 cup
soft brown sugar	100g	4oz	^{1}/$_2$ cup
salt and pepper to taste			
butter	150g	5oz	1^1/$_4$ sticks
dry breadcrumbs	100g	4oz	^{3}/$_4$ cup
single cream (half and half)	60ml	4tbs	4tbs

Butter a shallow ovenproof dish generously and line the base and sides with half of the breadcrumbs. Layer the apples and turnips alternately starting with the sliced turnips; dot each layer with butter. Pour the cream over the apples and turnips, add extra milk if necessary—the liquid needs to just cover the vegetables. Season and sprinkle with sugar. Sprinkle the remainder of the breadcrumbs on top and bake for ^{1}/$_2$ hour at 180°C (350°F/Gas 4).

Cranberry coleslaw

M ost Canadian Christmas menus include a cold salad either jellied or plain. This is a luxurious coleslaw made festive with the addition of tart red cranberries and grapes.

cranberries, finely chopped	175g	6oz	^{3}/$_4$ cup
sugar	50g	2oz	^{1}/$_4$ cup
finely shredded cabbage	450g	1lb	2 cups
orange juice	100ml	4fl oz	^{1}/$_3$ cup
celery stalks, chopped	2	2	2
green pepper, chopped	^{1}/$_2$	^{1}/$_2$	^{1}/$_2$
green or black grapes seeded and halved	175g	6oz	^{3}/$_4$ cup
mayonnaise or salad dressing	50ml	2fl oz	3tbs

Mix the cranberries and the sugar. Moisten the cabbage with the orange juice. Add the sugared cranberries, celery, green pepper and grapes. Toss lightly with mayonnaise or salad dressing. Chill for ^{1}/$_2$ hour.

Wild rice stuffing

Wild rice comes from the shallow marshes of Northern Ontario and Manitoba. It retains its lovely nutty texture when cooked. This is ideal for making the day before Christmas as the flavours improve with keeping and it reheats well.

wild rice	275g	10oz	1¹/₄ cups
chicken stock	900ml	1¹/₂ pints	4 cups
salt	5ml	1tsp	1tsp
white wine	175g	6fl oz	³/₄ cup
butter	45ml	3tbs	3tbs
large onion, finely chopped	1	1	1
mushrooms, finely chopped	225g	8oz	1¹/₂ cups
green pepper, finely chopped	¹/₂	¹/₂	¹/₂
red pepper, finely chopped	¹/₂	¹/₂	¹/₂
celery stalks, washed and chopped	6–8	6–8	6–8
egg, beaten (if using for stuffing)	1	1	1

Cook the rice with the salt in the chicken stock and wine until all the liquid is absorbed (about 40 minutes). Sauté the onion, mushrooms, green and red pepper and celery in the butter. About 10 minutes before the end of the cooking time add all the vegetables to the rice and cook until tender. If you are using the wild rice as a stuffing for your turkey, bind the cooked rice with the beaten egg. Alternatively, serve as an accompaniment to roast turkey.

Candied sweet potatoes

In Canada sweet potatoes usually make an appearance on the Christmas menu in one form or another. This recipe is for baked sweet potatoes with their natural sweetness enhanced by the addition of maple syrup and butter.

sweet potatoes	6	6	6
salt and pepper to taste			
brown sugar **OR**	75g	3oz	¹/₃ cup
maple syrup	50ml	2fl oz	3tbs
juice of 1 orange			
cinnamon	2ml	¹/₂ tsp	¹/₂ tsp
butter	50g	2oz	¹/₂ stick

Peel the sweet potatoes, boil until *nearly* tender and cut lengthwise into thick slices. Place in a buttered shallow baking dish and season with salt and pepper. Sprinkle with the sugar or maple syrup.

Pour the orange juice over the potatoes. Dot with butter, dust with cinnamon and bake, uncovered, in a pre-heated oven at 190°C (375°F/Gas 5) for 25 minutes.

Very sherried onions

Very quick, very easy and very delicious.

pickling onions* (small, white onions)	450g	1lb	1lb
water to cover			
sugar	15ml	1tbs	1tbs
vinegar	15ml	1tbs	1tbs
salt and black pepper to taste			

single cream (half and half)	250ml	9fl oz	1 cup
sweet sherry	45ml	3tbs	3tbs
butter, melted	45ml	3tbs	3tbs

Boil the onions until just tender (about 15 minutes) in the water, sugar and vinegar. Arrange the onions in a shallow, buttered, ovenproof dish and season with salt and freshly ground black pepper. Pour the cream, sherry and butter over the onions. Bake, uncovered, in a pre-heated oven at 180°C (350°F/Gas 4) for 25 minutes.

* Not pickled onions

Jellied cranberry salad

Jellied salads are a Canadian and American favourite. They couldn't be easier to make and the addition of walnuts in this recipe gives a pleasant crunch.

packet of raspberry jelly (jello)	150g	5oz	5oz
hot water	100ml	4fl oz	1/2 cup
cold water	175ml	6fl oz	1/2 cup
small orange, minced, skin and all	1	1	1
cranberry sauce	150ml	1/4 pint	1/2 cup
pineapple chunks	75g	3oz	1/3 cup
chopped walnuts	50g	2oz	1/4 cup

Mix the jelly with the hot water. Stir to dissolve, then add the cold water. Leave till starting to set, then add the minced orange, cranberry sauce, pineapple and walnuts.

Pour into a lightly oiled mould and set. Turn out and surround with lettuce or cucumber slices and garnish with orange slices. This is delicious with ham as well as poultry.

Apple and pecan salad

It is the spiced mayonnaise that makes this salad so good.

crisp lettuce, coarsely shredded	1	1	1
rosy apples, unpeeled and finely sliced	2	2	2
green grapes	75g	3oz	1/3 cup
chopped pears	100g	4oz	1/2 cup
pecans, lightly toasted	100g	4oz	1/2 cup

Spicy mayonnaise

mayonnaise	100ml	4fl oz	1/2 cup
sour cream	100ml	4fl oz	1/2 cup
peach or apple chutney	45ml	3tbs	3tbs

Mix the mayonnaise ingredients and chill well.

Mix the salad ingredients. Just before serving drizzle with the spicy mayonnaise and toss lightly.

Holiday pudding

In the best colonial tradition, most Anglo-Canadian families round off their Christmas meal with plum pudding and mince pies. One Canadian family however, much preferred their light, spongelike pudding made with carrot, apple and potatoes. Served with brandy sauce, cream or hot orange-and-brandy sauce it does make a delicious alternative to plum pudding.

suet	250g	9oz	1 cup
OR			
margarine	175g	6oz	3/4 cup

plain flour	150g	5oz	1¼ cups
salt	5ml	1tsp	1tsp
bicarbonate of soda	5ml	1tsp	1tsp
cinnamon	5ml	1tsp	1tsp
allspice	5ml	1tsp	1tsp
nutmeg	5ml	1tsp	1tsp
vanilla	5ml	1tsp	1tsp
white sugar	175g	6oz	¾ cup
raisins	250g	9oz	1 cup
chopped walnuts or almonds (optional)	75g	3oz	⅓ cup
mixed dried fruit	175g	6oz	¾ cup
currants	175g	6oz	¾ cup
cherries (red and green)	75g	3oz	⅓ cup
raw carrots, grated	150g	5oz	¾ cup
raw apple, grated	150g	5oz	¾ cup
raw potatoes, grated	150g	5oz	¾ cup
eggs, beaten	2	2	2

Put the suet, flour, salt, spices and sugar in a bowl and mix well. Add the fruit and nuts, then the grated apple, carrots and potatoes. Lastly add the beaten eggs and mix really well. This is the point when each member of the family may give the mixture a stir and make a wish. Put in a greased pudding basin, put in the top of a double boiler, cover and steam for 2–2½ hours, taking care that the saucepan doesn't boil dry.

Serve with hot orange-and-brandy sauce.

Orange and brandy sauce

juice of 2 oranges and the grated rind of one of them			
caster sugar (US: granulated)	15ml	1tbs	1tbs
cornflour (cornstarch) dissolved in	5ml	1tsp	1tsp
cold water	100ml	4fl oz	⅓ cup
brandy to taste			

Mix the cornflour and water and add to the rest of the ingredients. Thicken over a low heat but do not boil.

Newfoundland partridgeberry syllabub

Partridgeberries, also known as mountain cranberries or lingonberries, are found in abundance all over the island of Newfoundland. These slightly tart, rich red berries combined with a feather-light syllabub make a refreshing dessert for a Christmas meal.

partridgeberry (cranberry) sauce	60ml	4tbs	4tbs
juice and rind of 2 oranges			
caster sugar (US: granulated)	50g	2oz	¼ cup
white wine	150ml	¼ pint	½ cup
double cream (US: whipping)	300ml	½ pint	1¼ cups

Finely grate the rind of one of the oranges and add to the cranberry sauce. Divide the sauce equally between 6 stemmed glasses. Dissolve the sugar in the juice from the oranges. Add the wine, cream and rind of the second orange and whisk until you have light fluffy peaks. Spoon into the stemmed glasses and chill for ½ hour before serving.

~ EXTRA RECIPES ~

Curried squash bisque with apricot

Butternut and acorn squash are just two of the great variety of squashes available to the Canadian cook. With the addition of apricot and just a hint of curry this makes a rich, creamy and very warming soup to come home to after midnight mass, or to serve on Boxing Day (26 December).

dried apricots	175g	6oz	3/4 cup
water	300ml	1/2 pint	1 cup
acorn or butternut squash cooked and mashed	450ml	3/4 pint	2 cups
butter or margarine	45ml	3tbs	3tbs
small onion, finely chopped	1	1	1
curry powder	15ml	1tbs	1tbs
chicken stock	600ml	1 pint	2 1/2 cups
milk	450ml	3/4 pint	2 cups
single cream (half and half)	50ml	2fl oz	3tbs
almond flakes	25g	1oz	2tbs

Soak the apricots overnight in the water. In a large heavy-bottomed saucepan melt the butter or margarine and sauté the onion. Add the curry powder and cook for a minute or two more to release the flavour. Add the squash, apricots and chicken stock. Bring to the boil, then reduce the heat and simmer, covered, for 15 minutes.

When the soup has cooked, blend in batches to a smooth purée. Return to the heat and add the milk and the cream *but do not allow to boil*. Serve piping hot with a swirl of cream. A sprinkling of almonds adds a luxurious touch.

Tourtière

This tasty spiced pork pie is traditionally served by French Canadians at their midnight réveillon on Christmas Eve.

minced pork	450g	1lb	1lb
medium potato, boiled and mashed	1	1	1
potato water reserved from cooking the potato	150ml	5fl oz	1/2 cup
onion, grated	1	1	1
clove of garlic, crushed	1	1	1
mace	2ml	1/2 tsp	1/2 tsp
thyme	2ml	1/2 tsp	1/2 tsp
sage	2ml	1/2 tsp	1/2 tsp
small pinch of dry mustard			
small pinch of ground cloves			
ground black pepper to taste			
salt	5ml	1tsp	1tsp

Combine all the ingredients apart from the mashed potato in a large saucepan. Bring to the boil, reduce the heat and simmer uncovered for about 20 minutes, stirring occasionally. When the liquid is nearly all absorbed, remove from the heat and stir in the mashed potato. Chill the mixture.

Pre-heat the oven to 200°C (400°F/Gas 6) and prepare the pastry.

Pastry

plain flour	350g	12oz	3 cups
salt	5ml	1tsp	1tsp
margarine	75g	3oz	1/3 cup
lard	50g	2oz	1/4 cup
butter	50g	2oz	1/2 stick
cold water			
milk or beaten egg			

Cut the fats into the flour and salt and rub in with your fingertips until the mixture resembles breadcrumbs. Add a sufficient amount of cold water (about 45ml or 3tbs) to form a firm dough. Knead lightly on a floured board. Roll out two thirds of the pastry to cover a 20cm (8in.) pie dish generously. Gently press the pastry into the greased pie dish and trim the edges. Roll out the remaining pastry 2.5cm (1in.) larger than the pie dish. Fill the dish with the cooled meat mixture. Moisten the edges of the pastry with egg or milk and put the pastry lid on top, pinching the edges well together. Trim the edges and, using the extra pieces, arrange pastry leaves around a steam hole made in the centre. Glaze with egg or milk and bake for 40 minutes.

Egg-nog cheesecake

This recipe marries two Canadian Christmas favourites, egg-nog and cheesecake. It makes a lovely end to either a Christmas Eve buffet or a Boxing Day (26 December) meal.

Crumb crust

Graham cracker or digestive biscuit crumbs	100g	4oz	3/4 cup
butter, melted	30ml	2tbs	2tbs
caster sugar (US: granulated)	15ml	1tbs	1tbs

Mix the crumb crust ingredients and press into a loose-bottomed flan tin (spring form pan). Chill.

Filling

caster sugar (US: granulated)	100g	4oz	1/2 cup
eggs, separated	2	2	2
gelatine softened in	20ml	1 tbs heaped	1 tbs heaped
cold water	50ml	2tbs	2tbs
white rum	30ml	2tbs	2tbs
orange juice	60ml	4tbs	4tbs
rind of one orange			
nutmeg, freshly grated	2ml	1/2 tsp	1/2 tsp
cream cheese	300g	11oz	11oz
whipping cream	75ml	3fl oz	1/3 cup

Decoration

double or whipping cream	100ml	4fl oz	1/2 cup
chocolate, grated	25g	1oz	1oz

Holly leaves

chocolate	50g	2oz	
holly leaves	6	6	

Whisk the egg yolks and sugar until light and fluffy. Heat the softened gelatine gently to dissolve in the rum. Beat into the egg mixture along with the orange juice, orange rind and the nutmeg. Add the cream cheese and beat until smooth. Fold in the whipped cream and lastly the beaten egg whites. Taste at this point; you may like a little more rum/nutmeg/orange rind. Pour into the chilled crumb crust and chill—overnight if possible.

Whip the cream and use to pipe rosettes round the cake. Sprinkle the rosettes with grated chocolate.

If you really want to go to town, make chocolate holly leaves by melting chocolate in a double boiler, then brushing it on to the shiny uppersides of holly leaves. Freeze for 5 minutes or until set and then gently separate the leaves and the chocolate. They then need to be chilled for a further half hour just to firm them up before you use them to decorate the cheesecake.

Sparkling ruby punch

It's usual for Canadian hosts to greet their Christmas guests with a glass of festive punch. This punch is alcohol-free and tailor-made for drivers and children!

apple juice	1.2 litres	2 pints	5 cups
cranberry juice	1.2 litres	2 pints	5 cups
juice of 1 lemon			
ginger ale	1.2 litres	2 pints	5 cups

Mix the juices together. Just before serving add the ginger ale (Canada Dry, of course!).

Apple Kir

This one is for adults only. It has a lovely colour and is very elegant in champagne glasses.

apple concentrate	75ml	3fl oz	1/4 cup
crème de cassis (blackcurrant liqueur)	75ml	3fl oz	1/4 cup
dry white wine or champagne	750ml	1 1/4 pints	2 1/2 cups

Mix together. If you are using champagne, add it just before serving. This is *Kir royale*.

U S A

The USA enjoys a giant commercial bonanza at Christmas, with the store-owners rubbing their hands in glee as the dollars roll in. Surely nowhere in the world is there such a glorious show of decorations, trees, lights and gifts as here?

However, the visitor soon detects that beneath the superficial preoccupation with the material trappings of the festival, there lies a groundswell of delight in the birth of Jesus.

Despite the fact that the United States today is a melting pot of nationalities, the overwhelming majority of Americans who profess a faith are Christian. Recent statistics show that there are seventy-two million Protestants, fifty-one million Roman Catholics, 3.8 million belonging to Eastern churches, and 0.9 million to Old Catholic, Polish national Catholic or Armenian churches. With a population of more than 286 million, that's a large proportion of Christians!

The early American settlers in the seventeenth century were English, Dutch and French and they joined the native American Indian inhabitants already living in this vast, rich land. In the nineteenth century many more ethnic groups came, including Russians, Poles, Irish, Germans, Italians, Czechs, Africans and Mexicans. With the great diversity of background, it's not surprising that so many different Christmas traditions exist. Some of the customs brought in from Europe have survived intact, while others have been modified.

Nowhere is this more obvious than in the food eaten. The various ethnic groups brought with them their own countries' cuisines but modified them to fit the foods available. The United States has a wealth of food, and grows so much grain that it has been called the granary of the world. This abundance, together with a wealth of imagination, has made much American cookery superb. Travelling round the United States today, an observant visitor will notice that the food on offer varies not only with the nationality of the cook's forbears but also with the region of America.

Christmas was, of course, unknown in the Americas until 1492, when Christopher Columbus was shipwrecked, then rescued by the Indians, all on Christmas Day. He named his fortress and the adjoining village 'La Navidad' in honour of the day.

In 1620 the first Pilgrim Fathers arrived from England on the *Mayflower*. In the Plymouth and Massachusetts Bay colonies the celebration of Christmas was forbidden at first. The Puritan belief was that Christmas festivities were not discussed in the Bible and so shouldn't be allowed. Christmas was to be spent the same as any other day of the year. The laws were not repealed until the nineteenth century. In spite of the mixed feelings, Christmas was a big day for most new Americans. The Indians called the pioneer Christmas 'The Big Eating' and, in some French-settled areas, 'Kissing Day' because the French trapper families kissed each other when they exchanged gifts.

One of the first culinary signs that Christmas is coming in New York is after Thanksgiving when the dairies start selling egg-nog. American egg-nog has developed in a different way from the original English egg-nog which itself was a descendant of syllabub. Made with milk, cream, eggs, sugar and nutmeg, alcohol such as rum or bourbon is added before serving. In the eighteenth century in the deep South you might have seen eggnog served in grand fashion from a silver bowl surrounded by fruit and decorative greenery. In the nineteenth century egg-nog was served with free lunches by some restaurants in Christmas week. An American favourite, egg-nog today is drunk cold and preferably from crystal glasses.

Depending on their cultural background, some families have an Advent wreath with four candles on the table. Each week during Advent another candle is lit—perhaps by one of the children—before family prayers. Another symbol of Jesus' presence is the star and in Palmer's Lake in Colorado they erect a 500 feet diameter star on Sundance Peak which can be seen for twenty miles around. In Bethlehem, Pennsylvania, a star is lit up on South Mountain in early December. In Alaska, there are echoes of Eastern Europe as boys and girls carrying lanterns on poles hold aloft a large star covered with bright paper as they go round the houses. Singing carols, they're offered refreshments and the next night they return, dressed as Herod's men, in search of Jesus.

Starting the day after Thanksgiving, there's a notable change in many children's attitudes as they start doing chores with little whining or arguing. Story and song tell them that Santa knows when they've been bad or good, 'so be good for goodness' sake'. Two weeks or so before Christmas, children begin making decorations for the tree, popping corn and stringing it into garlands, restringing beads and making Christmas cards.

The old are not usually forgotten: in friendly neighbourhoods people take extra care to make sure they're warm and looked after and children visit to do any extra little job such as posting mail.

Christmas cookies in the United States come in many different shapes and sizes. Baked goods, such as cookies and fruit cakes or carrot cakes, are taken to neighbours, friends and relatives as pre-Christmas gifts. Sometimes cookies are hung on the Christmas tree and children enjoy themselves by shaping decorations from an inedible flour, salt, oil and water dough, baking, then painting and varnishing them. Other mid-December cooking may include a fruit-and-nut cake to keep for the festivities later, or special dishes that can be popped into the freezer, such as one of the many sweet or savoury pies that are so much a feature of American winter meals. In Chicago—4,600 miles from Poland—the second largest Polish population of any city after Warsaw can buy their much loved *kielbasa* (Polish garlic sausages), lovingly made specially for Christmas by Polish women, and eaten alone or in fragrant Christmas *bigos* (see page 107 for recipe).

Churches are decorated with poinsettias and candles just before Christmas and many have a manger scene with the figures of Mary and Joseph standing by the crib. In many areas of the country, it's customary for the adult choirs of some churches to prepare an evening worship service of Christmas songs, music and readings. Churches of different denominations hold these services on different nights usually Sundays—during December so that congregations can enjoy each other's efforts. Sometimes the children enact a nativity play during the evening. Many children are invited to a special Sunday School party before Christmas called a 'Happy Birthday Jesus' party.

Some Americans consider Christmas Eve more important than Christmas Day, reminding us of their eastern and south-eastern European backgrounds. They celebrate the evening with a festive meal after their candlelit church service. Others attend a midnight service before having their Christmas meal.

On Christmas Eve children all over the United States put out their stockings for Santa

Claus to fill when he comes down the chimney or through the front door. He may find a glass of milk and some cookies too. It's possible to rent a Santa to come to the door and children may have visited a store Santa already for a taste of the joys to come.

Santa Claus as we know him today is very much an American figure, though he originally entered American customs as good old St Nicholas with the Dutch settlers of the seventeenth century. His name is derived from the Teutonic Sanct Herr Nicholas and the Dutch *Sinterklass* but his rotund figure and his smiling face, moustache and beard were probably inspired by Jan Duyckinck, the pipe-smoking caretaker of the home belonging to a New York professor of biblical studies. The professor, Dr Clement Clarke Moore, wrote the universally loved Christmas poem 'The Night Before Christmas', about St Nicholas bringing presents in a reindeer-pulled sleigh, for his daughter.

Santa's sleigh first appeared, with one reindeer, in an earlier children's book called 'The Children's Friend: A New Year's Present, to Little Ones Five to Twelve', by Washington Irving, but Santa himself was then a thin man more like the saint of the old world Dutch tradition.

Clement Moore, an expert in folk beliefs, chose eight reindeer because of the eight-legged horse named Sleipnir which carried the Norse god Odin through the skies on his gift-bringing missions in ancient Norse mythology. In Moore's book, not only had Santa grown fatter, but the number of reindeer had grown to eight, each with its own name. The reindeer came into the picture because the Scandinavians believed that the first sign of winter was when the 'Old Man of Winter' came south, driving his reindeer herds before him. This Old Man, the 'personification of winter', became known throughout northern Europe by many titles, including Winterman, King Frost, King Yule, Old Winter, Grandfather Frost, and Father Christmas.

A few Pennsylvania 'Dutch' families (who are actually German or *Deutsch* in origin) still tell their children about 'fur Nicholas' or 'Pelznickel'—a once frightening though now more jovial figure dressed in fur who brings presents for good children but a switch for naughty ones.

On Christmas Eve it's the custom for Clement Moore's poem to be read aloud to the children. In some homes, part of Dickens' classic children's story 'A Christmas Carol' is read with its jovial warning to show generosity and kindliness at Christmas. Carols or Christmas songs are sung, and some exchange presents tonight, while others wait for Christmas Day itself.

Christmas morning finds children waking early to discover stockings bulging with little presents, fruit, nuts and sweets, if they're lucky. Some must have breakfast before opening their presents from under the Christmas tree. In view of the Christmas feast to come, some families have a surprisingly large breakfast. In Georgia, for example, waffles or pancakes may be served with a mixture of peanut butter and maple syrup, with coffee or juice to wash them down.

Morning services range from the sedate to the exultant, depending on the denomination and the locality. The manger scenes are completed with the inclusion of the baby Jesus in the crib. At home, preparations for the Christmas meal are in full swing. There is no traditional American Christmas dinner as such, but most people have a very special meal of their favourite foods. The main meal is likely to be eaten late in the afternoon, so children have a snack to tide them over while the meat cooks. The two menus supplied for a Georgian and a New England festive meal show the intriguing contrasts of Christmas food in the USA.

In Georgia, a typical celebration meal may be served as a buffet, with pumpkin soup sprinkled with herb croûtons or a creamy peanut soup to start off.

On the buffet there may be an oyster pie. A suckling pig is an old favourite, a reminder of Scandinavian Yule feasts of the distant past. Roast beef and turkey are perhaps more popular, the turkey served with cranberry relish and lots of vegetables and a cornbread dressing cooked separately. Sweet potatoes are used to make one of a dozen dishes such as a 'soufflé' which is a sheer delight. Besides roast potatoes, Brussels sprouts and French beans cooked in bacon fat, there may be a couple of salads including a colourful jellied one such as cranberry soufflé salad or egg-nog Christmas salad.

With the main dish will be eaten a selection of breads. In true southern style, cornbread, southern biscuits, ryebread and Parkerhouse rolls are served together in the bread basket.

As for dessert, pecan pie seems to come out tops with most people as it has for over two hundred years. Made with a cream cheese pastry its sweetness is just right for Christmas Day.

In New England the culinary picture is different. Seafood is a perennial favourite for the starter. Lobster, served simply with a light mayonnaise, is perfect, or else little clam 'meringues' made by adding clams to a mayonnaise sauce, mixing with stiffly beaten egg whites, and cooking on rounds of toast.

Turkey—with any one of many dressings such as sausage and oyster—roast beef, glazed ham or a large chicken will follow, accompanied by a large selection of vegetables such as baked acorn or butternut squash sweetened with maple syrup and flavoured with butter, potatoes mashed with garlic and sautéed in butter, a purée of lima beans, and a broccoli and cauliflower stir-fry. As in Georgia, there will be different breads.

The meal draws to a close with a wide choice of desserts such as pumpkin-cheese marble tart made with pecan nut pastry, carrot cake swathed in cream cheese frosting, blueberry pie and mincemeat tart. It's said by some that if you serve some sort of mince pie on Christmas Day, you'll have good luck for a year, but a guest who refuses it will have bad luck!

In early January the lights come down, the glittery ornaments are packed away, and already the stores are gearing up for the next festival. But for many people the true joy of Christmas doesn't fade with the festivities, the hope and light of Jesus' birth shine on all year through.

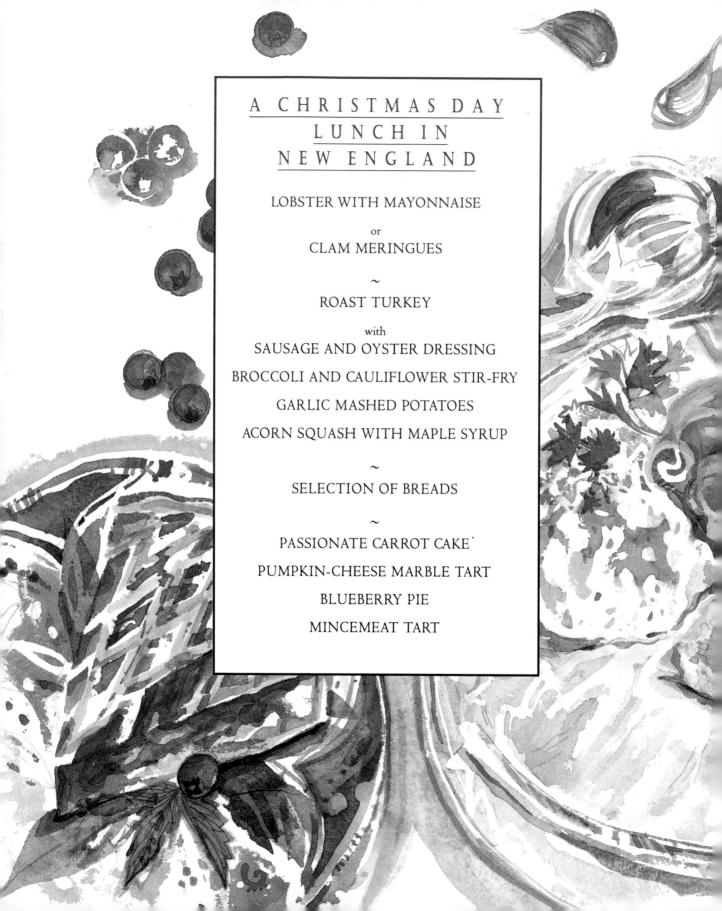

A CHRISTMAS DAY LUNCH IN NEW ENGLAND

LOBSTER WITH MAYONNAISE

or
CLAM MERINGUES

~

ROAST TURKEY

with
SAUSAGE AND OYSTER DRESSING
BROCCOLI AND CAULIFLOWER STIR-FRY
GARLIC MASHED POTATOES
ACORN SQUASH WITH MAPLE SYRUP

~

SELECTION OF BREADS

~

PASSIONATE CARROT CAKE
PUMPKIN-CHEESE MARBLE TART
BLUEBERRY PIE
MINCEMEAT TART

Lobster with mayonnaise

Lobster is expensive in northern climes in December, especially for a main course, but it makes an excellent starter for the Christmas Day meal. It's easier to buy lobster freshly cooked in the shell, but be sure to buy it from a fishmonger or supermarket fish counter you know to be reputable, and order it a week ahead to avoid disappointment. Don't be put off by having to 'dress' (split and prepare) the cooked lobster, because it's easier than you might think. However, your fishmonger would do it for you if you preferred.

This is one of the simplest of the many recipes for lobsters, and one of the most delicious. The mayonnaise recipe is foolproof and tastes delightful but it requires an electric blender. A good quality commercially made mayonnaise could be substituted.

freshly cooked lobsters	2	2	2
watercress			
mayonnaise (see below for recipe, or use 300ml bought mayonnaise)			

First prepare each lobster. Using a sharp knife, cut through the head and down through the tail. Open out the two halves and discard the dark thread of intestine which runs down the tail, and the small stomach sac which lies near the head. Leave the pink roe (the coral) and the greenish 'liver' (the fat or tomalley) near the head.

Twist off the big claws and crack them with a lobster cracker or by tapping with a hammer through a cloth. Carefully lift out the meat, remove the membrane lying down each claw, and reserve.

Twist off the small claws, or snip them off with scissors. Use a lobster pick or skewer to extract the meat, keeping the claws intact. Reserve the meat. Take two claws and fit the ends into each other to make a circle. When you have dressed both lobsters, you need to end up with four circles. Keep them to one side to use as bases on which to stand the four half shells.

Lift out the tail meat with a sharp knife and cut it diagonally into thick slices. Arrange these slices, rounded side up, in the opposite half shell. Put all the claw meat into the head shells.

Stand each half lobster on a claw circle on a serving dish and garnish with watercress. Serve the mayonnaise separately.

Mayonnaise

large egg	1	1	1
made (prepared) mustard	5ml	1tsp	1tsp
salt	2ml	$1/2$ tsp	$1/2$ tsp
pinch of white pepper			
sugar	2ml	$1/2$ tsp	$1/2$ tsp
oil (a mixture of mostly corn oil with some olive and/or walnut or hazelnut oil)	300ml	$1/2$ pint	$1 1/2$ cups
fresh lemon juice	30ml	2tbs	2tbs
white wine vinegar	10ml	2tsp	2tsp
boiling water	20ml	4tsp	4tsp

Put the egg, mustard, salt, pepper, sugar and 60ml (4tbs) of the oil into an electric blender. Cover and blend until smooth. Uncover and continue blending, slowing adding 150ml ($1/4$ pint/$1/2$ cup) of the oil and the lemon juice. Add the remaining oil and the vinegar, continuing to blend until the mayonnaise is thick. Stir in the boiling water and the mayonnaise is ready to serve.

Clam meringues

The only resemblance clam meringues bear to the sweet white confections normally known as meringues is their slightly puffed up shape. If you can't get clams, use cockles instead.

slices wholemeal bread, toasted	8	8	8

fresh or canned clams	100g	4oz	4oz
butter	50g	2oz	1/2 stick
plain flour	50g	2oz	1/2 cup
milk	200ml	7fl oz	3/4 cup
salt	2ml	1/2 tsp	1/2 tsp
pinch of black pepper			
mayonnaise	45ml	3tbs	3tbs
medium egg whites, stiffly beaten	2	2	2
shake of cayenne pepper			
chopped fresh parsley	10ml	2tsp	2tsp

Pre-heat the oven to 180°C (350°F/Gas 4). Cut each slice of toast into a round shape and put on a baking tray. Rinse the clams in cold water and drain. Baby clams can be left whole, but larger ones should be roughly chopped.

Melt the butter in a saucepan and stir in the flour. Cook gently, stirring, for one minute. Add the milk and stir vigorously as the sauce thickens. Remove from the heat and beat until smooth. Stir in the salt, pepper, mayonnaise and clams. Fold in the stiffly beaten egg whites gently and evenly.

Spoon the mixture on to the pieces of toast and sprinkle with cayenne pepper. Bake for 20 minutes. Sprinkle with parsley before serving piping hot.

Sausage and oyster dressing (stuffing, for roast turkey)

large onion, chopped	1	1	1
butter	100g	4oz	1 stick
fresh breadcrumbs	175g	6oz	1 cup
sticks celery, chopped	3	3	3

mixed herbs	5ml	1tsp	1tsp
fresh parsley, chopped OR	15ml	1tbs	1tbs
dried parsley	5ml	1tsp	1tsp
salt	2ml	1/2 tsp	1/2 tsp
pinch of black pepper			
canned oysters, drained and rinsed	350g	12oz	12oz
100% smoked pork sausage, such as Italian salami, skinned and chopped	100g	4oz	1/4 lb
water to bind			

Cook the onion in the butter until soft and golden. Remove from the heat and stir in half the breadcrumbs. Tip into a large bowl and stir in the remaining crumbs, celery, mixed herbs, parsley, salt and pepper.

Roughly chop the oysters and add to the mixture with the chopped pork sausage and enough water to bind everything together.

Use to stuff a turkey, or cook separately in a shallow greased casserole dish for the last hour of the turkey's cooking time. (See page 208 for roast turkey cooking instructions.)

Broccoli and cauliflower stir-fry

The beautiful green and white florets of broccoli and cauliflower look colourful on the Christmas table and taste crisply delicious.

broccoli	350g	12oz	1 1/2 cups
cauliflower	350g	12oz	1 1/2 cups
cold water	45ml	3tbs	3lbs
soy sauce	45ml	3tbs	3tbs
cornflour (cornstarch)	7ml	1 1/2 tsp	1 1/2 tsp

caster sugar (US: granulated)	5ml	1tsp	1tsp
corn oil	30ml	2tbs	2tbs
blanched whole almonds	50g	2oz	1/4 cup
celery, cut into thin diagonal slices	75g	3oz	1/3 cup
large onion, thinly sliced lengthways	1	1	1

Wash the broccoli and cauliflower and remove the leaves and thick stalks. Separate into florets. Cook in boiling water for 2 minutes and drain. Mix the water, soy sauce, cornflour (cornstarch) and sugar in a small bowl.

Put the oil in a large frying pan (or a wok if you have one) and heat it. Stir the almonds in the oil until beginning to brown. Stir-fry the vegetables for 5 minutes or until crisply tender but not overdone. Stir the soy sauce mixture into the vegetables. Cook and stir for 3 minutes and serve at once.

Garlic mashed potatoes

Paradoxically, these, smooth, creamy mashed potatoes have so much garlic that you can scarcely taste it.

heads of garlic (about 30 cloves)	2	2	2
butter	50g	2oz	1/2 stick
flour	50g	2oz	1/2 cup
milk	300ml	1/2 pint	1 1/4 cups
salt	2ml	1/2 tsp	1/2 tsp
pinch of pepper			
potatoes	1125g	2 1/2 lb	2 1/2 lb
butter	75g	3oz	3/4 stick

whipping cream	60ml	4tbs	4tbs
parsley, chopped	60ml	4tbs	4tbs

Peel and crush the garlic and cook very gently in the butter for 5 minutes, taking care not to brown it. Add the flour and cook gently for 2 minutes, stirring constantly, to make a roux. Remove from the heat. Put the milk in a small pan and bring to the boil. Add the milk, salt and pepper to the roux to make a thick white sauce and beat well until smooth. Cook, stirring, for 1 minute, and remove from the heat.

Peel and quarter the potatoes and cook in boiling water until tender. Drain, add the butter, and mash well until the butter has melted and the potatoes are smooth. Add the sauce, cream and parsley and stir thoroughly. Add more seasoning if required.

Acorn squash with maple syrup

There are many different varieties of marrow (squash) around at Christmas and their colour and shape add greatly to the appearance of any meal. For this recipe use any squashes small enough for one person, such as custard marrows or acorn squashes. Maple syrup, cinnamon and other spices, and streaky bacon make the baked squash taste wonderful.

small marrows/squashes	4	4	4
dark brown sugar	50g	2oz	1/4 cup
cinnamon	2ml	1/2 tsp	1/2 tsp
pinch of grated nutmeg			
pinch of salt			
butter, melted	50g	2oz	1/2 stick
maple syrup	150ml	1/4 pint	1/2 cup
streaky bacon slices	8	8	8
boiling water to put in base of pan			

Pre-heat the oven to 180°C (350°F/Gas 4). Cut each marrow (squash) in half and scoop out the seeds with a small spoon and discard. Mix together the sugar, cinnamon, nutmeg, salt, melted butter and maple syrup in a bowl. Put the marrow halves cut side up in a shallow baking dish and put equal amounts of the mixture into each. Lay the bacon slices over the marrow halves, one to each. Pour boiling water into the dish until 2.5cm (1in.) deep. Bake for 30 minutes or until the marrows are tender.

Passionate carrot cake

F rosted with a tangy cream cheese icing, this moist, wholesome carrot cake makes a festive dessert or a Christmas teatime treat. Tiny marzipan or fondant carrots are surprisingly quick to make and together with walnuts look very attractive decorating the pale cream iced cake.

wholemeal (wholewheat) flour	225g	8oz	2 cups
baking powder	10ml	2tsp	2tsp
salt	5ml	1tsp	1tsp
cinnamon	10ml	2tsp	2tsp
eggs, well beaten	4	4	4
corn oil	300ml	1/2 pint	1 1/4 cup
vanilla essence (extract)	5ml	1tsp	1tsp
caster sugar (US: granulated)	350g	12oz	1 1/2 cups
grated carrot	750ml	1 1/4 pints	2 1/3 cups
walnuts, chopped	175g	6oz	3/4 cup

Cream cheese frosting

cream cheese	75g	3oz	3oz
butter	50g	2oz	1/2 stick
vanilla essence (extract)	2ml	1/2 tsp	1/2 tsp
icing (confectioner's) sugar, sifted	100g	4oz	1 cup
walnut halves	6	6	6

Little carrot decorations

made marzipan OR	50g	2oz	1/4 cup
fondant icing	50g	2oz	1/4 cup
orange food colouring			
stick of angelica	1	1	1

Pre-heat the oven to 180°C (350°F/Gas 4). Prepare a 23cm (9in.) cake tin (pan) by greasing the inside, then lining it with greaseproof paper and greasing the paper. Mix the flour, baking powder, salt and cinnamon in a bowl. Stir the eggs, oil and vanilla essence (extract) in a large bowl. Fold the flour mixture and the sugar alternately into the egg mixture, and mix thoroughly but gently. Stir in the carrots and walnuts. Spoon the cake mixture into the tin (pan). Bake for 1 hour 15 minutes to 1 hour 20 minutes, or until a skewer comes out clean. Remove from the oven, wait for 5 minutes then remove from the tin and cool.

Put the frosting ingredients into a bowl and beat well till smooth. Use to cover the top and sides of the cake by swirling it over with a large knife. The surface doesn't have to be smooth.

Mould six tiny carrots from marzipan or fondant coloured with orange colouring. Arrange round the cake and stick two shreds of angelica at the base of each carrot. Intersperse the carrots with walnut halves.

Pumpkin-cheese marble tart

S wirls of pumpkin and cream cheese give this tart its name and the nutty pecan pastry gives it a lovely crunchy base.

Pecan pastry

plain flour	100g	4oz	1 cup
pecans or walnuts, ground	25g	1oz	1/4 cup
pinch of salt			
butter or margarine	50g	2oz	1/2 stick
vegetable cooking fat	15ml	1tbs	1tbs
egg yolk	1	1	1
cold water	30ml	2tbs	2tbs

Pumpkin-cheese filling

cream cheese, softened	225g	8oz	8oz
vanilla essence (extract)	2ml	1/2 tsp	1/2 tsp
caster sugar (US: granulated)	75g	3oz	1/3 cup
plain flour	15ml	1tbs	1tbs
pinch of salt			
egg, beaten	1	1	1
milk	30ml	2tbs	2tbs
canned or mashed cooked pumpkin	175g	6oz	3/4 cup
brown sugar	75g	3oz	1/3 cup
pinch of cinnamon			
pinch of allspice			
pinch of mace			
milk	50ml	2fl oz	1/4 cup

Decoration

pecan halves	12	12	12
pecans, chopped	10ml	2tsp	2tsp
whipping cream, whipped	50ml	2fl oz	1/4 cup

First make the pastry. Mix the flour, nuts and salt and rub in the butter and vegetable fat. Beat the egg yolk and water together and add to the flour mixture. Stir with a fork until the dough forms a ball. Knead very lightly on a floured board. Roll out the dough to a circle 28cm (11in.) diameter, and place this carefully in a greased 25cm (10in.) flan (pie) pan, neatening the edges. Bake in a pre-heated oven for 7 minutes at 200°C (400°F/Gas 6) and cool.

Make the filling by beating the cream cheese and vanilla essence (extract) till fluffy. Add the sugar, flour and salt and mix well. Add the egg and milk and stir in carefully. Remove 100ml (4fl oz) of the cheese mixture and set aside. In another bowl, mix the pumpkin, brown sugar and spices. Stir in the reserved cream cheese mixture and the 50ml (2fl oz/1/4 cup) of milk.

Fill the flan case by alternately spooning the pumpkin and the remaining cream cheese mixture into it. Gently swirl the two mixtures into a marbled effect using a spatula.

Bake at 190°C (375°F/Gas 5) for 25–35 minutes or until the filling looks set. Cool, then decorate with pecan halves round the outside and a swirl of whipped cream sprinkled with chopped pecans in the centre.

Blueberry pie

T his all-American pie is a great favourite at Christmas. Filled with succulent bluish-black berries, and topped with a shiny, golden, latticed pie-crust, it goes well with dollops of thick cream, vanilla ice-cream, plain live yoghurt, or fromage frais. The berries are sometimes known as bilberries, huckle-berries or whortleberries.

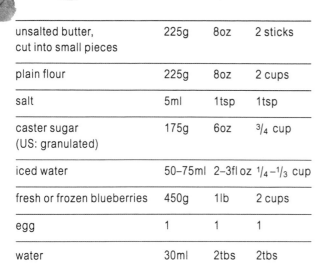

unsalted butter, cut into small pieces	225g	8oz	2 sticks
plain flour	225g	8oz	2 cups
salt	5ml	1tsp	1tsp
caster sugar (US: granulated)	175g	6oz	3/4 cup
iced water	50–75ml	2–3fl oz	1/4–1/3 cup
fresh or frozen blueberries	450g	1lb	2 cups
egg	1	1	1
water	30ml	2tbs	2tbs

Put the flour and salt into a large bowl and rub in the butter with your fingers until the mixture resembles fine breadcrumbs. Mix in 50 g (2oz/1/4 cup) of the sugar. Stir in just enough iced water to bind the pastry. Divide the ball of pastry into two, wrap in plastic wrap, and chill for 2 hours.

Pre-heat the oven to 180°C (350°F/Gas 4). Roll out half the pastry on a clean, floured surface, and use it to line a greased 20cm (8in.) pie dish.

Mix the blueberries with the remaining sugar and put in the pie-shell. Roll out the other half of the pastry and cut into 3cm (3/4 in.) strips. Make a lattice-work top with the strips. You'll find it easiest to lay half the strips in one direction across the pie, securing them at one end by crimping them into the edge of the pie-shell with a fork, and then to weave the remaining strips through them at right angles. Crimp all the strips into the edge of the pie-shell, then cut off their proud ends.

Mix the egg and water and brush this as a glaze over the latticed pie top.

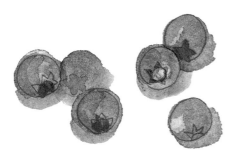

Mincemeat tart

You can use commercially prepared mincemeat for this tart but, if you have the time, this home-made recipe is particularly delicious.

Pastry

plain flour	225g	8oz	2 cups
pinch of salt			
butter	100g	4oz	1 stick
white vegetable fat/lard	50g	2oz	1/4 cup
caster sugar (US: granulated)	10ml	2tsp	2tsp
egg yolk	1	1	1
water	30–45ml	2–3tbs	2–3tbs
caster sugar (US: granulated), for sprinkling	15ml	1tbs	1tbs
water to brush pastry top			

Mincemeat

eating apples, peeled, cored and chopped	100g	4oz	1/2 cup
candied citrus peel, chopped	25g	1oz	2tbs
raisins	50g	2oz	1/4 cup
currants	75g	3oz	1/3 cup
sultanas (golden raisins)	75g	3oz	1/3 cup
glacé cherries, halved	50g	2oz	1/4 cup
grapes, peeled, seeded and quartered	75g	3oz	1/3 cup
almonds, blanched and shredded	50g	2oz	1/4 cup

grated rind and juice of 1 lemon			
pinch of mixed (pumpkin) spice			
brown sugar	75g	3oz	1/3 cup
melted butter	25g	1oz	2tbs
brandy or sherry	50ml	2fl oz	1/4 cup

First make the pastry. Stir the flour and salt into a large bowl. Add the butter and vegetable fat or lard, cut into small pieces, then rub into the flour with your finger tips until the mixture resembles fine breadcrumbs. Stir in the sugar. Mix the egg yolk and 30ml (2tbs) water, and quickly stir into the flour and fat mixture to make a dough. Add more water if necessary. Cover the pastry dough with plastic wrap and chill.

Pre-heat the oven to 190°C (375°F/Gas 5). Put a 7 inch (18cm) flan ring on a backing sheet and grease both. (Or grease a pie pan.)

Prepare the mincemeat by mixing all the ingredients together.

Use three quarters of the pastry to line the flan ring or pie pan. Fill with mincemeat. Roll out the remaining pastry until it forms a circle a little larger than the flan ring, and cut an 8cm (3in.) hole in the middle. Moisten the uppermost edges of the pastry lining the flan ring. Put the circle of pastry on top and crimp round the edges with a fork or your fingers. Cut off the excess pastry. Brush the surface of the pastry with water and sprinkle with sugar. Bake for 30–40 minutes or until the pastry is golden brown. Serve with whipped cream.

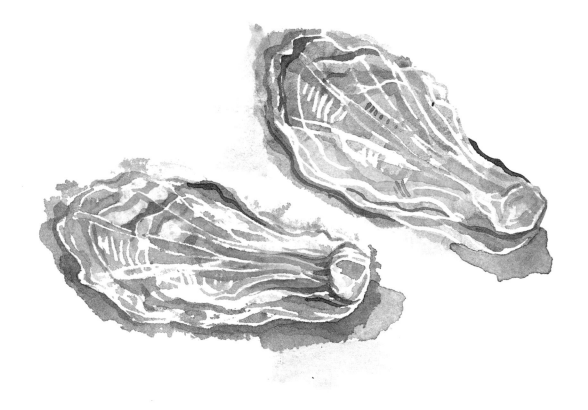

A CHRISTMAS DAY BUFFET LUNCH IN GEORGIA

PUMPKIN SOUP WITH HERB CROÛTONS
or
CREAMY PEANUT SOUP

~

OYSTER PIE

~

ROAST TURKEY
with
CORN BREAD DRESSING
and
CRANBERRY RELISH

or
ROAST SUCKLING PIG WITH APPLE AND
CITRUS SAUSAGE DRESSING

SWEET POTATO SOUFFLÉ

BACON-FRIED FRENCH BEANS

BRUSSELS SPROUTS

ROAST POTATOES

CRANBERRY SOUFFLÉ SALAD
or
EGG-NOG CHRISTMAS SALAD

CORN BREAD

~

PECAN PIE

LEMON COCONUT CAKE

CORN PUDDING

Pumpkin soup with herb croûtons

This creamy-yellow smooth soup looks especially festive if you serve it in the pumpkin shell. Herb croûtons complement the delicate flavour of the pumpkin perfectly.

small pumpkin OR	1	1	1
tinned pumpkin	450g	1lb	2 cups
butter	25g	1oz	2tbs
small onions, finely chopped	2	2	2
chicken stock	1.2 litres	2 pints	5 cups
peeled potato, cubed	175g	6oz	1/3 cup
sugar	25g	1oz	2tbs
lemon juice	15ml	1tbs	1tbs
paprika	5ml	1tsp	1tsp
whipping cream OR	250ml	9fl oz	1 cup
single cream WITH	150ml	1/4 pint	1/2 cup
double cream (US: whipping)	150ml	1/4 pint	1/2 cup

If using a pumpkin, slice open the top and scoop out the pips (seeds). Remove the pumpkin flesh with a spoon, leaving about 12mm ($1/2$ in.) next to the skin and taking great care not to break the skin. Measure out 500g (1lb) of this flesh. Any surplus pumpkin flesh can be used to make pumpkin cream cheese marble cheesecake.

Melt the butter in a large saucepan and gently sauté the onion until softened. Add the pumpkin, chicken stock, potato, sugar, lemon juice and paprika and bring to the boil. Cover and simmer for 35 minutes. Liquidize the soup or pass it through a strainer into a bowl, pressing the pulp with a wooden spoon to extract as much soup as possible. You can either return the pulp to the soup or discard it. The soup does taste delicious complete with the pulp but aim to get the consistency as smooth as possible.

Finally, add the cream and reheat, stirring, until hot enough to serve but not boiling. Serve in the pumpkin shell or a soup tureen. Offer herb croûtons separately.

Herb croûtons

These aromatic crunchy cubes of bread fried in butter go well with any creamy soup. Sprinkle on top at the last minute to preserve their texture.

large, thick slices of wholemeal bread, preferably not too fresh	2–3	2–3	2–3
butter	50g	2oz	1/2 stick
basil or oregano	2ml	1/2 tsp	1/2 tsp
thyme	2ml	1/2 tsp	1/2 tsp
pinch of salt			

With a sharp knife remove the crusts from the slices of bread and cut the bread into cubes 12mm ($1/2$ in.) wide, or less if you can do so without the bread crumbling.

Melt the butter in a shallow pan and add the cubes of bread. Fry gently, stirring frequently, until golden-brown but not burned. Sprinkle with the herbs and salt and stir well. Drain on kitchen paper and serve.

Creamy peanut soup

If you like peanuts, try this unusual soup which is good enough for a feast.

butter	50g	2oz	1/2 stick
medium onion, chopped	1	1	1
stalk of celery, chopped	1	1	1

plain flour	30ml	2tbs	2tbs
good chicken stock	1.2 litres	2 pints	5 cups
smooth peanut butter	175g	6oz	³/₄ cup
single cream (half and half)	175ml	6fl oz	³/₄ cup
peanuts, chopped, to garnish	15ml	1tbs	1tbs

Melt the butter in a frying pan and add the onion and celery. Sauté until the onion is softened but not brown. Stir in the flour. Add the chicken stock, stirring, and bring to the boil. Rub through a sieve or liquidize. Add the peanut butter and cream, stirring well. Reheat but don't boil. Sprinkle with chopped peanuts.

Oyster pie

When oyster pies were first cooked in the United States, oysters were cheap. Nowadays such a pie makes a very special party dish suitable for Christmas Eve. If you prefer to make individual open tartlets, perhaps for a starter on Christmas Day, this recipe will do just as well, and you need only half the amount of oysters, which makes it easier on the purse. You could of course substitute mussels for oysters. The potato pastry used here complements the shellfish well, but you could use shortcrust or flaky pastry.

shelled oysters or mussels	450g	1lb	1lb
white wine	100ml	4fl oz	½ cup
potato pastry (see below)			
wholemeal breadcrumbs	100g	4oz	³/₄ cup
parsley, chopped	15ml	1tbs	1tbs
anchovy fillets, chopped	25g	1oz	2tbs
spring onions (green onions), chopped	6	6	6
black pepper			

egg, beaten	1	1	1
juice of 1 large orange			
double cream (US: whipping)	200ml	7fl oz	³/₄ cup

Cook the shelled oysters or mussels by poaching in their juice and the white wine for just two minutes. The drained liquid can be used to make a white sauce to serve with the pie.

Make up the potato pastry and use two thirds of it to line a greased pie dish. Mix together the drained oysters or mussels, breadcrumbs, parsley, anchovies, spring onions and black pepper and spoon into the pie. Top with the rest of the pastry and decorate with pastry trimmings stuck on with beaten egg. Brush with beaten egg. To the remainder of the egg add the orange juice and the cream and mix well. Make a hole in the centre of the pie and pour this mixture into the pie. Bake in a pre-heated oven at 180°C (350°F/Gas 4) for 40–45 minutes or until the pastry is done. Cover the top of the pie with foil for the last 15 minutes to prevent burning.

Potato pastry

A tasty pastry for oyster pie, and a useful pastry for a change for any fish or meat pie. Use instant potato from a packet for consistent results.

instant potato mix small (60 g) packet	1	1	1
plain flour	350g	12oz	3 cups
butter, cut into small pieces	100g	4oz	1 stick
lard, cut into small pieces	100g	4oz	½ cup

Make up the instant potato mix in a large bowl as directed on the packet. Add the flour and the fats and rub in well until the fats are incorporated evenly. Cover and chill till needed.

Corn bread dressing (stuffing)

The moistness of corn bread combined with onion, sausage, liver and a little Madeira makes for a stuffing you'll never forget. It's not surprising that corn bread stuffing is one of America's favourites.

butter	100g	4oz	1 stick
onions, finely chopped	225g	8oz	1 cup
sticks of celery, chopped	4	4	4
sausage meat	450g	1lb	1lb
the turkey liver			
corn bread, coarsely crumbled	250g	9oz	2 cups
water chestnuts, finely sliced	75g	3oz	1/3 cup
pinch of salt			
freshly ground black pepper			
fresh thyme OR	10ml	2tsp	2tsp
dried thyme	5ml	1tsp	1tsp
fresh sage OR	10ml	2tsp	2tsp
dried sage	5ml	1tsp	1tsp
Madeira or sherry	60ml	4tbs	1/4 cup
double cream (US: whipping)	60ml	4tbs	1/4 cup

Melt 75g (3oz/1/3 cup) of the butter in a large frying pan and sauté the onions and celery for 5–8 minutes until very lightly browned. With a fish slice (slotted spatula), lift them into a large bowl, letting any fat run back into the pan. Put the sausage meat into the pan and cook gently, stirring, till lightly browned. Lift into a sieve to drain away as much fat as possible. In the same pan, melt the rest of the butter and add the turkey liver. Cook for 3 minutes, then remove it and chop it coarsely. Add it to the onions. Next add the drained sausage meat, corn bread, water chestnuts, salt, a little black pepper, thyme and sage. Stir, then mix in the Madeira and cream. Use to stuff the turkey or cook in a separate baking tin and serve in scoops.

(See page 208 for roast turkey cooking instructions.)

Cranberry relish

Try this uncooked cranberry and fruit relish sweetened with marmalade and honey with your turkey. You'll be surprised at how delightful it is.

fresh cranberries, washed	225g	8oz	1 cup
small apple, peeled, cored and quartered	1	1	1
orange, washed, quartered and seeded. Don't remove the peel.	1	1	1
fennel, sliced	25g	1oz	2tbs
orange marmalade	45ml	3tbs	3tbs
honey	20ml	4tsp	4tsp
walnuts, chopped	25g	1oz	2tbs

Mince the cranberries, apple, orange and fennel or blend them in a food processor. Add the marmalade, honey and walnuts and stir well. Chill until ready to eat.

Suckling pig with apple and citrus sausage dressing

Roast pork and ham at Christmas time have been popular in Europe and the United States for hundreds of years. In the South some families like to cook a whole suckling pig. Brief your butcher in advance if you want to try this recipe, and remember to check the size of your oven to see if it will take a whole suckling pig! The citrus flavour of the stuffing given here counteracts the slight fattiness of the meat.

suckling pig	5–6kg	10–12lb	
(This will be about 50–60cm (20–24in.) long, and will feed at least 10 people.)			
apple and citrus sausage stuffing (see recipe)			
corn oil and salt to rub pig			
whole apple or orange	1	1	1
prunes or large cranberries	2	2	2
some greenery			

Fill the pig with the stuffing and skewer or sew it up. Weigh the roasting pan, then put the stuffed pig into it and weigh it again. Use bathroom scales to do this easily. Place a crumpled ball of foil in the pig's mouth to keep it open. Cover the tail and ears with foil. Rub the skin with oil and salt. If you have room in the oven, tie the back legs together pointing backwards from the tail, and tie the front legs together pointing forwards. If not, tuck the legs under the pig and secure with skewers or string. Put into a pre-heated oven at 230°C (450°F/Gas 8) and cook for 15 minutes, then lower the temperature to 160°C (325°F/Gas 3) and continue roasting until tender, allowing 25–30 minutes per 0.5kg (1lb) stuffed weight. Baste frequently.

Take the pig out of the oven and remove all the foil. Put the whole apple or orange in the pig's mouth and—if you like—small prunes or cranberries in the eyes. Decorate with a wreath of greenery round its neck.

Apple and citrus sausage dressing (stuffing)

The ingredients for home-made sausage are simply incorporated into this delicious stuffing recipe which goes so well with roast pork. Start the night before you want to cook the pig.

grated rind and juice of 2 lemons			
grated rind and juice of 2 oranges			
whole oats	100g	4oz	3/4 cup
wholemeal breadcrumbs	375g	13oz	2 cups
large cooking apples, not peeled, but cored and finely chopped	4	4	4
dried thyme	10ml	2tsp	2tsp
lean ham, diced	225g	8oz	1 cup
onions, finely chopped	3	3	3
butter, melted	75g	3oz	3/4 stick
egg, beaten	1	1	1
water			

Put the grated rind and juice of the oranges and lemons into a bowl and add the whole oats. Leave to soak overnight.

The next day, in a large bowl mix together all the ingredients, including enough water to make the stuffing hold together. Use to stuff the pig.

Sweet potato soufflé

The sweetness of this dish marries well with roast pork and the joy to the cook is that it can be put in the oven with the roast three quarters of an hour before you eat, so there's no last-minute hassle.

sweet potatoes	600g	1lb 5oz	1lb 5oz
caster sugar (US: granulated)	50g	2oz	1/4 cup
grated rind of 1/2 a lemon			
brandy	15ml	1tbs	1tbs
pinch of ground nutmeg			
pinch of cinnamon			
small pinch of salt			
butter, melted	50g	2oz	1/2 stick
egg yolks	2	2	2
single cream (half and half)	150ml	1/4 pint	1/2 cup
pecans, chopped	25g	1oz	2tbs
egg whites, well beaten	2	2	2
marshmallows	100g	4oz	1/2 cup

Cover the sweet potatoes (in their skins) with cold water in a large pan and bring to the boil. Boil for 25 minutes, then drain. When cool enough to handle, peel and purée the potato flesh. Add all the ingredients except the egg whites and marshmallows to the potato purée and mix well. Beat the egg whites until stiff and gently fold into the potato mixture and pour the mixture into a buttered ovenproof dish. Lay the marshmallows on top and bake in a pre-heated oven at 180°C (350°F/Gas 4) for 45 minutes.

Bacon-fried French beans

French beans are relatively scarce and expensive in the winter but you can use frozen beans for this recipe. The bacon-flavoured beans go well with roast pork.

streaky bacon rashers (slices), de-rinded	225g	8oz	1/2 lb
French beans (fresh or frozen), topped and tailed	450g	1lb	3 cups

Lay the bacon rashers on a baking tray and cook in the oven at 180°C (350°F/Gas 4) for about 15–20 minutes until brown and crispy but not burnt. Pour the fat carefully into a saucepan and add the French beans and enough water just to cover them. Bring to the boil and simmer for 5–10 minutes or until just tender but not overcooked. Crumble the bacon rashers. Strain any remaining water from the beans and put into a serving dish. Sprinkle with the crumbled bacon.

Cranberry soufflé salad

Brightly coloured little savoury jellies or congealed salads add to the razzmatazz of the Christmas table in the southern states. These are a warm pink colour.

very hot water	225ml	8fl oz	1 cup
unflavoured gelatine, 11g/0.4oz envelope			
sugar	30ml	2tbs	2tbs
pinch of salt			
mayonnaise	100ml	4fl oz	1/2 cup
lemon juice	30ml	2tbs	2tbs
grated lemon rind	5ml	1tsp	1tsp

whole cranberry sauce (can or jar)	450g	1lb	16oz
orange, peeled and diced	1	1	1
walnuts chopped	50g	2oz	1/4 cup

To decorate

lettuce			
mayonnaise	30ml	2tbs	2tbs

Put the water into a bowl and sprinkle on the gelatine, sugar and salt. Stir with a fork until disolved. Whisk in the mayonnaise, lemon juice and lemon rind. Pour into a shallow, rectangular tin and freeze for 10–15 minutes or until firm at the edges. Spoon into a bowl and beat till fluffy, then fold in the cranberry sauce, orange and walnuts. Pour into individual moulds and chill until firm. Loosen each jelly by holding the mould upside down under hot running water for a few seconds, then turn out on to a bed of lettuce. Swirl a teaspoonful of mayonnaise on top of each one.

Egg-nog Christmas salad

You can make your own eggnog for this layered creamy-yellow and pink jellied (congealed) salad (see page 317 for egg-nog recipe), or you can use a commercially prepared variety if available. If you can't buy cans of crushed pineapple, chop pineapple chunks or rings instead.

can (425g/15oz) crushed pineapple	1	1	1
fresh lime juice	45ml	3tbs	3tbs
unflavoured gelatine, 11g/0.4oz envelope			
eggnog	350ml	12fl oz	1 1/2 cups
sticks celery, chopped	3	3	3
packet (135g/4 1/2 oz) raspberry jelly (jello)	1/2	1/2	1/2

boiling water	450ml	3/4 pint	2 cups
cranberry sauce	275g	10oz	1 1/3 cups
lettuce			

Drain the juice from the tin of pineapple into a saucepan, and heat to boiling. Remove from the heat. Put the lime juice in a bowl and sprinkle the gelatine on top. Stir with a fork and leave for 5 minutes to soften. Add to the boiling pineapple juice and stir until dissolved. Remove from the heat and allow to cool. Add the egg-nog and chill in the fridge until beginning to set. Gently stir in the drained pineapple and celery. Pour into a 1500ml/2 1/2 pint mould and chill until firm.

Dissolve the raspberry jelly in the boiling water and add the cranberry sauce. Chill until it begins to set, then pour over the layer of jellied eggnog. Chill until set.

When ready to serve put a bed of shredded lettuce on a serving dish. Loosen the jellied salad by holding the mould upside down under running hot water for a few seconds, then turn out on to the bed of lettuce.

Corn bread

Corn bread is traditionally southern but has been exported throughout the United States as it's so scrumptious. Light and slightly gritty in texture, it's quite unlike ordinary wheat bread but more like cake. Cook it as a loaf or as corn bread muffins, or even use it to make a delicious dressing (stuffing) for turkey.

plain wheat (white) flour	175g	6oz	1 1/2 cups
baking powder	15ml	1tbs	1tbs
salt	5ml	1tsp	1tsp
white or yellow water-ground corn meal (sometimes known as polenta flour or maize meal)	275g	10oz	2 1/3 cups
caster sugar (US: granulated)	25g	1oz	2tbs

butter, melted	100g	4oz	1 stick
eggs, beaten	4	4	4
milk	225ml	8fl oz	1 cup
single cream (half and half)	50ml	2fl oz	3tbs

Pre-heat the oven to 200°C (400°F/Gas 6). Grease a 20cm (8in.) square heavy baking dish well with butter or oil and put it into the oven. Sift the wheat flour, baking powder and salt into a bowl. Stir in the corn meal and sugar. Pour in the melted butter and mix until the mixture looks like breadcrumbs.

Beat the eggs and milk together in another bowl, then mix well into the flour mixture. Stir in the cream. Take the baking dish from the oven and spoon the corn bread mixture in. The consistency should be like a thick paste. Bake for 25–30 minutes or until a skewer inserted into the centre comes out clean. Cool for 5 minutes then remove from the tin. Serve in large squares or slices.

Pecan pie

Pecan trees grow in profusion in the southern states and if you have a sweet tooth, the combination of pecans and syrup in this pie will delight you. This pastry uses cream cheese which gives it a lovely crumbly texture and contrasts with the sweetness of the pie filling.

Cream cheese pastry

butter	75g	3oz	3/4 stick
cream cheese	75g	3oz	3oz
plain flour	225g	8oz	2 cups
water to mix			

Filling

eggs, beaten	3	3	3
egg yolk	1	1	1
dark corn syrup or golden syrup	175ml	6fl oz	2/3 cup
brown sugar	100g	4oz	1/2 cup
butter, melted	75g	3oz	3/4 stick
plain flour	25g	1oz	1/4 cup
vanilla essence (extract)	2ml	1/2 tsp	1/2 tsp
pecans, chopped	275g	10oz	1 1/4 cups
pecan halves, to decorate	50g	2oz	1/4 cup
whipping or double cream	150ml	1/4 pint	1/2 cup

Beat the butter and cream cheese in a large bowl until smooth, then mix in the flour. Add a little cold water if necessary to make the pastry cling together. Chill, covered, for 1 hour.

Mix together the eggs and egg yolk, syrup, sugar, butter, flour and vanilla until smooth, then stir in the nuts.

Roll out the pastry on a lightly floured surface and line a greased pie dish. Trim to fit and then fork or crimp the edges. Pour the filling in and bake at 180°C (350°F/Gas 4) for 40–50 minutes. Remove from the oven and decorate with pecan halves, pressing them into the pie slightly. Cool. Serve with whipped cream.

Lemon coconut cake

Layers of sponge cake sandwiched and covered with a tangy, lemon, quick American frosting, and sprinkled with toasted coconut, make this mouth-watering confection.

plain flour	200g	7oz	1 3/4 cups
baking powder	10ml	2tsp	2tsp

pinch of salt			
butter or soft margarine	100g	4oz	1/2 cup
caster sugar (US: granulated)	225g	8oz	1 cup
medium eggs, well beaten	2	2	2
milk	150ml	1/4 pint	1/2 cup
vanilla essence (extract)	2ml	1/2 tsp	1/2 tsp

To decorate

quick lemon American frosting (see recipe)			
dessicated (flaked) coconut	100g	4oz	1/2 cup

Pre-heat the oven to 180°C (350°F/Gas 4). Grease two 20cm (8in.) sandwich tins (round cake pans), put a circle of greaseproof paper in the base of each, and grease the paper.

Sift the flour, baking powder and salt into a medium bowl. Cream the butter or soft margarine with the sugar in a large bowl until very light and fluffy. Gradually beat in the eggs. Gently stir in the flour alternately with the milk and vanilla essence (extract).

Pour the mixture into the prepared tins (pans) and bake for 25–30 minutes. Cool on a wire rack.

Spread the coconut evenly on a baking tray and cook in the oven until beginning to brown, taking care not to burn it. Leave to cool.

Use a third of the American frosting to sandwich the two layers of cake together. Swirl the remainder quickly over the top and sides of the cake with a palette knife. Before the frosting sets, sprinkle the top of the cake with half the toasted coconut and carefully press the remainder round the sides.

Quick lemon American frosting

caster sugar (US: granulated)	175g	6oz	3/4 cup
egg white	1	1	1
heated lemon juice	30ml	2tbs	2tbs
pinch of cream of tartar			
grated lemon rind	10ml	2tsp	2tsp

Put all the ingredients into a bowl and place over a saucepan of gently simmering water. Whisk with a hand or electric whisk until the mixture thickens and soft peaks form when you lift the whisk. Use while still warm to fill and frost the cake.

Corn pudding

If you wish you can serve corn pudding as a savoury dish with the turkey or pork, instead of as a dessert. In this case, leave the sugar out and add 2ml (1/2 tsp) of salt and a shake of pepper to the flour.

eggs, beaten	2	2	2
flour	25g	1oz	1/4 cup
creamed sweetcorn 425g/15oz cans	2	2	2
caster sugar (US: granulated)	75g	3oz	1/3 cup
melted butter	30ml	2tbs	2tbs
evaporated milk	400ml	14fl oz	1 3/4 cups
pecan nuts chopped	50g	2oz	1/4 cup

Mix all the ingredients in a bowl and pour into a greased casserole dish. Stand the dish in a roasting tin and pour water into the tin until it reaches halfway up the sides of the dish. Bake at 150°C (300°F/Gas 2) for 1 1/4–1 1/2 hours.

CHRISTMAS: A COOK'S TOUR

~ EXTRA RECIPES ~

Turkey tetrazzini

This simple and tasty dish is an unusual and easy way to use up leftovers of turkey after Christmas. Turkey Tetrazzini is a variation of chicken Tetrazzini which, according to the cookery writer James Beard, was created and named after a renowned Italian *coloratura* soprano. Signora Tetrazzini was a famous gourmand who loved to sing and eat in San Francisco in the early years of the twentieth century. She had an amazing girth and a passion for pasta, on which this dish is based.

butter	25g	1oz	2tbs
green pepper, deseeded and chopped	1/2	1/2	1/2
small onion, chopped	1	1	1
pimentos	15ml	1tbs	1tbs
pinch of pepper			
large pinch of salt			
mushroom soup 425g/15oz can	1	1	1
grated cheese (New York or mild cheddar)	150g	5oz	3/4–1 cup
chicken stock	100ml	4fl oz	1/2 cup
mushrooms, chopped	75g	3oz	1/3 cup
cooked turkey meat, diced or shredded	675g	1 1/2 lb	3 1/2 cups
thin spaghetti, boiled but not too soft	225g	8oz	8oz
a little paprika			

Melt the butter in a frying pan and sauté the pepper and onion for 5 minutes. Mix all the ingredients in a large bowl. Put into an ovenproof dish and sprinkle with paprika. Cover and bake at 180°C (350°F/Gas 4) for 45–60 minutes.

Poinsettia balls

Poinsettias—those flame-like Christmas flowers—originated in Mexico. They were named after the first American minister to Mexico, Dr Joel R. Poinsett, who made them popular in the United States. In Mexico they are called flowers of the Holy Night and the legend goes that a peasant girl named Cuernavaca had no gift to take into the cathedral on Christmas Eve. An angel came and told her to pick a stem of an insignificant green, leafy plant to take up to the altar. On her way there, a priest was about to send her out of the church when the top of the leafy stem suddenly turned a radiant red!

These little round nut-covered cookies are decorated with glacé cherries shaped into poinsettias.

plain flour	175g	6oz	1 1/2 cups
pinch of bicarbonate of soda (baking soda)			
pinch of nutmeg			
pinch of salt			
butter or margarine	100g	4oz	1 stick
honey	50ml	2fl oz	3tbs
egg yolk	1	1	1
orange peel, finely grated	7ml	1 1/2 tsp	1 1/2 tsp
orange juice	20ml	4tsp	4tsp
egg white, beaten till frothy but not stiff	1	1	1
pecans, chopped	175g	6oz	3/4 cup
glacé cherries cut into 6–8 segments or 'petals'	150g	5oz	1/3 cup

~ 316 ~

Mix the flour, bicarbonate of soda, nutmeg and salt. In another large bowl, beat the butter until softened and then beat in the honey. Add the egg yolk, orange peel and juice and mix well. Add the flour mixture and beat till thoroughly incorporated. Cover and chill for 3 hours or more. Shape into 2.5cm (1in.) balls. Roll in egg white, then in the nuts. Place well apart on an ungreased baking tray. Put 4–5 cherry petals on each ball in a poinsettia shape. Bake in a pre-heated oven at 160°C (325°F/Gas 3) for 15–18 minutes. Remove and cool.

The recipe makes about 36.

Divinity candy

This candy is white with red and green flecks and is also known as 'sea foam'. If you can't get pistachio nuts, almonds will taste just as good, though they don't look the same. It's best to choose a dry day to make divinity candy. If it's wet or humid, cook it longer and leave it to set for a day or so before cutting it up.

granulated sugar	450g	1lb	2 cups
golden (dark corn) syrup	150ml	1/4 pint	1/2 cup
water	100ml	4fl oz	1/2 cup
egg whites	2	2	2
vanilla essence (extract)	5ml	1tsp	1tsp
glacé cherries, finely chopped	50g	2oz	1/4 cup
pistachio nuts, finely chopped	50g	2oz	1/4 cup

First line a baking tin or dish 25 x 15 x 5cm (10 x 6 x 2in.) with foil, then grease the foil well with melted butter.

Put the sugar, syrup and water into a large heavy-based saucepan and heat, stirring, until the sugar has dissolved. Continue heating until a little of the mixture dropped into a bowl of cold water forms a hard ball.

This will take about 15 minutes. If you have a sugar thermometer, it should reach 125°C (260°F).

Beat the egg whites in a large bowl until stiff but not dry. Next, pour the candy mixture slowly in a thin stream on to the egg whites, beating constantly with a wooden spoon or—better still—with an electric mixer.

Add the vanilla essence (extract) and continue beating until the mixture holds its shape in a ribbon when you pour some on to itself. By this time it will have lost some of its gloss. This will take about 5 minutes.

Stir in the cherries and nuts and pour into the prepared tin or dish. Leave till firm and then cut into pieces. Store tightly covered.

Egg-nog

This recipe contains either alcohol or vanilla essence (extract), to suit all tastes.

eggs, well beaten	4	4	4
caster sugar (US: granulated)	50g	2oz	1/4 cup
rum, bourbon, brandy or sherry OR	100ml	4fl oz	1/2 cup
vanilla essence (extract)	2ml	1/2 tsp	1/2 tsp
cold full cream milk (half and half)	900ml	1 1/2 pints	3 cups
double cream (US: whipping)	50ml	2fl oz	1/4 cup
grated nutmeg			

Into the bowl of beaten egg stir the sugar and alcohol or vanilla essence (extract). Gradually whisk in the milk and double (US: whipping) cream. Strain the eggnog into glasses and chill. Before serving, sprinkle a tiny bit of the grated nutmeg into each glass.

INDEX